TAKEDOWN

TAKEDOWN

INSIDE THE HUNT FOR AL QAEDA

PHILIP MUDD

UNIVERSITY OF PENNSYLVANIA PRESS

PHILADELPHIA

Published by
University of Pennsylvania Press
Philadelphia, Pennsylvania 19104-4112
www.upenn.edu/pennpress

Printed in the United States of America
on acid-free paper

2 4 6 8 10 9 7 5 3 1

Library of Congress Cataloging-in-Publication Data

Mudd, Philip.
Takedown : inside the hunt for Al Qaeda / Philip Mudd. — 1st ed.
    p.   cm.
Includes bibliographical references and index.
ISBN 978-0-8122-4496-0 (hardcover : alk. paper)
1. United States. Central Intelligence Agency—Officials and
employees—Biography. 2. United States, Federal Bureau
of Investigation—Officials and employees—Biography.
3. Qaida (Organization) 4. Intelligence officers—United
States—Biography. 5. War on Terrorism, 2001–2009.
6. Terrorism—United States—Prevention. 7. Terrorism—
Government policy—United States. I. Title.
[DNLM: 1. Mudd, Philip.]
JK468.I6M83   2013
363.325'163092—dc23
    [B]   2012038313

This book is for my father.
I suppose it is the way of most sons never
to tell their fathers that they love them.
But perhaps they can write it. Thank you,
papa, for everything you gave us,
and everything you taught us.
Break out a deck of cards.

Contents

Preface   ix

1   The 9/11 Aftermath   1

2   A Return to Langley   27

3   The Spreading Threat: Moving Beyond
the Core of Al Qaeda   70

4   The Second War: The Intelligence Problem of Iraq   90

5   A New View at CIA: Deputy Director
of the Counterterrorist Center   104

6   The Years of Threat   135

7   Watching Threats at Home: The FBI Calls   145

8   One More Transfer: Intelligence at the Department
of Homeland Security   191

Index   199

Preface

THE ORANGE BOWL, Miami's iconic, rickety football stadium, was the venue for the glory years of Miami football—from the hometown Dolphins' perfect year of 1972, and their Super Bowl runs of the 1970s, to the rise of the University of Miami Hurricanes and their first collegiate national championship in 1982. When my parents moved the family, five kids, to Miami from Washington, D.C., in the mid-1960s, they bought season tickets to the Dolphins and held them for a few decades. My father often lent the tickets out, but he occasionally returned to Dolphins games after I left for college. It was part of growing up for me, watching the Dolphins in searing heat, and attending that first Hurricanes national championship victory in the Orange Bowl. It was there that my career started, and this story begins.

Months into graduate school studying English literature at the University of Virginia, things weren't going entirely smoothly. The students were too good—not competitive in a negative way, just too smart, too focused, and too driven. My grades weren't good, David Letterman was a great diversion on late-night television, and I soon understood that I would never be able to pursue a doctorate and settle into a professorship. As I searched for the next step, teaching kids to love literature seemed like a good option: until three-dozen high schools rejected my resume, all in similar letters that I taped to the refrigerator door. After earning a Master's degree in literature, I found myself working at a tiny newsletter publishing company in the suburbs of Washington. Not much of a career, wearing my dad's old suits, wide 1970s lapels and all, and commuting to a high-rise office building in suburban Bethesda, Maryland. Making $13,500 a year. It was clear this wasn't the future.

Until my father called. He told me that Al, our old seatmate at the Dolphins games and a man I had known from my childhood, had seen an employment advertisement in the *Wall Street Journal*. It was the years of Reagan budget bumps for defense, and the CIA was growing rapidly. They needed new people, and they were hiring. Only a month or two into the newsletter job, I already knew it wasn't for me. Not knowing anything about the CIA, it nonetheless sounded a lot more interesting than what I was doing. It was international, with the allure of travel and working with an organization with a brand name that inspired awe across America, and around the world. And despite my lack of depth on international affairs, I, like any reader of the daily *Washington Post*, had a regular diet of global events on my doorstep every morning. It seemed interesting. And it had to pay a lot better than my newsletter job.

There was no online *Wall Street Journal* in 1984, obviously, and no way I could think of to contact the CIA. Without Google, how did a prospective applicant submit a resume? Dial information and ask for the CIA switchboard? So, as an enterprising twenty-three-year-old, I hopped in my rickety Chevrolet Chevette, resume in hand, and drove right up to the front gate of CIA headquarters, in the leafy suburb of Langley, Virginia, off the George Washington Parkway that runs along the Potomac River. Security around CIA headquarters increased in later years, after terrorism at home in America became a concern and two CIA employees were murdered near the front gate. But when I drove up, I immediately found myself before the guard station at the entrance. No concrete barriers, no visitor center. I'll never forget it. "What do you want?" the armed guard asked. And, like naive college graduates the world over, I thought I had a good explanation for a rash drive across town to one of the most secure facilities in Washington. "I understand you are running newspaper advertisements for new employees, and I have my resume here," I answered, through a rolled-down car window.

It is hard to imagine what that guard thought, but I had no other option I could think of in order to offer my application to a place I'd only ever heard of in movies and books. I didn't have the *Journal* ad, which presumably had a forwarding address for resumes. He directed me to a nondescript building in nearby Rosslyn, Virginia, directly across the old Key Bridge from the exclusive townhouses of Georgetown. So I drove there, left the resume with a receptionist, and drove home, thinking that would be the end of that. A secretary at the entrance took my resume and said they'd "be in touch." That was the kiss of death for a job seeker, especially with a track record of three-dozen turndowns from high schools across the northeast.

A month or two later, I returned home to find a flashing red light on my answering machine—the old boxy type that now probably exists only in museums. I rolled the tape and knew instantly, despite my ignorance about intelligence, national security, or Washington itself, that this was the CIA. Declaring only his first name—Bob? John? Jim? I don't remember, except that it was not memorable—a voice on the other end of the line left a short, vague message, and a phone number. Please call, he asked, sounding appropriately nondescript. I was excited, hoping this was the way out of a first career step I knew would never work.

Another trip in my Chevette, whose engine at this point had the unfortunate habit of regularly cutting off entirely in 65-mile-per-hour traffic on Washington's beltway, the commuter highway that encircles the city. Another reason for a new job and a new salary: time for a new car, something to replace an inherited family heirloom that was turning out to be a deathtrap. Like many potential new hires, I was so excited, and so worried about getting caught in traffic, that I arrived perhaps 90 minutes early. I drove farther down the parkway, past the CIA complex, to stop at a fast-food restaurant for breakfast and coffee, and returned in plenty of time.

A battery of interviews followed. Psychological tests. A polygraph with a humorless questioner. Face-to-face conversations with managers. A test or two on general familiarity with world events, for which I'd prepared by trying to read the *Washington Post* every day. Despite the seriousness of the process, and the intimidating prospect of joining an intelligence organization, my enduring memories are humorous. I've had more polygraphs at this point than I remember—never fun, but not usually memorable. That first one was. I walked in thinking it might be a good idea to build rapport with the polygrapher. At twenty-three, I didn't know any better. So I told her that I was from a family of convicted felons, the Mudd family. All true: my great-great grandfather was the doctor who had set the leg of John Wilkes Booth, the assassin of President Abraham Lincoln. Booth broke his leg after jumping from the second floor of Ford's Theater, in Washington. He then rode a horse to the home of Dr. Samuel A. Mudd, a Confederate sympathizer who had met Booth before the assassination.

Needless to say, the polygrapher was not amused. Many people know the old Civil War story of Booth's escape; she did not. The first step I had to take to find my way out of this hole was to explain why I had mentioned that I was from a family of a convicted felon. That took some time—she was not a Civil War buff. The second step was to endure the humorless polygraph that followed. No smiles. No rapport building. More like "Do you have anything in your background that might make you susceptible to blackmail?" kinds of questions. End of story. Lesson learned: never mess with polygraphers, a rule I kept during the many polygraphs that followed over the next quarter-century.

Without receiving any coaching on interview skills—I don't recollect even thinking about practicing how to answer the "what are your major strengths and weaknesses" questions—and with a naive idea that an interview was just a conversation with another adult, I also fumbled my opportunity for what was then known as the "CT" (career trainee) program. The interviewer posed the classic question: Can you describe one of your weaknesses? There began a conversation, an hour long, about procrastination, which I identified as a personal challenge I had faced in college and graduate school. Like every other student, presumably. But as the conversation dragged on, I continued to add detail, and we finished the entire hour-long interview having discussed only that one issue: procrastination. The CT program, at that time, was an avenue for the best and brightest recruits to undergo an extended training program. It was longer and with more experiences than the standard training exercises, and would prepare them for what promised to be fast promotions and promising careers. Following the interview, I was rejected. When I did join the Agency, I spent the first year or two meeting those who had made the cut, thinking that I had already slipped behind my peers in failing to get over the bar for that program.

Beyond interviews and the polygraph, there was one other minor hurdle that worried me. Shortly after I received the phone call and then proceeded through the interview process, the applicant office representative told me that a background investigator would appear at my employer to ask questions of my boss, the newsletter owner. I had one request: please let me know just a bit in advance, I asked. My boss doesn't know that I am considering leaving, and I want to tell him myself before a shadowy government investigator shows up unannounced to ask him questions about some odd, top-secret government job for an agency that the interviewing agent won't identify by name.

I returned from lunch one afternoon, some time later, to notice an older man (older to me, at least) waiting in the small sitting room of the newsletter offices. This was extremely rare: we were only a handful in the company, and we rarely had unannounced visitors. Especially visitors who said they would wait indefinitely for the owner. Who dressed in navy blue suits and white shirts. Who looked suspiciously like retired government employees now conducting background interviews.

I was petrified. Certain that this was the background investigator, I quickly realized both that there would be no advance notice and that I would have to approach my boss first, to announce to him, moments before he would host an interviewer, that I wanted to leave the business he owned. He was courteous, but both of us knew this job was not a good fit: within ten minutes, I had not only told him of my CIA interviews, but we had also progressed enough to agree that I would leave the firm, and my departure would come within two weeks. All this before he even spoke with the waiting investigator. Little did I know at that point, before the bulk of my background investigation had concluded, the high number of applicants who never make it through the review process. I quit the newsletter job thinking this background check was a formality, a box-checking exercise, which turned out to be a completely unfounded assumption, I later learned.

No applicant knows how long a background investigation will take. Six months? Nine months? A year? Longer? Two weeks after that fateful day, I was out on the street and unemployed, early in the summer of 1985, with nothing to do. My brother was living in a tiny apartment for the summer, plodding through Georgetown Law School and with his own summer break open. We decided, on the spur of the moment, to take a classic American road trip. New England sounded good: cooler weather, a great place to drive with an ancient station wagon. So we did.

Until Farmington, Maine, on July 4, 1985. Nothing serious, but another in the series of mild missteps that started a twisting, turning career of integration into a large bureaucracy, a dozen or so job changes, and ultimately assignments at agencies across Washington. My brother and I had decided that Washington was too hot, so we piled up the station wagon and headed out on a vaguely defined trip through the coast of Maine, by spectacular Acadia National Park, and along the rocky shore. At some point, we decided to head inland, toward Vermont and New Hampshire. That old station wagon had a big, pre-conservation engine that could really move. Assuming all rural police officers and sheriffs would be picnicking on the Fourth of July, I edged the speedometer toward 80 miles per hour in what turned out to be a 35-mile-per-hour zone. After some time, a cherry-red light appeared in the rearview mirror. Unshaven, in old Bermuda shorts, and shoeless, I stepped out of the car to find an extremely irate police officer. He yelled that he had followed us for some time, and directed me into his patrol car, after determining that I could not find the vehicle registration. I asked whether I could retrieve my shoes; he declined, in clear terms.

We found our way to the small police station, slowly talking along the way as he settled down. He initially told me he would charge me with three violations: for misdemeanor speeding, driving without a valid registration, and evading a police officer. (He said he had been following our speeding car for several miles.) He also got around to revealing—I don't remember how we transitioned into this subject—that he earned money on the side on a lower-rung professional wrestling circuit, using the persona of a police officer in the ring. Truth is sometimes stranger than fiction, I suppose. In any case, this was my first and only visit to a holding cell, after a photograph and fingerprinting. I felt like a felon.

In the midst of July 4 celebrations, it took some time to find the county clerk so she could come into the jail to collect my bail money. An elderly lady finally appeared, took my money, and approved my dismissal. Months later, I pled (via mail) no-contest to the charge. Luckily, my brother's presence meant that he could drive the car to the station, following the police vehicle, and he drove me away from the Farmington police station to continue on our summer lark.

I was concerned, during the swearing-in ceremony the week I officially joined the Agency, that I might be the only person in the large audience collected in the CIA's "Bubble" (the auditorium next to the entrance of the main headquarters building) who would check "yes" in the box "Have you been arrested or convicted since you started the background clearance process," but the speeding ticket must have gotten by the CIA administrator processing those sign-in papers. Nobody seemed to notice. Another crisis averted.

Nine months after the CIA clearance process began, after the interviews, psychiatric evaluations, polygraph, investigators questioning old friends and visiting neighbors, I walked through the front doors of CIA headquarters in Langley, Virginia. I look back incredulous at how little I really knew about a career change that would define my professional life. Still unanswered were basic questions about what job I would actually have—what is an analyst, after all, and what do they do every day?—and how long I would stay at it. I assumed in those first days and weeks that it would be for a maximum of two years. I'll try this, I figured, but I have no real idea what it is, aside from the fact that it looks interesting and pays better than my last job. But it'll never stick. It did stick, though, after many years of meetings with heads of state and briefing the president in the Oval Office, answering questions in the well of the Congress of the United States, traveling around the world, and seeing some of the most remarkable people doing some unusual and interesting things. It wasn't until twenty-five years later that I left.

This is the story of what I learned, after growing up and moving up in the CIA and then taking part in the campaign of my generation: the counterterrorism fight after 9/11. It is not only the story of what one lone junior officer did, as a Washington-based analyst multiple levels below senior decisionmakers in Washington. It is the story of what I saw, one bit of history that might help create a mosaic among hundreds of thousands of other stories, and just one angle on a complex counterterrorism campaign that is now into its second decade and that has defined the U.S. intelligence community and U.S. foreign policy. It is not a story about CIA secrets, which we were all sworn to protect when we entered the service, nor is it a critique of the many senior policy and intelligence officials with whom I worked. Observers who have spent more time watching Washington than I lament how divisive this city has become. This book was purposefully written to avoid participating in the nasty infighting here in Washington, or attacking senior officials from the safe seat of a former intelligence official who never faced the pressure of elected office himself. If that renders the book less useful, so be it.

This, then, is not a comprehensive history. Instead, it is only a simple snapshot, one slice of what it's like to be on the ground floor of something so big that no single person will ever see or understand all the angles. Like many of us who have left, I do not believe I will ever go back. But it was a heckuva ride along the way.

CHAPTER 1

THE 9/11 AFTERMATH

THE EISENHOWER Executive Office Building stands next to the West Wing of the White House, across the avenue inside the White House complex that passes by the permanent TV stands where commentators on the nightly news can report with the White House residence and the West Wing as a backdrop. "Old EOB," as it is known, is often described as a wedding-cake building: an ornate edifice with black-and-white checkerboard marble floors and high-ceilinged offices. The building is lovely but too elaborate, too expensive, too spacious for a world in which scrutiny of government spending would mean that no one would think of designing a modern-day version. It is a relic of another age, when heels echoed down marble halls and decisions were considered behind mahogany desks without the speed of electrons or the 24-hour press of media, Congress, and life in the capital.

For me, it was a wonder to come to Washington as a junior government official—at the CIA—and find myself, fifteen years later, walking to work every day along the executive avenue that runs beside the West Wing. It seemed more of a TV show set, not a daily commuting route. Walking outside you might see some foreign leader you'd only ever heard of in the news getting out of a limousine to walk through the West Wing doors, a nationally recognizable correspondent you'd only ever seen on TV, or a senior government official whose name had only ever been the title page of a document. All this coming to life in the compound that represented the political heartbeat of a political city that is at the power center of the globe.

But it was not a wonder to live in that city on that day. On a remarkably clear morning that rivaled the best early fall days swampy, humid Washington can offer, we thought that our office building might be the next target. During a chaotic few hours on September 11, we went quickly from a buzz about what appeared to be a tragic but isolated airplane hitting a tower in New York—I first thought it might be a wayward Cessna—to twin strikes by commercial airliners that had us believing there might be many more in the air.

I met an old friend on that crisp, energizing morning at a local institution, Swing's Coffee, across the street from the office. Swing's coffee was good, but it never seemed out-of-the-ordinary special. Picking a new Starbucks over the old Swing's, though, would have seemed like sacrilege, so a few of us regularly met there. We would trade insights about issues in the Middle East and South Asia, which was my portfolio at the National Security Council, or talk about what was going on in Washington, one of ten thousand similar conversations that make up the information exchanges that are the heartbeat of policymaking in the city. New York does money; Washington does power, policy, and politics. None of us was rich, but we all had interesting jobs. Many of us working these issues had known each other for years, and we all talked. Washington seems big, and daunting, to a newcomer, but it shrinks quickly in foreign policy circles.

When I returned to the Old EOB office from the coffee shop, it was humming with the news that a plane had flown into the one of the World Trade Center towers. We all flipped on TVs, watching that tower while the regular workday waited. For those few desperate minutes, the mood was not yet frantic: the short-lived assumption was that this was a one-off event, a tragedy, certainly, but not a national emergency. Quickly, the second impact changed everything. It seemed like a dream, the rapid realization that this could be no accident, no coincidence. Then, within minutes, someone spread the word in our office—after the second strike and the rapid realization that this was an orchestrated terrorist strike on America—that we might be the next target for a commandeered aircraft approaching Washington. It made sense, with the White House next door, and the lack of hard information meant that we could only speculate during the moments before evacuation.

The mundane thought crossed my mind, during those first frenzied moments, that even the seconds of searching for a wallet and car keys might be the difference between life and a suicide airliner striking the building. It seems absurd, in retrospect, but that one thought captures the chaos and confusion, and the sense of unknowing, that came to characterize the rest of that day, and ensuing days and weeks. So after that warning passed down the halls and into offices and cubicles, I joined the stream leaving the building and spilling out onto Washington streets as disorderly as any Hollywood disaster movie. Tens of thousands of people were milling around, security forces were deploying around the White House grounds, and cars clogged the tight streets. There was a pervasive sense that an event of unimaginable magnitude had happened, but there was also an overwhelming dread that we had witnessed only the start of a series of events. I tried to pass any location that might have live television coverage, but there were masses on the streets, and the din made hearing any TV impossible. It was a sea of humanity, swirling with no apparent direction.

Even then, watching crowds pass, it was hard not to draw the inescapable conclusion that we were witnessing a Pearl Harbor-scale event. I do not remember contemplating, during those minutes, that the strikes would not only change my life and those of other government workers but also change the country—the entire world. Like many, I was focused on getting out of the city, where the streets were jammed, and hearing from my family—in particular, my brother, a prosecutor in lower Manhattan out of reach because of overburdened cellphone circuits. I couldn't call him for hours, time ticking away in a vacuum of information in which none of us knew how what exactly was happening in New York. I knew he wasn't in the Trade Center buildings, but no one could have avoided the thought that perhaps he'd been caught in falling debris.

The news of the Pentagon strike added to the chaos, and then stories, later proven false, broke of an event at the State Department, not far away and near my route home, across one of the bridges connecting Washington to suburban Virginia across the Potomac River. Soon, as I tried to circle back to the Executive Office Building compound, the White House grounds and the Old EOB appeared to be off-limits, even for staff. Security in SWAT gear were everywhere. A coworker and I, a colleague from the White House, found our way to her car and left an underground parking lot, seemingly one of the last cars allowed to move out of that garage. We slowly found our across the Potomac, passing the billowing smoke from the Pentagon easily visible down the river to the south of the city. Another reinforcement of the dawning realization that images once reserved for Hollywood had made it to real-life in Washington. What is this? I remember thinking. And what are we in for? And, even then: how will this change things? Already, there was less a sense of chaos than of sadness; early estimates of loss of life were astonishing.

The next hours were surreal: spending the afternoon and evening at the home of my closest friends in Washington, watching the horror unfold on their television. I had initially gone to my house, but it just didn't seem right to hear about this tragedy alone. It was still a disaster movie set, with us remaining incredulous, as the towers tumbled and the realization grew steadily that this was not only real, but the tragedy of a generation. My peers and friends in the world of intelligence and security had spent decades witnessing major breaking events around the world, and trying to understand and explain to policymakers how events overseas might affect the United States, but none of us could have pieced together that evening what our world would later hold. How national security would lurch forward, from earlier decades spent warning of political unrest ten thousand miles away or developments in ballistic missile systems to the new reality. And whether a group named Al Qaeda, whose leaders wanted to return to a world thirteen centuries ago, might stage another "terrorist spectacular" that would have civilians jumping to their deaths from burning buildings in America.

The intelligence industry I had been a part of for fifteen years was later faulted for a failure of imagination on a grand scale, and for missing "dots" that, if connected, might have exposed two of the bombers in the United States, both allegations that led to reshaping the entire U.S. intelligence community and that still haunt the CIA today. But it seems hard to imagine that before 9/11 any analyst should have been able to create a narrative that would have been compelling enough to lead others to believe that this nightmare scenario was real, and to change foreign policy so dramatically. It is not that reasoned intelligence analysis could not have pieced together such a story; we learned a painful lesson about understanding this adversary that day. But no one would have believed the scenario that unfolded with enough conviction to take the kind of action needed to fight this threat—global military and intelligence operations, along with diplomacy—that came to convulse the planet. Living the reality was harder to fathom than any fiction I had read. There was no thought of these implications then, though: only reflection on the enormity of what had just happened, what it meant, and what we would do about it. And a sense of horror at the senseless loss of life as humans jumped from buildings. For later generations, those hours and days will be not fully describable, despite book after book and countless documentaries. There is no way, now, to translate that sense of emptiness that was the byproduct of murder on such a massive, bloodthirsty scale.

⬿

THE NEXT days are a blur now. I suppose we returned to the office a day or two later; I can't remember how quickly, and I can't even remember what we felt, and what we discussed, when we returned to the White House compound. It is as if the overwhelming magnitude of that first day erased the memories of the next.

There was, clearly, a small cadre of staff at the White House working on how to respond. But I was not part of that group, and those of us outside that circle did not have an understanding of what the president and his advisers were contemplating. It seemed apparent that military action would be imminent: with the Taliban refusing to sever its links to Al Qaeda, which had used the Afghan safehaven to create the expanding network that had led to the 9/11 attacks, there seemed little option other than mounting an effort to oust the Taliban and clean out Al Qaeda. The alternative—missile strikes from offshore, for example, or a more restricted effort against Al Qaeda with covert assistance and proxies—would have had limited effect on the group, and Americans, along with allies around the world, were prepared for the sacrifice of a major military intervention. But with the history of the Soviet quagmire in Afghanistan, and a decade of disinterest in the country following the Soviet withdrawal, it was hard to imagine how decisive action could come without great risk of America ending up on the same path as the Soviets. Like many, though, I did know that I wanted a piece of the fight, whatever it would come to be.

Weeks later, my small world started to draw closer to the center of the counterterrorism campaign that exploded on that day. As U.S. intelligence agents and special forces allied with anti-Taliban elements in northern Afghanistan known as the Northern Alliance and began to sweep south in a remarkable offensive, other agencies in Washington contemplated the political problem that had confounded policymakers since the departure of the Soviets from Afghanistan in 1989 and the collapse of the Soviet-backed Afghan government in the early 1990s. That question quickly became front-and-center: how to piece together a credible central government in a country long riven by ethnic splits, convulsed by brutal militia violence, and unaccustomed to control by a central government. How to make a miracle out of a morass, fast and on-the-fly, after more than a century of failed interventions by British colonial forces and then the mighty Soviet Red Army.

In retrospect, it seems clear that the only response a president could authorize and lead was the one that followed: a large military campaign that would put tens of thousands of troops on the ground for years. Surprisingly, I don't remember having that clear sense in the days after the attacks; history has a way of making what was in late 2001 a hazy future path seem as if it was pre-ordained, or inevitable. Despite that initial haziness, the outlines of what was to follow started emerging soon enough.

A senior diplomat, ambassador James Dobbins, had served earlier in nation-building roles, developing a reputation for trouble-shooting in ambiguous environments—the Balkans and Haiti—that required toughness to deal with the hard realities of political factionalism and idealism to believe that those factions could be brought together to find a future. He was selected to lead a small U.S. government team that would have the task of sorting out how a new government might emerge in Afghanistan, one that not only pulled together long-warring factions but also might meet approval from governments around the world—Pakistan, Russia, Iran, the Central Asian states—all with different and sometimes competing agendas in Afghanistan. And he would have to move quickly. No one would have predicted how fast the Northern Alliance and its American partners would sweep south, into the Taliban heartland, and it did not take a crystal ball to figure out that there had better be a diplomatic effort quickly to determine what political process would fill the Afghan void.

I received word early on that Dobbins's team would have members drawn from U.S. government agencies with overseas missions—State Department, Pentagon civilian brass, military, and CIA. And I told Langley, the location of CIA headquarters, that if there was to be a CIA officer detailed to the team, I wanted to be that person. The timing was right for the assignment: I had already been contemplating next steps in my career before the 9/11 attacks, and it seemed to make little sense to stay on at the National Security Council now that the new counterterror campaign would require so many people to take new positions. Despite not having cleared my departure with my colleagues at the White House, not having met Dobbins, and not knowing anything about what his mission might entail, I wanted to be on his team. This was weeks after thousands had been murdered, and any officer in any government service would feel a need to join or support the effort to respond, and maybe to play a bit part in ensuring that this would not happen again. A role in the Dobbins mission would open the door to a place in what was to become the campaign of a generation. It would also, for a career analyst more accustomed to producing written reports in Washington for policymakers, offer a seat at a diplomatic table that might never be repeated: the launch of an effort that would be part of American history. Much to my surprise, I got the call to join up. It seemed like a blessing to me; I was to become the CIA liaison to Dobbins's team. I did not know that this one move would lead to a decade in this counterterrorism fight. There was no way to anticipate what followed.

Those of us on the team knew about South Asia, but we were novices at the nation-building game. Many of us who had watched Afghanistan and the broader South Asian scene for decades underestimated Dobbins: "He doesn't know this turf in Afghanistan." "This is complicated, and he doesn't know the players." "This is too complex to learn so quickly—they should have chosen someone with experience in this part of the world who could be on the ground running immediately." Some members of the team were, like me, career watchers of South Asia who assumed, incorrectly, as it turns out, that the only knowledge that counted would be regional knowledge. Discounting the importance of knowing statecraft, understanding Washington at senior levels, having the connections, confidence, and authority to pull levers, experiencing how other broken states grew out of disarray, we radically underestimated Dobbins's prospects and the power of his personality. Whoever picked him got the right guy.

Those of us early doubters were, we now know, hopelessly wrong. Combining the shrewdness of a tough, longtime diplomat with the experiences of weaving together complicated and competing interests in his earlier assignments, Dobbins proved to be a prescient choice. He succeeded in an environment that had encouraged failure, a place where the Soviets had been forced to withdraw and successive British invading forces more than a century before had been made to abandon. It was a remarkable performance, pulled off in a hazy policy environment where there were no clearcut paths, no precedents, with a ragtag team, in little time, and with a hodgepodge of resources.

I still remember some of the first conversations, as members of the interagency team started appearing in makeshift State Department offices: in the midst of global diplomacy, a national security emergency, and a human tragedy now hard to fathom, we had many conversations about the basics. How the heck are we going to get out to the region, and quickly? Where do we get transportation? And how can we be mobile once we get there? When we first left Washington, I don't even recall knowing where we would end up on that trip, or where we would go as the trip evolved, or when we would return. It reminded me of a short tour I had once had working on the program to support Afghan rebels, years before. Then, in the largest CIA covert action program ever, in a bloody campaign against the arch-nemesis Soviets, trying to ship weapons from a remote location, the questions for weeks were so much less exotic than what you read in novels. Where are all the pallets for this going to come from? We have the military materiel to ship—can we get it onto the ship? Whoever said "don't sweat the small stuff" didn't have to find a military aircraft for diplomatic transport at a time when the military was itself engaged in a huge, rapid mobilization.

The diplomatic team under Dobbins started coalescing early, meeting at the Department of State in the Foggy Bottom section of downtown Washington and quickly sensing that, to get this job done right and quickly, we had to get on the road. Dobbins took charge immediately, using each of us to reach back into our own bureaucracies and determining, with this grab-bag handful of interagency officers, whom he could depend on for what. We all had strengths, we all had weaknesses. He didn't waste time, nor did he mince words, in sizing up what each of us brought and using us as he saw fit. In short, if you could help, he'd depend on you. If you couldn't, he wasn't interested in niceties. "Direct" would understate his personal style. There was a scramble to find aircraft that could fly us to Central Asia and Pakistan, but not a clear sense of where we might find ourselves even a month out. And then there was the task of finding the foundations of a new Afghan political authority, which might take many months, with prospects of success that would never get near fifty-fifty.

The military transport aircraft eventually did appear. We spent the following weeks shuttling across Europe and into Central and South Asia, a wandering crew looking for consensus from potential foreign partners and Afghanistan's neighbor states on who might emerge from the chaos to become a focal point for new political hope in Afghanistan. The adventures along the way were memorable, such a cluster of unique incidents that they seem fanciful in retrospect. We went to the residence of the former king of Afghanistan, Zahir Shah, in Rome, our vehicles passing black-clad security personnel posted at the approach, including some sitting in trees near the former king's compound. Inside, we found a pleasant group of people with an idea of returning their rapidly aging king to Afghanistan, a long-lost monarch who was not well and who hadn't been to his home country in decades. And there was talk among that Rome group, unreal in the most unreal of times, about him returning not just as a figurehead or a steadying force but as a serious player helping run a government—an idea, even then, that seemed as far-fetched as it was charming. The former king did return to Afghanistan some time later, but he was frail, and his role was not significant. He was never destined to play a major role in running Afghanistan; he couldn't have. But those days, and those dreams of hangers-on, offer a glimpse of the myriad plans and plots being hatched, around the world, by expatriates looking to play their own role in a country long abandoned by foreign powers.

We talked to powerbrokers in the former Soviet states of Central Asia, passing the antiseptic, gray, hulking buildings on Soviet-era boulevards to talk to brusque men accustomed to wielding power by brute force. We talked to the Pakistanis, who had long viewed Afghanistan as their western backyard and the military "strategic depth" at their nation's back, important to stabilize so they could focus the lion's share of their army on India, their foe on the eastern border. In one meeting with a senior Pakistani Foreign Ministry official, the wealth of strikingly beautiful artifacts decorating his house in Islamabad appeared almost like the collection of an officer who had served a lifetime as a colonial administrator in one of his country's dominions. But they were Afghan artifacts; neighboring Kabul was moving farther from Pakistan's controlling orbit as the world demanded a new government, and there was commentary around the globe that the Pakistanis might not let go of their dream of a friendly, stable Afghanistan so easily. Would they continue to view their neighbor as a place where they pulled the strings, at the expense of accepting the less palatable solution of a regionally and internationally accepted government that might not be quite as amenable to Pakistani demands?

The Pakistanis had worked so long to stabilize the border, and they were so close to seeing the Taliban, allies of Pakistan, take over the entire country. We forget now, in the midst of regular, open criticisms of Pakistan's performance during the past decade, that it was not even certain then which side of the fence it would sit on. I suspect that President Pervez Musharraf knew that he had little choice, and he made a foreign policy U-turn—watching the Taliban face a crushing Coalition force—that must be about as stark as any in the history of foreign policy. One day the patron of the Taliban, as it moved north and was chipping away at the last resistance. Weeks later, accepting a foreign invasion that would sweep away many years of dreams of Pakistani diplomats, intelligence officers, and military men who were driven to help their Taliban allies succeed. Pakistan's choices from those days are forgotten in the West, but they tell the tale of why, even today, Islamabad remains an ally of the Coalition but with a deep, hard to fathom relationship with Taliban remnants. Old habits die hard.

In one of the most bizarre personal twists for me at that time, we found ourselves in Peshawar, near the tribal areas of Pakistan, talking to Pakistani leaders there even as the fighting raged across the border. We had a security detail with us. I mentioned to one of them that I had recently bought farmland due west of Washington, D.C., in the rolling hills of Virginia's Shenandoah Valley. Really, he answered. There's somebody else on the detail who has land out there. So in the midst of a dusty Third World town, many thousands of miles from home, I sat down with one of the Diplomatic Security officers on the detail. After fewer than ten questions, it was clear: not only did he have land in the same area, but he had a piece of the same farmland I had bought, and we shared a property line. We were neighbors, meeting for the first time halfway around the world. Both with a vision of living in a sleepy, isolated American village; both passing through a South Asian warzone.

As the diplomatic whirlwind continued, it was surprising to many of us how quickly a consensus grew around an urbane politician from the majority Pashtun ethnic group of southern and eastern Afghanistan. Everywhere we went, people talked about the same man: his name, Hamid Karzai, cropped up in every capital. It was like manna from heaven. We had only weeks to assess and then assemble what was to become a transitional government, and the consensus emerged so clearly that there appeared to be no other path. There were later intense debates and differences over Cabinet positions in Kabul—whether men representing the different ethnicity of the Tajik Northern Alliance should have a greater or lesser share of "power" ministries in the Cabinet, for example—but Karzai's name as the potential leader of this fractious group was always at the top of the list of presidential candidates. There is an inordinate amount of public scrutiny today about Karzai, and whether he is up to the task. As with so much of what I have seen during the past decade, these conversations appear to me to be missing the point. What was the alternative? What would you have done? Find a different candidate? Who? How? And for how long? We live in a country where we want others to see the world as we do, and to act as we would. Karzai acts as an Afghan, one whose interests often do not coincide with ours. There was no perfect solution then, and there is none now. He was the best we could see.

I met Karzai with Dobbins a few times in Kabul, along with other members of the emerging Afghan coalition that grew out of the disparate groups fighting the Taliban after 9/11. He seemed to me to match the stories we had heard: articulate, thoughtful, and soft-spoken, not at all the rough-hewn warlord you might expect to emerge from one of the world's bloodiest civil wars. And he was the consensus candidate, unquestionably.

It was quickly evident that we had to speak not only to parties with a stake in Afghanistan's future but to Afghans inside the country as well. How to assist in cobbling together a new government of Afghans, in Afghanistan, without visiting the country, especially given that we were already in the region and just a short flight away? These Afghans had been fighting, first against the Soviets, then among themselves, and now alongside a Coalition, losing lives in this new war for the sake of ousting the Taliban. It was hard to argue that the diplomatic team there to help couldn't manage, even for a few hours, to visit the warzone. There were obviously questions about security, but, to a person, the team was enthusiastic about a trip. Dobbins told the team that he wanted to go in—initially just for a day-trip, it turned out—to begin to draw in leaders from Afghanistan's legendary warring factions. I had a modest role in his team, but at that time, in fall 2001, the CIA had a huge role in providing covert support to the Afghan elements that ousted the Taliban. I had spent a career as a deskbound analyst in Washington; it was the operations officers on the other side of CIA headquarters, and in the freezing expanse of Afghanistan, who were leading this fight. Like the rest of the team, I wanted to see this up-close. The sense of history unfolding then was almost palpable, knowing that what we were seeing would help decide the future of the country that was the focus of attention for people around the world.

Much of the initial work Dobbins requested involved transport: getting into and out of Afghanistan. This was not long after U.S.-backed Northern Alliance troops had taken Kabul but before the fall of the Taliban stronghold of Qandahar in southern Afghanistan, so it was not a typical diplomatic exercise. Before I left CIA headquarters for the assignment, I had met Hank Crumpton, chief of the CIA operational group working in the building, and with U.S. military and Northern Alliance partners to manage the campaign in Afghanistan. Hank was legendary: tough, decisive, not a man to suffer fools, especially in the midst of a hot war. Give Hank a job, stand back, and watch the fur fly. There is one guarantee: it would fly, efficiently. And it did. He was a master at overseeing the tactics and strategy of the covert war: like Dobbins, the right choice at the right time. Hank and I later became friends, but he was focused on the war in those days, not arranging flights for diplomats. And I could almost hear it in his voice, on the other end of a scratchy satellite phone call: Who is this analyst guy asking for a flight into Bagram? But he delivered. John McLaughlin, former deputy director and then acting director of the CIA, told me years later that Hank had asked him the same question: Who's the analyst calling for air support? McLaughlin filled him in, and I never knew of these exchanges at the time. It was yet another in the many examples of the CIA's strength: figure out what the mission is and deliver, quickly and flexibly, with a minimum of bureaucracy. Dobbins depended heavily on that mission flexibility, and we benefited greatly from Agency help during those days.

Afghanistan had gone through many years of Soviet-backed dictators and internecine civil conflict since the late 1970s, but there was still the vestige of a government. It made sense to pay homage to that remaining leadership, or at the very least to avoid alienating them, and Dobbins wanted to see Burhanuddin Rabbani, the putative president of Afghanistan and a longtime player in the country's complicated politics (and who would become the victim of a suicide assassin in 2011 when he was attempting to broker talks among Afghan factions). Hank and his team arranged the trip, via Uzbekistan, across the massive Hindu Kush mountain range. Flying over these mountains, many 20,000 feet or more, stuns the senses: it is as if the face of the earth is corduroy, with row after row of jagged snow-capped peaks followed by deep green valleys. I will never forget sitting in the cockpit, watching these massive peaks roll underneath, knowing that the villagers from another century we passed overhead were among the most isolated in the world, in tiny outposts deep in valleys, and wondering what they thought of yet another foreign force invading their country. Alexander the Great had gone through here, and legend has it that he left a line of blue-eyed descendants in the country as he made his legendary sweep across Asia. Now it was another invader, another in a long line of centuries of them.

We landed at Bagram Airfield, once a central node for Soviet air operations into Afghanistan but now a shell, with the windows of the air traffic control tower blown out and rusting materiel and hulks of steel everywhere in the desert dirt off the runways. It was a moonscape of military hardware, testimony to a land that had not witnessed peace for decades. As we deplaned, a line of Northern Alliance soldiers stood to salute us, with matching uniforms but often wearing what appeared to be basketball shoes, presumably donated by their American sponsors. Walking past the line, toward the waiting vehicles, it was hard not to contemplate the gap between a Washingtonian visiting from the security of a snug Western capital and a group of former guerrillas who had suffered hardships their allies would find hard to imagine.

But they appeared to be a spirited bunch, energized perhaps by their surprisingly rapid assault on the Taliban through the plains north of Kabul and into the Taliban's southern heartland.

The Rabbani meeting turned out to be another surreal moment, at least for a CIA officer who had served for a short period as a small part of the Langley team supporting funneling aid into Afghanistan in the post-Soviet days a decade earlier. The U.S. government once supported those dedicated to the ouster of the Soviet-backed government; we were now turning to those guerrilla groups of a decade before, after we had left them to fight among themselves, asking them to help us bring stability—and to trust us. The scene included a small group of Americans, led by Dobbins, who met Rabbani in a vacant room at the airfield. The meeting room's interior matched what we had seen of the control tower and the airfield—shattered windows and no lightbulbs—but Rabbani entered in robes so starched and white that they appeared to have been taken out of a dry-cleaning bag. Immaculate.

I will never forget the questions that loomed around us. The Soviets had been hounded out of Afghanistan by a tenacious Afghan opposition. But we were now here, with the southern capital of Qandahar still in Taliban hands, talking about steps forward for a new government. After years of the Karzai government, it is easy to forget now that American media were using the word "quagmire" to give a sense of reliving Vietnam, predicting that the United States was in for the same treatment the Soviets had received. Sitting there, with one of the leading figures responsible for the ouster of the Soviets, I was concerned about this as well, looking forward as both part of a team trying to project hope for the future and formerly part of a team that aided the same rebels in a civil war. I later learned that Al Qaeda had hoped for this outcome: they thought the Americans would prove softer than the Soviets. In their view, an American invasion was unlikely, but they would welcome American troops, whom they thought they could bleed, and humiliate, faster than the Red Army.

⌒

AS TIME went on during those weeks, Karzai's name continued to emerge as the most prominent potential leader to serve as the president of a new

Afghanistan, and a hodgepodge of Afghan factions and global powers, from Iran to Russia to the United States to Pakistan, were simultaneously coming to the same view. As support for him grew, there also was mounting talk about a meeting in Bonn, Germany, to bring together the disparate groups from Afghanistan and key countries to settle on a transition plan. The Bonn meeting was to negotiate an agreement for an interim government among previously warring factions and chart a new way ahead. The atmosphere is worth remembering: after so many years of civil war, we now had one faction (the Northern Alliance) representing several major ethnic groups, fighting another faction (the Taliban) comprised of rival Pashtun tribals. And Karzai, viewed by the northerners as a southerner. And not only leadership rivalries from Day One, with both sides coming out of decades of mistrust and war, but also questions about how to divide the "power" ministries to provide balance. Talk about confusing diplomacy, with a timetable for success that was measured only in days and weeks.

Our team went to Bonn with Dobbins, shuttling up to a castle conference center on a hill, eating excellent buffet food in a banquet hall while men with turbans and headgear of every description milled around us. The Christmas market of Bonn was underway, and Muslim representatives from Afghanistan were everywhere. Yet another otherworldly event, just months after the 9/11 attacks. Meanwhile, still fighting thousands of miles away, the Taliban was resisting as winter closed in, and villagers who would never know the luxuries of a Bonn castle were hoping that it would all just end. A peace conference in a cold European city; the smoldering remains of a still-warm civil war back in Afghanistan.

Dobbins, of course, provided the muscle for the diplomatic efforts, talking to all international groups—including the Iranians, a move that caused consternation among some in Washington—and a wide variety of Afghans. The Iranians had not had diplomatic relations with the United States since the fall of the Shah in 1979, but dealing with them made sense: after all, they shared a long border with Afghanistan, they were intensely interested in Afghanistan's future, and they had been covertly assisting some of the factions in the civil war before 9/11. Furthermore, the reality was clear, as it is today. Iran has active security services with long experience providing weapons and training to guerrilla forces, with the Lebanese Hezbollah the most prominent example, followed by the more recent case of Shia allies in Iraq who have proven devastating foes of the American invasion. If we cut them out of the Bonn process we would face the certainty that they would make life difficult, perhaps impossible, in Afghanistan. So Dobbins talked to them.

He stayed at the castle; most of the staff stayed at a hotel down the hill, driving up daily through the German forest to the castle, trading the few day passes each diplomatic group received and milling around among the participants, asking questions and taking the temperature, comparing notes every day. We assisted Dobbins in the limited ways we could, offering him what we heard in the hallways. But he was unquestionably the leader, the head negotiator, and the architect.

Peace still wasn't quite everywhere in the air, though. Unforgettable was the moment when one of the Afghan factional leaders, from a tribe known for its tough fighters, asked to meet with me. He spoke no English; I spoke no Pashto. So we had an interpreter—none other than Zalmay Khalilzad, a native Afghan who went on to become U.S. ambassador to Afghanistan and Iraq and then U.S. representative to the United Nations. Zal was always personable, always a master at talking to all sides of Afghanistan's political landscape. He spoke to them in their language, and he had grown up there. With this unique background he was priceless, both for his knowledge and for his engaging personality, able to speak to any number of Afghan players and gain their trust. He had also been my boss at the White House, a senior National Security Council staffer running the Middle East and South Asia office at the time I left for the Dobbins trip. We knew each other well, so the favor of translating in a side office at the castle seemed a natural. He had stayed in touch with various factions from his office at the National Security Council, sometimes frustrating more structured agencies across town because of his unscheduled, unscripted phone conversations with Afghan leaders who could speak to him in their language and who trusted him.

Some of the Afghans had discovered my CIA background, which turned out not to be of much interest to most of them. But one, a turbaned, gold-toothed tribal leader, saw the CIA connection as an opportunity. In the midst of a peace conference, as all sides discussed how to bring an end to one of the world's most vicious and persistent conflicts, he approached me quietly in the corridor and asked for a meeting. Not certain what to expect, we went into a small side room later, with Zal. Incredibly, it took me a few minutes to realize that a peace conference in Bonn was his opportunity to request a quick infusion of AK-47 assault rifles for a region of eastern Afghanistan. I couldn't figure out whether to be irate, or laugh, or walk away in disbelief. But it was our job to bring together factions, not to alienate anyone, so I put him off by telling him I'd bring the request back to headquarters. I don't remember how I followed up with him, after sending an incredulous note back to Langley, but having a conversation about weapons with a warlord in the midst of a peace conference stands out in my memory as a commentary on why peacemaking in this conflict has turned out to be such a task. We'll talk peace, was what I heard. But not until we shoot every enemy we have. It is hard, as some in Washington have said about the Arab-Israeli conflict, to bring peace to a people who want it less than the foreigners intervening in their land.

Karzai made the astute decision to stay in Afghanistan during the Bonn conference. A man who had spent much of Afghanistan's civil war in Pakistan, outside the fight in his homeland, now had to be sure to show his fighting mettle while others left for Europe. After all, the war was still on: it was not long after the fall of Kabul and then the Taliban heartland of Qandahar. Yet events were moving quickly during those first months, especially when measured against the experience of the Soviets and the reputation of Afghanistan as a quicksand for foreign militaries. Dobbins and the U.S. government, with allies collected at Bonn, had moved from "quagmire" in Qandahar to a banquet hall in Bonn in less than two months.

The Bonn conference was settling on the outlines of a new Afghanistan, though, and Karzai, the sole candidate to become the core of a future government, had to make some sort of appearance. So he was beamed in one day via a phone link to the hilltop castle. It might only have been a gesture, but this almost electrifying voice out of the medieval morass of Afghanistan helped seal his leadership role. The conference quickly went on to produce agreement on a process to form an interim government, only months after the 9/11 attacks. After Haiti and the Balkans, Dobbins had proved once again that talented, tough diplomacy pays. It was an unforgettable lesson in the power of diplomacy as a tool, used in concert with military and intelligence firepower and benefiting from the focus of a globe that was galvanized in a way we have not seen since. It was a textbook example of military and intelligence force backed up by diplomatic statecraft, all backed by focused presidential power.

The final pages of that early post-9/11 chapter in late 2001 were more memorable than Bonn: a return to Afghanistan to reopen the U.S. Embassy, which had been closed since the late 1970s, and then attendance at the show that was Karzai's inauguration. There was still extensive work to do as Karzai emerged and the new governing coalition took shape. It is worth remembering the deep divides that run through Afghan society, with ethnic Tajiks and Hazaras toward the north and the Taliban, ethnically Pashtun, arrayed across the south and southeast. To forge a new sense of nationality, Dobbins and the U.S. government pressed for cooperation among the ethnic factions, a government under Karzai that would be representative of different ethnic groups to show unity and maybe forestall another civil war. And this after the mainly Tajik Northern Alliance had led the late 2001 surge against the Taliban. Coming on the heels of the years of civil war, it was a tall order to create a workable inter-ethnic coalition out of wartime chaos. It took only one quick drive through some of the most damaged sections of Kabul, where one faction had rocketed the city so badly that it was reduced to rubble, to understand the mistrust that divided the factions. Their brothers-in-arms had been killed for years by some of the factions they were now asked to join in government.

This meant that some of the time during late fall 2001 involved meeting the Afghan players who were transitioning from fighting to jockeying for position in the new government. From the smell of rapid battlefield success in rolling back a half-decade of Taliban gains to the sudden realization that, with the new musical chairs of Afghan politics, leaders representing different factions and ethnicities would have to move quickly to secure seats and power for their constituents against rivals who were now also part of Afghanistan's future government and Karzai's cabinet. They would now need to swallow ethnic pride and compromise.

These meetings, led by Dobbins, included key players from the various ethnic groups. They included the former spokesman of the Northern Alliance, Abdullah Abdullah, who became foreign minister, and the soon to be defense minister Mohammed Fahim, a Tajik. It also included the new intelligence minister, who appeared to me to be one of the most thoughtful and impressive of the entire group, telling us that he had grown up on the streets and learned foreign languages in the alleys of hawkers and rambling shops around the bustling downtown Chicken Street markets. Much of this conversation continued to revolve around the sensitive issue of which faction, and who, would get the power ministries such as Defense and Foreign Affairs. There was also the question of how the Northern Alliance Tajiks, who had formed the bulk of the Northern Alliance and felt they had borne the brunt of the advance against the Taliban during the post-9/11 offensive, might cede some power to the southern Pashtuns, who had lived under Taliban rule for half a decade. Without a census that was even close to current or accurate, parceling out posts based on population was out of the question, and probably a potentially dangerous precedent anyway. Meanwhile, various diplomats were returning to Kabul to reopen their embassies.

The days included regular consultations at the old U.S. Embassy (which still lacked heating, as the cold and damp Afghan winter set in) with the other diplomats involved in piecing together the new government. This meant opening up the grimy old building, which had not had Americans there in a few decades since the descent into war, Soviet invasion, more civil war, and Taliban takeover.

The Embassy had been vacated quickly all those years ago, and we entered a time capsule. Former Afghan employees over the years had tried to protect the building, and they had done a remarkably good job. I was surprised to find, for example, that the library still had books that were decades old, on bookshelves that were still intact. Offices still had ashtrays on desks, reminders of an era when such offices were not off limits to cigarettes.

I visited one section of the building as we opened it up, with old calendars and magazines and a relic of the past, a few posters of scantily clad women in the communications area. Most surprisingly, I found one of the largest birdnests I had ever seen on top of one of the interior air conditioning units: the building had become home for birds that had made their way through a broken window, and the shelter of an office must have proved a perfect nesting area. Among the most unique experiences of that Afghan interlude had to be finding a large plastic garbage bag and stuffing a bird's nest, with its overwhelming stench, into the trash. We all pitched in, remarking on the odds and ends we found that showed how much time had passed since the building had served as an active Embassy. One day high diplomacy, the next garbage removal.

The Embassy also has a small annex, which the entire Dobbins team used for accommodations. The setup was modest at best, with one vaguely functioning shower and toilet and, like the Embassy, cold and damp during the early days of the Afghan winter. There was no complaining, though. We had it good. In the field next door, a band of U.S. military officers and enlistees who served magnificently, with courtesy, honor, and valor, sleeping in tents and bathing anywhere they could while we had the annex. Never once did they comment on the contrast between their field accommodations and what we had: despite its limitations, the annex was far better than a tent with no heat or running water. Initially, our entire small crew, perhaps a half-dozen, stayed in that tiny annex, with military-issued MREs—meals ready-to-eat, military rations in plastic bags. Diplomatic missions, it turns out, don't always happen in the cocktail party environments you read about.

Transportation, too, proved to be a persistent challenge. Aside from the mechanics of arranging aircraft, there was the issue of traveling securely around the city and getting into the air hub of Bagram Airfield, in the midst of a still-raging civil war and concerns about anti-aircraft fire from the surrounding mountains taking down our lumbering helicopters and transport aircraft. During the second of our two stops there, we landed at night, taxiing in on a dark runway, only to have the massive back hatch of the aircraft, typically used for larger transports of men or equipment, open in the pitch black to reveal a U.S. serviceman guiding our small band to our quarters. He led us in the dark, using only the light of a green-glowing chemical stick in his mouth. Driving into the capital by the main road, with not only potholes but small car-sized pieces of pavement blown out in many areas along the way, it was easy to get the sense of the intensity of the fighting, and how recently this road had witnessed war.

We found more reminders in the city that Afghanistan was nowhere near stabilized, though we could not have imagined that the capital would still witness suicide bombings and Taliban assaults years later, into the second decade of the war. For our protection at the Embassy, there was a small, rotating team of U.S. soldiers on the roof keeping a lookout. The roof had excellent visibility, into neighboring streets and the walled housing compounds typical in that part of the world, at a time when there was concern about rocket-propelled grenades or other rounds coming into the compound. Descending one day at the end of their shift, one crew of two soldiers said they'd had some small-arms fire across the top of the Embassy that day, probably AK-47 rifle rounds. None of us had heard this earlier, and we were curious about why we hadn't learned about it. "We think it was just a wedding celebration," was the response. I don't recollect feeling particularly relieved—what if they were wrong about the intent behind the rounds?—but the U.S. military support was great. They just never complained, never lacked courtesy, making the best of a hostile environment in a war no one had anticipated even four months earlier.

The Embassy annex was cramped, to say the least, and there were other accommodations in town that I quickly took advantage of. A nearby hotel was occupied by Agency officers, working with their Special Forces partners. As U.S. intelligence and military components led Afghan units into the capital in the testy days of Kabul's fall, the hotel seemed as good a location as any for their burgeoning presence. Like many experiences in the field, cooperation on the ground reflected little of any bureaucratic tensions that might exist between Washington agencies. These field officers, from different agencies with different training and missions, all slept under one grimy roof. I was an analyst who shared a room that included both Agency field personnel and Special Forces officers. Nobody asked any questions; I didn't know who they were, and they never approached me.

Both elements, intelligence, and military, brought strengths—the agility of the Agency, and its specialty of handling human source networks; and the ability of special forces personnel to operate in extremely difficult field conditions (winter in Afghanistan's hinterlands) and coordinate ground and airpower with information gathered through CIA operations. You couldn't have told them apart, at least not quickly. They were a team.

They also ate together in that facility commandeered in the days after the surprisingly rapid assault into Kabul. The food was hot, decent, and plentiful, the accommodations certainly not sterile but as clean as any in Kabul—and night-and-day different from the tough conditions the field officers were living in during their deployments side-by-side with Afghan units, in the cold and early snows without toilets, showers, hot water, or a clean bed. As an amateur cook, I made the mistake of asking for a quick visit to the cavernous kitchen that delivered our food. A quick look around was enough—too much attention might convince a visitor that eating was more of a risk than terrorist attacks. The huge space looked more like a cave, with large battered pots over burners, in an environment that seemed taken out of a medieval storybook, with cooks wearing leather aprons and hammering red-hot iron out of a kiln. But they did their jobs well: I only remember decent hot food, lots of it. And there were no stomach illnesses, after a career of travel that had often been interrupted by food poisoning in environments much more civilized than Kabul.

I also remember visiting the makeshift CIA center of activity in Kabul, a mishmash of computer terminals, outdoor gear, and staff who worked all day, every day. The mission demanded it—the war was still on, hot and heavy—and the conditions didn't exactly provide a lot of alternate entertainment, beyond books and shipped-in DVDs. It was around the days of Tora Bora—the mountain hideout for bin Laden and other Al Qaeda members who were fleeing to Pakistan—the time period many commentators look back on and ask "What happened? Why didn't we get him, if we thought we knew where he was?" Those same questions endure today, not only about what happened as Al Qaeda leadership fled across the mountains into western Pakistan, but about why Osama bin Laden remained at large for so long, and why his number two, Ayman al-Zawahiri, is still out there somewhere.

Spending my time with Dobbins's team, I was obviously not working at the CIA offices in Kabul, but the hindsight critiques of the Al Qaeda pursuit from those days through today miss key points about what the mission was, and is. The war for Afghanistan was still intense at the end of 2001, and much of the effort in the station was focused on supporting the forces that were pushing back the once-surging Taliban. Years later, the rapid progress ousting the Taliban is lost in the mist of a decade of back-and-forth with Taliban remnants, now resurging as Coalition forces slowly withdraw. But then, the fight was up in the air: ousting the group that had hosted the architects of 9/11 was a primary focus, and the hunt for Al Qaeda leaders was only a part of that mission.

Afterward, when counterterrorism operations shifted to the Al Qaeda players who had migrated to Pakistan, the mission was equally clear. Ensure that we do not have another catastrophic event on U.S. soil. Destroy Al Qaeda's safehaven; break up plots; find, fix, and finish plotters. As it turns out, the key plotters managing Al Qaeda operations after the Afghan exit were not bin Laden and Zawahiri. Those two, at the top of the Al Qaeda hierarchy, proved over time to be more symbolic leaders, providing strategic direction, cajoling their underlings, weighing in on key decisions, but not day-to-day overseers. Statesmen in their own eyes, trying to galvanize a global jihadist movement by focusing on issues such as the plight of Palestinians, intervention in Darfur, and even global warming. Always on the run, they feared that too much contact with the Al Qaeda organization, especially as operational leaders were captured or killed, would expose them to foreign spies, missiles, or militaries. They went underground. Not in caves, as we saw with the raid in Abbottabad, in which bin Laden was killed by U.S. forces, but effectively isolated from regular contact with the organization.

Later in the counterterrorism campaign, the focus was not just on the two at the top, or even primarily directed against them, but also on those who posed the most significant tactical threat to the United States, the series of operational commanders and their subordinates and facilitators who were trying to piece together the next major plot: Khalid Shaykh Mohammed, Hamza Rabia, Abu Yahya al-Libi, Abu Faraj al-Libi, and the rest of them. The list goes on, mostly Al Qaeda leaders whose names are unrecognizable to most Americans. But they were once all key players, all critical to plotting against the U.S. homeland, and now, all dead or captured. The measure of success was not just who was captured or killed, or whether bin Laden and Zawahiri were gone, but whether operations broke plots and destroyed networks that could sustain long-term training and planning resulting in another strategic strike. In that sense, looking forward from the 9/11 attacks, I think the focus on these operational figures was well founded: virtually no one, in 2001, would have bet that the United States would not have witnessed another 9/11-style event by now. In this most critical sense, the operational focus was successful. Bin Laden took nine-plus years to take down, and Zawahiri is still out there, but their organization poses nowhere near the strategic threat it did a decade ago, and its leadership is decimated beyond recognition. Just the sense of slippage in the Al Qaeda organization that any reader can sense from bin Laden's guidance from Abbottabad is sufficient evidence of the counterterrorism campaign's success.

⟿

BUT WE were focused on Karzai, and on the tenuous agreements being forged about his new, inclusive government. During that second visit to Kabul in December 2001, for the negotiations about posts in the government, we all participated in the ceremonial reopening of the Embassy, watching the raising of the American flag by the U.S. military on a cold, damp day. The symbolism, to me, seemed striking. Less than four months earlier, before the crisp morning of the eleventh of September, Afghanistan had been forgotten, a smoldering pile of Cold War embers that had died out in the national consciousness as it was consumed by endless civil wars that were leaving the Taliban slowly in control of the country. Now, not long before Christmas Day, the Taliban was on the run, a Northern Alliance surge southward had progressed beyond what many observers had ever imagined or hoped for, and an Embassy abandoned many years earlier was open for business. Quite a day.

The Embassy building itself was even open for business. Ambassador Dobbins continued to greet various diplomats in upstairs offices, yards away from where he was staying in the dilapidated, dingy annex. The offices were not well appointed, the plumbing didn't work, and the rooms were cold. But the Americans were back, along with our allies. And the push to finish the horse-trading that resulted in the Karzai government was in high gear.

Far more spectacular than the opening of the Embassy was the Karzai inauguration, scheduled for late that December. There was a swirl of activity beforehand, questions about which warlords felt slighted and which would agree to appear on the podium, even to the day of the inauguration. And then there was the event. We drove up to a massive hall, with bright colors and native headgear from across Afghanistan in an array that was fascinating, almost festive. Despite the language barrier during the ceremony, it was such a historic occasion that sitting in the hall felt like living history. Ismail Khan, a fabled warlord from the Persian-influenced western part of Afghanistan, appeared, after lingering doubts about whether he would acknowledge Karzai as president. Karzai spoke. The ceremony was elaborate and the streets were milling with guests dressed in tribal costumes; the effect was like a set for *Raiders of the Lost Ark* against a *National Geographic* photo spread.

As we drove up, there was some trepidation, at least on my part, in a country that had seen the capital ripped apart by rocket attacks from rival militias, that we might witness a terrorist strike on the inauguration grounds. These were idle concerns. All went smoothly, in a chaotic country unaccustomed to hosting political inaugurations in the capital. Suicide bombers, long known in devastating attacks by Lebanese Hezbollah and Tamil rebels in Sri Lanka, were still all but unknown in South Asia, but I couldn't help wonder that day whether a car bomb might hit the ceremony, where security was not a priority. Years later, of course, the international scourge of suicide bombers would seep into Afghanistan, and the bloody path to the years-long Taliban fight that now defines the NATO presence would come home to this new fight in ways no one then would have imagined. Like other terrorist methods in this age of Internet and immediate access to news and ideas—beheadings, Mumbai-style small arms attacks, backpack bombs made from beauty parlor chemicals—suicide bombings spread among the loose network of terrorists as the cheapest, most effective way to gain attention.

There were other guests mixed in with this colorful array, though these were more unobtrusive visitors. The CIA had assisted Karzai as part of its post-9/11 mission to support anti-Taliban militias. Early in the fight, he had infiltrated into southern Afghanistan, the heartland of the Taliban and the southern Pashtuns who form their base. The fighting was still intense when he went in, airstrikes were a constant threat, and there was at least one reported instance where Karzai's protectors had shielded him from aerial bombs. Tough moments in southern Afghanistan during the early weeks after the fighting with U.S. forces and the Northern Alliance had forged a bond between the country's future president and hardened field operatives from the Agency, who were side-by-side with the tough Afghans opposing the Taliban in the south. Karzai hadn't forgotten. Some of the key team who had been around him received a handwritten note from him, a sincere thank you for the risks they took to help him in those chaotic days. So they were there as well, in the background, quietly witnessing what they had helped achieve. Later they faded back into the scenery, a short respite in an otherworldly inauguration ceremony before returning to the grit of the fight on the ground.

After charter flights around Europe and Central and South Asia, the team had been on the road, on and off, for many weeks. We had seen airtime in all manner of aircraft, including sitting in the middle of a cavernous transport plane, dwarfed by a cargo area designed more for tanks than people. Dobbins clearly had experience in these kinds of environments: on one of our early nighttime flights, he quickly took out his bedroll after we boarded and immediately fell asleep on the floor of the metal cargo bed. None of this mattered—morale was high, and it seemed almost unbelievable that Afghanistan had seemingly moved so quickly, belying the worries about quagmire and contrasting so sharply to the Soviet experience. Meanwhile, we all also had an eye on Christmas Day. Transportation out of Afghanistan was always a touch-and-go affair, and we were wondering whether we would make it home in time for the holiday. We did, just in time, after the inauguration ceremony on the 23rd. We all knew the first chapter of the lengthy U.S. diplomatic mission in Afghanistan had been completed—there was a broadly accepted coalition government in power, for a transitional period.

Flying through Uzbekistan and then into New York, I found myself, less than 48 hours later, on the Metro North commuter train out of Manhattan's beautifully restored Grand Central Station to visit my brother for Christmas in a small town north of the city. The scenes across New York were classically American: glittering lights near stations at the wealthy suburbs as we slipped by, passersby in holiday clothes, and windows with gifts celebrating the holiday. After the dust and constant sense of insecurity in Kabul, the contrast was hard to absorb. On the train during that trip north, marking the end of what I knew would be one of the most fascinating experiences of my life, a woman in her holiday best and her small daughter, the two of them clearly back from a last-minute shopping visit to Manhattan, looked at the dust on my bags, my rumpled clothes, and a pair of tired eyes. "Coming home from the holidays?" she asked. "Yes," I answered, "heading up to see my brother." "Where are you flying in from?" "Afghanistan," I responded. She didn't seem to know what to say. Less than four months after 9/11, a diplomatic mission that had once seemed unreachable was already now slipping into memory.

CHAPTER 2

A RETURN TO LANGLEY

I HAD NO job when I returned to Washington after Christmas, and the flurry of activity the previous months had kept me largely insulated from the changes the Agency had recently undergone. Aside from working on transportation for the Dobbins team and speaking to a few of the people managing the CIA fight in Afghanistan, I hadn't stayed in any sort of contact with the building. The shift of focus, personnel, and resources to the counterterrorism mission was substantial, and the Agency was already a different place, as I quickly found. I first heard of where I might be headed in the days after my return from the Karzai inauguration while staying at my brother's house north of New York City and taking in the quiet after the mayhem of Kabul. From raw Kabul to freezing Westchester County, enjoying life in a tiny village with a traditional Italian deli next door and an old Protestant church across the street. Even after short trips, it was always good to get home to simple pleasures—Italian subs, breath freezing on early morning runs on dirt roads by old mansions, and the sense of freedom from fear and insecurity that goes from transitioning to America from a warzone. Not to mention a regular sleep schedule and a large golden retriever to wake me up every morning.

My old boss and mentor, Winston Wiley, knew me from days before 9/11 when we had both worked in what had been a much smaller Counterterrorist Center. He had risen quickly, becoming second-in-charge of analysis at the Agency, where I served as his special assistant. He had then moved up to take command of the analytic wing, several thousand strong. The Agency had a few organizational pillars from its inception. One core element, then called the Directorate of Operations (now the National Clandestine Service, or NCS), was responsible for the people in the overseas field who recruited and ran secret agents. Its counterpart component was the Directorate of Intelligence (DI), a mostly Washington-based group of specialist analysts responsible for reviewing intelligence coming in from the field and writing reports that made sense of intelligence and world events for policymakers in Washington.

I had grown up in the DI, the component responsible for producing analyses for consumers around Washington. We wrote "finished" intelligence—carefully researched, written, and edited analyses of global issues. Our mission was at the other end of the domain from that of field operators, who collected "raw" intelligence; that is, they talked to a source or a foreign security service, and drafted reports based on what the source said. Analysts tended to be more introverted, interested in research and delving into the details of complex problems. Collectors were people-oriented, more focused on determining how to spot, assess, develop, recruit, and handle human sources.

From the outside, it might appear that the core skills required of analysts are straightforward: develop expertise in a particular area, and write about that area to help a policymaker understand a complicated problem, such as a foreign nuclear weapons program or an insurgency halfway around the world. In retrospect, the skills that were drilled into me, and many other analysts, were more nuanced and more difficult to learn. The first and most basic was a relentless drive to write clearly, quickly, and succinctly. I thought I knew how to write when I received my master's degree in English Literature from the University of Virginia. Looking back, I now believe it took close to a decade to build real writing skills. Not just the clarity of a sentence—using verbs, that were precise, avoiding adjectives and adverbs, eliminating waste—but more subtle weaving through three pages of text, telling a story for a reader who needs detail but doesn't have the time to read detail. Along with briefing skills—how to speak to any audience, anytime, about anything you're responsible for, possibly on short notice—learning to write professionally was an art among the Agency's analytic ranks. Managers were tough, always demanding cleaner drafts, more precise language, and, with many layers of review, asking the same questions from different angles.

Even harder, though, was the art of learning how to ask the right questions, especially on problems that had already been worked over dozens of times. Newer analysts often believe they are responsible for simply capturing the knowledge they have. Instead, what I discovered, over years, centered on the importance of framing the question properly from the outset. At its simplest, for example, was learning that the question started with what the policymaker needed to know, not regurgitating what I knew. Over time, each piece of paper became, for me, a chance to write the story I thought would combine what the policymaker needed and enough art to believe that the answer was crafted so well that no one else could capture it better. The pain of learning how to do this, under layers of management who were sometimes brutal in providing feedback—but also often brutally brilliant—took more than a decade.

We needed more analysts to write on the counterterrorism problem, and we needed them fast. There was no time to train them on how to understand terrorism and terrorist groups. So Wiley had, immediately after 9/11, shifted about two hundred personnel to dramatically expand the number of analysts working on counterterrorism. Overnight this transformed the analytic wing and put counterterrorism analysis on a par with more traditional global problems, such as nonproliferation and major regional issues, that were the powerhouses of the CIA's analytic component. Rare in government, he was an aggressive decisionmaker, willing to move quickly in the face of rapidly changing events. Though the 9/11 attacks were a watershed, then and now, in how the Intelligence Community operates, his rapid shift of so many analysts caused a lot of commentary in the CIA's analytic bureaucracy, and I started to hear murmurs of this when I returned from Afghanistan. This transfer of personnel was a lesson in confronting a problem at a time of adversity: in for a dime, in for a dollar. Not too much studying, not too much overthinking, all no doubt with the understanding that in large organizations, if you wait too long to move, you'll lose the momentum of the moment. He made the most of that moment, and analytic managers who lost pieces of their "rice bowls" had neither the time, nor the will, nor the ability to object. In any case, with nearly 3,000 dead and an intelligence battle coming on, no one would think to do so, at least not in September 2001. The Agency was transitioning to war, and fast. While the CIA is not the most command-oriented bureaucracy in

Washington, instead known for an independent streak that can be troublesome for politicians, what it lacks in ease of management it makes up for in agility.

⌐

I HAD been gone for a year, initially on the White House National Security Council assignment and then on the Dobbins mission, and I had little idea how the analytic arm had changed. Despite years in the service, I'd been on the road so much that I had lost track of what was emerging in the Directorate of Intelligence in the wake of the 9/11 organizational shifts. What I returned to was already significantly different from what I'd left twelve months before. I was not even aware of that first, fundamental step, the establishment of a separate counterterrorism office during the post-9/11 months. In CIA terms, an analytic office is the biggest subcomponent in the business, equivalent to the analytic firepower the agency applies to the country's biggest threats. It wasn't, however, just this organizational designation that was significant: the beefed-up numbers of analysts who were now dedicated to the problem told the story. Wiring diagrams are fine—they help define organizations, and they identify what bureaucracies value—but in any large entity, people are the real measure of leadership focus. Later, many would raise questions about whether the pre-9/11 commitment that preceded this buildup had been significant enough; now, though, those questions were in the future, and the new numbers were substantial.

The already unquenchable thirst among policymakers and CIA executives for knowledge about Al Qaeda, and the mushrooming quantity of knowledge that was pouring into Langley, had led, within weeks of 9/11, to this explosion in the number of analysts, operations specialists, and other personnel working the counterterrorism problem. I received a call, over that Christmas, from Wiley, telling me that this new analytic arm had been created and explaining quickly what was going on at the Agency and in the Al Qaeda fight. He talked about the expansion of the new management structure as well; as the analytic cadre expanded, the number of managers required to oversee this new beast had also grown. Even with my year-long absence from events in Langley, I understood the magnitude of what he was talking about during that phone call. Would I, he then asked, take over as second-in-charge of this expanding counterterrorism analytic effort? This was a much larger enterprise than I had previously managed, and after the Dobbins assignment, it was a job that was still in the belly of the beast. There was only one answer.

This attraction of managing at a higher level came with the growing understanding of the upsides and downsides of management for me at the CIA once I moved into a management position. There was the straightforward part: try to produce quality analytic product. Manage the organization (budget, personnel, never my strength). But there were also the sometimes more challenging but blurrier responsibilities. There was the high end: what should the vision be for such a new analytic entity, and how should that vision be executed? And the less high end: how to deal with a highly talented analyst who cannot manage to work in a group environment?

Overlaid on this was the culture of management at CIA, at least at that time. We had broad latitude to determine which terrorism stories we should tell, and how we should tell them. Clearly, we had to cover key issues such as emerging threats. But on broader problems, we could develop our own storylines. We also had the latitude to participate in executive decisionmaking—at the level of the CIA director—and White House, media, and Congressional happenings that I sensed among my peers at other agencies. This is not to say the job was particularly fun—it often was not, especially given the nature of terrorism—but it was interesting and challenging, and the latitude given to managers at the Agency offered a sense that we could make a difference.

I knew he was serious, and that the effort he had described was serious. In 1999, while I was serving as his assistant during his tenure as second-in-charge of analysis, he had shifted me, over objections of favoritism, to manage the Iraq analysis group. This had taken some stomach on his part: I did not have management experience at that time, and this was a jump two levels up the management chain. The internal electronic chatline of CIA analysts included a few highly negative comments about the move—some screened from the database, which reached all analysts, because they were so ugly—but Wiley proceeded nonetheless. So I knew now, several years later, that he wasn't going to mince words. Not all his moves were the right moves, but he never lacked for boldness. And he didn't mind taking on trouble.

The offer he made that winter didn't require much decision making on my part. Almost four months after 9/11, it was abundantly clear that we were in a period of war that not only rightfully focused the entire U.S. govern-ment, and the world, but it was also the war of a generation, for a people that had never seen such an event on U.S. soil. And analysis that could make some sense out of the global problem of terrorism would be critical for U.S. security, especially given the facts that this problem required intense analy-sis—Al Qaeda was not an easy beast to understand—and that intelligence was among the most prominent tools the president was using to fight the threat. The uncertainties of how the U.S. might confront the terrorist threat were huge when the Dobbins mission to Afghanistan kicked off; now, months later, it was increasingly clear that this campaign would be big and long. It was consuming America.

So I agreed immediately, taking Amtrak's Northeastern regional train down to Washington to return to a building I hadn't much seen for a year and stepping into the office in a rapidly outfitted section of CIA's original, 1960s-era headquarters building shortly thereafter. The office was led by Pattie Kindsvater, whom I didn't know at the time but who became a friend. Initially, though, it was one of those management experiences that took some work: she was heading a busy office with growing pains, and her boss (Wiley) had just pushed an unknown deputy on her who didn't have a lot of experience and had been out of sight of CIA headquarters for the entirety of the post-9/11 months, which must have seemed like dog years at that point. Furthermore, my position hadn't been announced formally when she and I first met, after my return. So there were a few quietly awkward days of occupying an outer office in the midst of her staff, without portfolio, while the bureaucratics of the new assignment were put in place. It was a bit odd. But she never complained to me about Wiley's choice. Not once then. And not once later.

Pattie had far more managerial experience than I, providing a steady hand as the office grew and offering counsel and guidance to me without ever seeming overbearing. We were complementary: she provided structure and a broad knowledge of office management at a senior level, and she added a steely sense of purpose. Because she had run the much smaller counterter-rorism analytic unit before 9/11, she knew the strengths and weaknesses of the core of more experienced analysts we had, those who were now writing some of our most important analysis and providing the analytic weight anchoring the much larger cadre of newly assigned analysts who joined them. I added to Pattie's experience my background working on Middle Eastern and South Asian issues, which had been a focus for me for more than fifteen years at that point, and I had spent more time working with the Congress and media. We shared some of the substantive duties, such as the daily review of the cats and dogs that made up the now-famous Threat Matrix, everything from serious threats reported by penetrations of Al Qaeda to random reports from write-ins who didn't know what they were talking about, or simply made up threats. Over time, we grew as colleagues and friends, quickly switching off duties such as the weekend visits into the office to review the matrix.

The threat information then was voluminous and dominating, contributing to a pervasive sense that every day might bring a new attack by a surprise cell in the United States or somewhere else in the world. We had an office rhythm, even during the busiest of times, but the backdrop was always threat. It shadowed us every day, coming from traditional intelligence sources and from left field, each day a new experience that required lots of on-the-fly decisions. I remember driving in Washington, listening to local news radio, when reports started streaming in about an aircraft violating airspace around the Capitol. The incident turned out to be a wayward private pilot who no doubt landed to a reception he never forgot. But those initial radio reports, along with a thousand other false leads and sources talking about real attacks, meant that life seemed surrounded by questions about whether we had missed something that might signal the next 9/11-style strike.

This sense of imminent threat was reinforced by the accessibility of all the senior managers in the Center at all times of the day and night; we all had secure phones and secure faxes that could transmit classified material to our residences, so even without driving in to review the threat matrix, we received frequent calls about new threats rolling in from officers on the night and weekend watch. Or there would simply be new questions from policymakers that required quick attention. The world of terrorism, especially during those first years, was inescapable anywhere you went, from TV to radio to newspapers to friends, a feeling I will never forget and never want to live through again. Speaking to many colleagues in the years afterward, including those of us who have left the service, I suspect many of us share the view that those years were among the more interesting during the long careers we enjoyed, but nonetheless they were years we would just as soon forget. Or, better yet, not have lived at all, like all Americans. Driving home at night, remembering the images showing faces of those who had died at the Trade Center and now were featured in the pages of the *New York Times*, wondering whether there would be thousands more: those were times that brought immediacy to a world of intelligence that seemed a long way from the more studied world of strategic assessments of Soviet intentions that had dominated agency analysts when I joined, in the Reagan years of the 1980s.

∽

WE ALSO shared oversight and editorial review of terrorism analysis for what is the Holy Grail in the analytic wing of the Agency: the daily analytic articles that are briefed to the president in his personalized morning intelligence package, long known as the President's Daily Brief and referred to by its acronym, the PDB, or sometimes simply "the book." For decades, the Agency has provided a similar package of intelligence every morning, changing the style and format over the years to reflect the personality of each president. The items in the PDB package range from strategic analysis—the evolution of a foreign country's nuclear program, for example—to tactical, such as a quick-turnaround overnight update, with photographs, from a missile test in that same country. Not everything provided to the president is what is referred to as "finished" intelligence—formally prepared short or long memos that have gone through strenuous, painful analysis, coordination among analytic colleagues, and management and editorial review. The package may also contain what intelligence professionals call "raw" reporting, unanalyzed information directly from the best-placed and most sensitive human sources, or intercepted phone calls transcribed by specialists but not yet scrutinized by the army of intelligence analysts in Washington. Or satellite photographs of a missile launch. Or open source reporting, summaries of global media reporting and editorials dissecting a presidential visit, for example.

Every morning, a group of intelligence briefers fans out, as they did before and after 9/11, across Washington to present this information personally to the government's most senior officials, from the secretaries of defense and state to the national security adviser, chairman of the joint chiefs of staff, attorney general, FBI director, secretary of homeland security, and others. The core briefing package remains the same: the update the president might receive on breaking events in the Middle East would be the same for all the "principals," as his most senior advisers are called. In Washington, power starts with the president, and most readers want to know what the president is reading. Each individual briefer has the latitude to adjust the package by selecting articles that are of most interest to the principal, so the briefer for the FBI director might determine that an appraisal of trade prospects overseas does not meet the threshold for the director but that an assessment of shifts in Mexican drug smuggling across the Southwest border should be near the top of the morning briefing pile. This is customer service, national security style.

Each of these "principals" also has the authority to request follow-up, typically in writing but occasionally via a quick oral response or a visit from an analytic expert. The briefers return to Langley and gather to provide a collective backbrief later in the morning, assessing among themselves how well the analytic "pieces" went over and cataloguing requests for additional analysis. The responses to these questions can range from simple—what's the name of the foreign official who's mentioned in this intercepted phone call?—to far more complex, perhaps the changing dynamics among drug cartel leaders south of the border. And, by tradition and protocol, the answers typically are provided quickly, often overnight and almost always within a few days. The analytic cadre takes this daily exercise extremely seriously: analysts might agonize afterward if their meticulously prepared submission to the PDB is subjected to the "flip," the term used when senior customers quickly glance at a piece but flip the page to the next article without giving the first item a serious read. In this world of Washington, where access to power is the currency of the city, even email responses to a casual question from a briefer will go through multiple layers of review.

In the years after 9/11, after I returned to Langley, Pattie and I were responsible for overseeing the material going into the PDB that related to terrorism and counterterrorism. This might seem like a simple task—to sign off every afternoon and evening on a few pages of written material—but it could easily chew up several hours a day. The day-to-day preparation for the resident's "book" had a rhythm of its own: start the day with our own internal package of overnight intelligence in the Counterterrorist Center, everything from breaking news overseas to reports from sources inside Al Qaeda to updates on what detainees at CIA's overseas detention facilities were saying. We then hosted our internal staff meeting, during which senior analytic managers, all of whom had grown up as analysts themselves, came to the conference room to discuss whether there were breaking events we needed to cover or more strategic issues we thought merited consideration by the government's most senior decisionmakers. And since the analysis changed quickly on breaking events, we might not see a final version of a PDB piece until midnight or later. It was common to suggest in the morning that we cover one angle on a story, only to find later in the afternoon or evening that the story had already changed, and the focus of the analysis going to the president had to change accordingly.

Pattie and I switched off PDB review duty, week on, week off, heading upstairs after our internal morning management meeting to participate in the broader conversation among all senior analytic managers about planning the next morning's PDB package, a ritual among CIA senior analytic managers that has been going on for decades. Especially in the years after 9/11, we knew, every day, that we had to come to the table with interesting topics to present—there was an unwritten rule, and rightly so, that we would not publish a PDB during those years without saying something new about terrorism. Not just reportorial pieces arraying facts, but new ways of assessing the terrorism problem that was consuming all corners of the federal government. And after months and years went by, finding new and interesting ways to provide context to old problems we'd reviewed endlessly became an especially challenging proposition for us when we had a readership—including President George W. Bush, who was highly engaged in receiving our analysis and acting on it—who had heard it all. This was an evolving creative challenge: analysis wasn't just the profession of presenting what was going on, or what might happen, it was the art of finding perspectives that experienced readers might not have considered. When we, and they, thought we'd seen it all.

Other elements of this process also shared this pulsing, newsroom-like feel that was fed by the daily requirement to feed the beast, the PDB, and respond to questions from senior officials across Washington. Often, we would present a few sentences outlining a few new analytic articles early in the day, providing the lead concept and a quick synopsis at the Agency-wide analytic meeting held every day in the conference room of the Agency's senior analytic team. With that initial roundtable among all the Agency's senior managers, the roster of daily items that would eventually be distilled for the president's book could be assembled in its first rough form. Some terrorism articles didn't pass muster in the broader analytic meeting; Agency managers knew, collectively, that we had a responsibility to ensure that pieces unrelated to terrorism went in the PDB briefing, and a lot of ideas Pattie and I presented didn't pass muster. And despite the urgency of counterterrorism issues then, not all pieces required this type of quick, one-day turnaround: as in a newsroom, there was always a mix of daily events, such as a significant terror strike somewhere around the world that would require us to comment, but there were always more strategic, stand-back pieces, ranging from assessments of the state of global efforts against terrorist fundraising to appraisals of how different countries were performing against local terrorists.

After years of practice, this process remained a crapshoot. Despite all the attention frontline and mid-level management focused on the pieces analysts wrote, invariably, one or more of the daily articles would come up to Pattie and me requiring substantial work or, less often, in such rough condition that we "spiked" them, determining they were poorly written, lacked coherence, or simply were not of sufficient interest to be salvaged. We had a superb group of senior managers, though: day in and day out, over years, they came up with different stories to tell, different angles to explain. But when you're trying to tell a story for the hundredth time, with a new twist that you think will work, sometimes you come up empty. And we often did.

Helping an office grow in the midst of an exploding global conflict is not something that anyone is trained for, and it is not an environment that allows for a steady, staged rollout. We were no exception. Most of our office management, in the midst of this rapid expansion, had been stepped up at least one level in the management chain from their previous experience, including the head of the office, Pattie, and me. And while there was a small core in the office who had worked the terrorism problem for years, including some very talented Al Qaeda analysts, terrorism analysis before 9/11 had not been at the top of the list of sought-after assignments, and this initial core was stretched. Most new analysts came into the Agency as specialists in either a geographic part of the world or what we called a "functional" area, such as missile or nuclear analysis. Almost none joined as counterterrorism specialists, a corner of analysis that was not taught in universities, and those who did took years to build expertise. Far more often, analysts learned on the job, quickly: sifting through masses of data and rapidly applying the craft of analysis to a new problem they had never anticipated working on when they earned degrees in history, international affairs, the politics of foreign countries, or, like me, English literature. So we learned on the fly about the management challenge of leading and administering at higher levels of responsibility than we were accustomed to and about the substantive tangle of al-Qaeda, its leaders, and its plans and intentions.

Pattie led the office with a clear vision, a wealth of management expertise in our weakest areas, such as personnel and budgeting, and generally how to set up the organization. She also brought a more than generous spirit toward those of us under her who were learning on the job, sometimes painfully. We had, for example, the issue of dealing with many analysts who had signed on to the Agency because, after years of academic or language training on the outside, they wanted to spend a lifetime focused on their core area of expertise, a particular geographic region, for example, or a foreign weapons system. They were serious and committed specialists—years of building expertise reflected not only a professional interest but a passion. And they had not come anticipating an overnight shift to an Al Qaeda problem where they not only knew little but also felt, professionally, that their work would lack the depth we needed. They wanted to add value and, at that time, I am not certain how many of them knew how quickly they would become major contributors.

The vast majority took to the task with open-mindedness and an understanding of the magnitude of the problem the United States faced, and many grew to become experts in their new field, finding it rewarding, fast-paced, critically important, and fascinating. They were told early on that their service would be for a specified period of time (a year), and that they could return to their original positions afterward to apply the expertise that they had brought to the Agency as new hires. This was not simply a gesture to accommodate analysts: for those with language skills and overseas experience, shifting them away from the analytic areas they covered might lose the Agency training and experience that was irreplaceable. Over time, we could backfill them with new hires who brought area expertise.

But we needed lots of analysts, fast, to handle the rising flood of information, and the recruitment process for the new ones, with its background checks and polygraph, takes many months. Furthermore, the training and seasoning to progress from entry level to journeyman takes years, so there was no quick or easy fix for the requirement to assess the mountains of new intelligence, as the massive U.S. intelligence collection systems shifted from traditional targets to focus on terrorism and added critical data from partner services. For many months, we struggled to create an office that had the professional draw of working on the most crucial topic in the building and the kinds of management support any employee could expect: clarity in promotion processes, an experienced management cadre, and expertise that would surround a new analyst over years of development.

Almost all the analysts responded well to this environment, though they rightly asked, as months passed, that the office complement its growing efficiency in assessing terrorism with growth in its administrative backbone. We had a year to make an impression, after which many had the option to return to their home offices, and whether we could create an attractive enough work environment to avoid a massive exodus was a constant topic of conversation. As a new office, we had questions about morale, and whether the new analysts felt that the career they might build in this new subject area would eventually become as well structured as what they might find in more well-established offices. A bit surprisingly, though, in the end a large number of these post-9/11 transfers from within the Agency, a higher percentage than we could have hoped for, stayed.

I remember only one person who was removed from the job for cause, the only time in my recollection that I was involved in firing an employee. He had started to show signs of irrational behavior, including writing odd emails to the CIA director that caught the attention of the director's security staff, but the problem had, as far as I could tell, less to do with wartime pressures and more to do with the employee's personal and emotional problems. The new crew of analysts succeeded. Nonetheless, the fact that this was the only removal I remember is not, in my view, a positive: with such a large workforce, it goes without saying that some employees filter through who lack the skills for the job or are missing the emotional or mental capability to work well in large group environments. But the hoops managers have to jump through to remove employees in the federal government are so incredible that you would need an overwhelmingly compelling case to proceed with the process. Not to say that evaluations of employees leave no room to reward excellence—the best are promoted faster, and the weakest fall behind, in a promotion process that is quite competitive and serious—but firing problem employees was one of the clearer examples I remember of the frustration of working in a large government bureaucracy.

There were a few analysts who were talented, and had a place in the Agency's highly skilled analytic workforce, but who didn't do well in the new counterterrorism environment they joined. In this small minority, some were so deeply expert in their original areas that they felt their expertise was wasted on new subject matter where they could not contribute as much. Others did not handle the pressure well. A yet smaller number were just chronic complainers, and we released a few rather than allow their complaints to fester. Some, of course, were right: they were underutilized, as we tried to apportion assignments to fill gaps. Any organization will face personnel challenges in volatile times.

Meanwhile, I was making my own mistakes while learning management at this level—several hundred people in contrast to my previous experience of a few dozen—and Pattie wisely gave me the chance to stumble now and then. So I did. High among these errors, and irritatingly evident in retrospect, was agreeing to counsel too many problem employees who probably should have spent more time talking to their immediate management chain. This was not a case of opening a door to an employee who needed to talk; it reflected more a mistake of accepting too many appointments with employees who presumably thought they could get an easier hearing than they had received or thought they would receive at lower levels. Many of us were learning similar lessons on the fly. In a profession measured by how well we understood and could decipher for policymakers and senior CIA executives what was happening with Al Qaeda and in the greater counterterrorism campaign, it was a simple lesson: as new organizations grow, administrative structures and new managers learn the ropes, organizations struggle. But with Pattie's steady hand, we evolved. I remember mistakes but not profound errors.

⤳

MORE NOTICEABLE outside the office was the learning curve we struggled with to understand a global counterterrorism problem of great complexity, in the face of consumers across the U.S. government who demanded answers to a dizzying variety of questions on terrorist money flows, Al Qaeda leadership, the development of global terrorism cells inspired by Al Qaeda foreign capabilities against Al Qaeda targets, Al Qaeda intent and capability regarding weapons of mass destruction (WMD) pre- and post-9/11 invasion, and other subjects too numerous to list. Most prominent in this learning curve, early on, was management of the deluge of tactical threat information that flooded into Washington—from CIA, National Security Agency technical eavesdropping, FBI domestic leads, Defense Department intelligence. The threat matrix was created as a tool to provide a tactical snapshot of the threats that flowed in every day, from people calling an FBI office to report suspicious activity to intercepted phone calls from terror cells overseas. Mixed it was, and is, representing a healthy dose of the trivia of terrorism. Poison pen letters, for example: disgruntled employees falsely claiming a coworker is a terrorist, or spurned lovers attempting to retaliate against an old girlfriend by anonymously fingering her new boyfriend as a terrorist plotter. Or, harder to weed out, sources who think they can improve their standing and salary by claiming they've heard of a new threat, from an individual they won't identify. Also thrown in were the highest-end threats, serious, solid information from credible sources or hard leads from foreign services who might be following individuals with known linkages to Al Qaeda. In between were some of the most difficult threats, amorphous comments about the next "big one"—a major attack—or references to the next strike from sources with proven access but lacking enough specificity to allow for helpful analysis or action.

The matrix laid out a chart summarizing these threats in spreadsheet form, listing sources, the threats themselves, and follow-up as experts from around the U.S. intelligence community gathered multiple times daily, in a classified videoconference session, to discuss how to handle individual threats. Some could be discarded quickly. Poison pen letters, for example, often quickly lead to a perpetrator who thinks he's anonymous only to realize that he's been identified in less than 48 hours and, now faces federal charges for leading the feds on a wild goose chase. One example: go ask someone referenced in a letter—say, the girlfriend of an individual named as a dangerous "terrorist"—

the simple question who might harbor enough of a grudge against her to finger her new boyfriend. Presto, threat resolved: my old boyfriend, she'd say. He has a temper problem.

Other threats, though, might persist for months, such as a threat "thread" or "stream"—a series of connected intelligence reports—that a human source spins out over time until his credibility is discounted. Or a snippet provided from a valid source who continues to prove trustworthy but who has only episodic access to threat information. He might accurately report what he hears, but his limited access later proves to represent only rumors from training camps that are circulating widely among potential recruits but do not represent fact. Or a reference to an unnamed operative sent to the West for an unidentified mission, with almost no identifying information, a lead that might never be resolved.

The collective response to these threats by intelligence agencies in Washington has grown much more efficient since 9/11. Handoffs of threats between agencies, sharing with state and local officials, more rapid capability to weed out below-threshold nonsense—the process is increasingly streamlined. After years of video coordination and thousands of threat leads, this is one of the untold stories of the campaign against terrorism: the transition from the harried days of threat matrix management a decade ago to the standard policies and procedures of today.

This relatively smooth operation was not always so. Early on, keeping track of the volume of threats alone was a challenge, along with coordinating follow-up among agencies to see how quickly we could resolve threats, either determining that they were valid or learning enough to remove them from the list. Not to mention ensuring that agencies shared what they knew efficiently, quickly balancing the need to protect sensitive sources that could easily lose access with any exposure with the need to ensure that those who need to know—from Washington to the West Coast—receive the intelligence. Despite the constant media leaks that might give ammunition to the few remaining intelligence officers who were reluctant to share, this shift from the mantra "need-to-know"—restrict information carefully, even too carefully, in other words—to "need-to-share" happened quickly. Bureaucracies evolve their hard-wired cultures in ways that are hard, or impossible, to break, but the transition from "need-to-know" to "need-to-share" was one of the fastest, and most remarkable, transitions of bureaucratic culture I ever saw. It happened almost overnight: no one wanted to sit on threat information that another agency might find valuable.

The matrix process also required follow-up, tracking efforts not only to check good leads, and determine who had what across Washington, but to wash out bad information and to notify agencies when a threat came off the list so that those agencies with responsibilities to put in place defensive measures didn't have to respond to threats that were no longer valid. In instances far too frequent to mention, a source was fabricating what he had heard, a fragment was misheard, or a reference that appeared to be threatening turned out to be benign. The threat matrix, in other words, was a matrix of threats, fabrications, half-truths, vague warnings, and spurned poison-pen lovers, all packaged so that the agencies responsible could systematize the separation of the limited bits of wheat from the massive loads of chaff.

To add another set of eyes to the process, we required at least one senior executive to review the matrix every evening, including weekends, to try to ask every question we could think of before someone up the line, or at an outside agency, asked to try to avoid missing anything. CIA executives, and their counterparts at other agencies across town, reviewed the matrix to nail down even minor details and follow-up, in the days and months before procedures were as well oiled as they are today. Every day, we handled questions such as whether foreign countries that might be affected by the threat had been advised. Whether all relevant agencies in Washington had been informed. Whether a broader warning, outside U.S. government circles and out to the general public, was warranted. Whether private sector entities—or, in rarer cases, individuals—needed a specific warning. And whether incoming threat information might affect the newly established color-coded threat warning system. This system died with some derision and almost without a whimper in 2011, but when it was established, every move in the color code meant high-level meetings around town, large Congressional briefings for members who would go home for the weekend and answer questions from constituents, and endless media inquiries.

The matrix was part of what became not only a tradition inside the Agency but a well-known element of the Washington war on terror outside: the 5 p.m. counterterrorism meeting every weekday evening chaired by CIA director

George Tenet. What we called "the 5 o'clock" included players from around the Agency, everyone from the director and his deputy, John McLaughlin, to the Agency's lawyer and public affairs adviser, representatives from the military, FBI, and other Washington agencies who were on loan to CIA, senior executives from the Agency's 7th floor executive corridor, and a cast from the Counterterrorist Center.

The meeting was often referred to as the "small group," a phrase that we often mocked because the number of people in the room regularly would surpass 30, some standing around the paneled walls of the director's conference room for meetings that often lasted an hour or more. Many viewed this meeting as a necessity: it was not just a session that updated the director, it was both a one-stop-shopping place to keep on top of the wide range of activities underway in the Center—everything from the conduct of the war with special forces in Afghanistan to updates on partnerships and operations with sister services to details about the next takedown of a terrorist we had been tracking. It was a decisionmaking meeting. Frequently, we would bring up an operational or analytic problem that sparked a discussion at the table, and the director or others would make a decision on the spot based on the discussion. Whether to call a foreign leader. Whether the president might need to see a particular piece of information. What to do about a new leak. How we should characterize new information about what Al Qaeda was up to.

Despite the number of people in the room, Tenet encouraged participation and conversation—this was not a formal exercise intended only to report to him. We "prebriefed" the meeting every day in the Counterterrorist Center before we went upstairs, but only for a few minutes, and then mostly to ensure that we would offer solutions to the director if we handed him a silver platter of problems. We also gathered beforehand so that we could ensure no surprises, to guarantee at least quick coordination for a Center that was already so large, and occasionally so fragmented, that leaders of different entities might not have spoken about a common problem before they walked into that prebrief. Often, one component would be prepared to raise an item linked to another component, in what was a remarkably free flow of ideas for the director, when the second component wasn't aware that the issue was even up for discussion that night. Not bad to have free flow and even disagreement at the table, even with the CIA director present; not good to have poorly prepared disagreements that resulted from lack of conversation or coordination.

Behind the scenes, Tenet's mercurial nature was legendary. Aggressive, Mediterranean in his passion for the business and in the way he attacked problems and dealt with people, he was a larger-than-life boss. He motivated us with vigor and intensity, and he was so oriented toward people that he knew most of us by name and by our strengths and weaknesses. This didn't always play to his advantage—some staff felt sidelined when his wide circle did not embrace them as personally as they saw others brought into the circle. But partly by force of personality, he brought morale back to an organization that had suffered under his predecessor.

John McLaughlin, the deputy director and then acting director, usually saw the President every morning during the week, and often on weekends, when the President was in town or at Camp David. They joined in presenting to the President the PDB, the summary of events around the world that we thought the President should know about or act on. These issues might range from weapons proliferation in Iran to economic crisis in Asia to drug trafficking in Latin America. And, of course, in the post-9/11 environment, terrorism and counterterrorism, the two issues that dominated what we called his morning "book," the PDB.

Director Tenet also regularly took along various staff from the Counterterrorist Center to participate in the White House briefings, to provide background and analysis on issues that required more back-and-forth or were not suited to the limited confines of a standard written PDB article. Senior operational executives, for example, went along for the briefings in the months after 9/11 to explain how the Agency was teaming up with the Northern Alliance in Afghanistan and to chart progress in the war. I went on a few of these trips with Tenet, always interested in how the president looked at the intelligence and surprised at how comfortable he appeared to be with Tenet. And, more than once, surprised that he asked my opinion. In one humorous exchange, at a briefing in the West Wing's Situation Room, or "Sitroom," we were providing a briefing on an issue to Bush and a circle of advisers when the president looked down the small briefing table, asking "What do you think?" Director Tenet began to respond, but the president cut him off. "No, George, him," he said, looking at me. The drive in the director's

SUV back to CIA headquarters allowed for a few good-natured barbs for a director who never minded letting us have our say in front of a president who was far more engaged, in my extremely limited exposure to him, than many media reports suggested. The director didn't mind us speaking up; he encouraged it.

Vice President Dick Cheney also had a keen interest in intelligence, and CIA staff members also occasionally traveled to his residence, at the leafy campus of the Naval Observatory in northwest Washington, to brief him. I remember sitting on the broad porch of the Observatory one sunny morning, waiting to speak with him about a significant operation we had run on a day he was taking his standard morning intelligence briefing at the residence. The operation I was to talk about involved playing a video, so I brought a laptop with the feed loaded and ready to go. As usual, the vice president's attention was fixed on the intelligence. We had preloaded two different versions of the video feed. Later I couldn't be thankful enough about the preparation we had done to ensure we had a backup. It was a most unpleasant feeling standing in the vice president's house, hitting the "play" button, and finding that the first version of the video wouldn't run. A few moments crept by with painful slowness; thankfully, preparation paid off, and the backup went off without a hitch.

Many of us who had been around the intelligence more than a few years knew, even then, that the access we enjoyed to present intelligence at the highest levels of government might never be seen again in our lifetimes. There had been jokes, years before, about the CIA's lack of access to the Oval Office, always one of the measures, among CIA employees trained to think of the president as their top consumer, of whether the Agency's standing is rising or falling. The president and his advisers had been avid intelligence consumers before 9/11, but after the attacks it became second nature to assume that if we needed help on something—pressure on a foreign leader, a serious Congressional problem, decisions about whether there would be public warnings stemming from threats to the Homeland—the president or the vice president typically would be willing and more than ready to help, and we'd have access to ask for this kind of help nearly every day.

Those PDB meetings, then, were not just information sessions. If we had a foreign leader who was proving particularly difficult on a high-level issue, for example, "the book" might feature a piece explaining the story so that the director could go on to address what we might do to solve the problem. The analysis in the PDB was purposefly designed to avoid giving the president the answers or prejudicing the discussion one way or another—in the intelligence world, analysts try to separate analysis from decisionmaking to ensure that the intelligence is not colored by their view of what the outcome should be. The PDB analyses framed issues, so the director or another policymaker could follow with a menu of options for the president, who could then make on-the-spot decisions with the policy advisers in the room with him.

Not infrequently, we received rapid responses from the Oval Office, in a rapid-fire war, within 24 hours. This is remarkable in a government operating in the most powerful city in the world with one of the world's largest federal bureaucracies. So the evening sessions might cover what we should write for the president in the morning; what operational updates we should prepare; how we might approach a difficult foreign security service or political leader; or how we should coordinate with a partner agency in Washington on an issue that would require the director's intervention.

The PDB briefings were presented by an analyst, typically a senior officer often from the Senior Intelligence Service—the CIA equivalent of a General Officer in the military—who was selected in a highly competitive process for what was viewed among analysts as one of the service's most prized positions. When the president traveled, this briefer and a secure communications package traveled with the presidential party, receiving the daily briefing via fax and filtering responses and questions back to headquarters for immediate follow-up. So we had a clear, daily sense on the masses of analysis we were passing to the Oval Office, about what worked well and what did not, and we could stay on top of the ever-changing list of topics that were on the president's agenda, crafting PDB articles that would help put his priorities into context with intelligence. We also paid attention to his calendar, trying to add items before travel, for example, that might match the countries he was visiting.

All of us at CIA headquarters reacted far too sensitively to those daily ups and downs—a presidential dismissal of an article was cause for extended conversations, some useful, many not. A number of us also knew, however, that this incessant focus on a few key consumers was not entirely healthy: what if the president was just having a bad day? And what about balancing this focus on the most senior officials with more attention to whether working-level officials felt well-served? But in the rapidly moving intelligence world, this daily feedback from the Oval Office was crucial. If intelligence helps a consumer understand a problem well enough to make a reasoned policy-making decision, then understanding the policy problems the top consumer was facing, particularly in a world as fast-moving as counterterrorism early in the decade, was essential. Furthermore, this access was a morale boost: any intelligence officer who can't get interested in coming to work in the morning when the country's leader is reading intelligence with that kind of voraciousness is just not in the right job.

↬

OFTEN THE material for the morning presidential briefings grew out of the previous evening's 5 o'clock sessions, where breaking items we presented to Director Tenet often led to analytic discussions about what the intelligence meant, and how we should write PDB articles to best capture what we thought would help policymakers understand what we were seeing. In these situations, Tenet let analysts say what they thought. Yet he also, by virtue of his constant access to the White House, obviously had a clear sense of what questions we might need to "tee up," as he would say, and how we could be helpful, to maintain the conversation's focus on priorities that might be important to the president. So we would regularly spend a part of the evening 5 o'clock kicking around how to tee up a problem appropriately: we would typically have just one page for a complex problem, so explaining complexity with nuance when the answer was derived from various intelligence bits was an art form.

Tenet's deputy, John McLaughlin, was a great help during this process, and one of the most impressive analysts and leaders I witnessed during more than two decades watching some of the best. Precise in language, incisive in breaking down analytic problems, and always courteous almost to a fault, many professionals viewed him as the ultimate analyst's analyst. We would often sit in the 5 o'clock, in the midst of some muddled conversation, and he would unscrew his fountain pen, write a few notes, and talk through with us how we might think about the problem. On the spot, he'd break down a problem into its components, explaining back to us what we had just said with simple clarity. Without ever once seeming supercilious, or distant, he was invariably right. And the director, recognizing a superior intellect when he saw one, almost invariably listened and deferred.

Helpfully, for planning purposes, these evening sessions were not entirely random (though the director, when a critical issue emerged, might encourage cross-table conversation that looked random, much to the chagrin of a few in the room). The sessions had a standard pattern. We started with the threat matrix and moved onto updates on the war in Afghanistan; global operations against al Qaeda; WMD-related issues; and terror finance analysis and operations. Each briefer would step quickly through key points during the short prebriefs we had every night. This was not a universally successful model. CIA is an agile organization with extremely talented professionals. But the flipside of this agility is that the Agency is an unwieldy bureaucracy. Its structure is relatively flat, with responsibility devolving down the food chain. So officers regularly said things to the director that had never cropped up in the prebrief. We did not try to prevent bad news from reaching him, but we were frustrated when the conversation would spin off in an unanticipated direction, wasting time.

These random conversations around the table often turned a bit chaotic. We didn't mind raising difficult questions at the meeting—that was, after all, part of the purpose of bringing us all together—but a rule of thumb in these situations was that you don't raise a problem without at least attempting to offer a solution or two. And we didn't always succeed on the latter. So periodically, after a particularly messy conversation, one of the 7th floor executives—Steve Kappes, for example, then the second-in-charge of operations—would pull me aside for a few short, clear comments. A former marine who was well known in the Agency for instilling discipline in an otherwise often undisciplined organization, his remarks were always on the mark after a particularly confused briefing: "Professor Mudd," he would begin, "we won't be having that happen again, will we?" Always looking for the nearest exit in these situations, my response was invariably "No, sir." And then exit, quickly. Invariably, a few of us would then return to our offices and discuss how to avoid future such mishaps. Despite attempts to abide by the "no problem without a solution" rule, and the "if you're going to raise a problem at the 5 o'clock, please mention it during the prebrief" rule, we never succeeded.

Director Tenet enjoyed this: he liked the give-and-take, and he liked to know what debates were stirring. We didn't. To this day, he still reminds me.

Tasks coming out of the meeting were common. The work they entailed was not a downside—there wasn't a lot of useless memo-writing in this fast-moving environment—but they were painful, especially as the months and years passed and some of our senior managers, especially those with young children, stayed in position. Countless were the Friday evenings when, heading into the second hour of a particularly drawn out 5 o'clock meeting (they were usually relatively short), we knew we had a problem that would require coverage in the morning's presidential brief. The gold standard for intelligence is acquiring and analyzing that which is significant enough to merit the attention of the most senior policymakers in government. The hundredth time that happens, though, the luster of access to the Oval Office loses a bit of shine. As the months, and then years, wore on, we grew tired, though the analysts and operators maintained a far sharper edge for far longer than I would ever have imagined when I first returned in January 2002.

Tenet and McLaughlin were far from the only players who intervened during those sessions. We also had regular comments from one of the legendary characters at the Agency during that period, the CIA's executive director, or ExDir, as he was known, roughly equivalent to a corporate chief operating officer. A. B. (Buzzy) Krongard was serving in the position then, a one-time investment banker recruited to join us by Tenet in an effort to add rigor to CIA's business practices. Buzzy was always direct and to the point, not to mention colorful, taking a step back from problems and bringing an outsider's ability to cut through bureaucratic answers that might make sense to long-timers inside the building but not to anyone coming in fresh from the outside. He reveled in the outsider's role, though he clearly also found the intelligence business fascinating, and he respected those of us who were long-time staff. Buzzy had no problem, in the midst of some now-forgotten debate, telling the director exactly what he felt. "Why the hell would we do that," he'd say, or "That doesn't make any sense." He spoke with a bluntness that forced us to consider his perspective. In any organization, having people with different perspectives, who have the experience and authority to toss a grenade on the table now and then, is critically important. It happened all the time at the CIA leadership table, and I witnessed director Robert Mueller, when I moved to the FBI years later, recruit people who played similar roles in his leadership team meetings.

My boss Pattie and I rotated the 5 o'clock briefing duty for the matrix, a responsibility that was later assumed by the National Counterterrorism Center (NCTC), the interagency entity charged with analyzing terrorism and threat information from all Washington agencies and presenting a consolidated analytic product. In the early days, though, there was no National Counterterrorism Center. Pattie and I were in the chair, week on, week off. So if Pattie had the nightly threat briefing, I had the review of whatever articles we might be presenting in the PDB the following morning.

Like the process to review the matrix, the nightly PDB review ordeal was not as simple or smooth as it might sound. An analytic item would be proposed and accepted by us and the 7th floor analytic leadership that had oversight over all global issues. An analyst then would complete a draft, understanding that the initial draft would often bear little resemblance to the final product after many layers of editorial changes. Managers through that chain would review the item carefully, and an independent staff of editors would comb it. Only then did Agency seniors review it, turning it over to the briefer and the director for presentation in the Oval Office and to other senior consumers around town. The president and advisers would then read it (or not) and respond, and the cycle would start again, every day.

This is the textbook version, but it never quite worked as the books said it should. Broad "think" pieces that did not require quick turnaround might follow a process vaguely similar to this, with analysts taking days or weeks in painstaking preparation that allowed for careful research and an editing process that transpired during daylight hours. But because terrorism stories developed so quickly, multiple times a week we would have articles begin emerging overnight, or through the day, that required a quick-turnaround analysis, even on issues that were notable enough to require considerable thought. Just as frequently, we faced requests from senior policymakers in downtown Washington that required rapid responses, either because the questions were time-sensitive or simply because the unwritten service tradition of Agency analysis mandates quick, quality turnaround.

The Agency-installed secure faxes and secure phones many of us had in our homes were the bane of existence for a CIA analytic manager. They allowed for late-night review from analysts who might stay past midnight to finish a piece and read off on the editorial changes. The printing and graphics standard for the book was, and is, very high. Production required us to put the book to bed, for the printers, by about 2 a.m. so that the printing plant could put together a clean, highly professional document. By that time, though, or even earlier, the intelligence briefers for the government's most senior officials would arrive so they could review what they would present later that morning at Defense, State, the White House, DHS, FBI, and elsewhere. And because some of the analytic pieces were complex, an analyst or two responsible for drafting the analysis might come in during those early hours to "brief the briefers," to explain the articles to the staff fanning out across town for the morning briefing of senior policymakers, who knew their customers well and who often could anticipate what might be asked.

The secure faxes were either a godsend or a nightmare, mostly the latter. They allowed those of us in management review to head home before the analytic piece was completed—all pieces went through many layers of review, as much for style and clarity as for substance—but they also meant that pieces often were not finished until 11 p.m. or midnight. If you could reach the senior manager responsible for review by fax, why bother to finish the article during regular work hours? So, more times than anyone could remember, the phone would ring with notification that a piece was ready. Those of us reviewing would switch on the at-home fax, the piece would (if the equipment worked, which was alarmingly hit-or-miss) appear, and a few words, maybe a few sentences, would be changed. Done. Night over. I remember countless times when a much-anticipated piece, prepared in anticipation of an Oval Office conversation the following morning, would arrive warm off the fax. And sighs of relief when the piece was in good shape, requiring little or no intervention.

Not so fast. Also common, and a recurring nightmare, was the piece appearing in rough shape, missing the key point, with a lead that wasn't supported in the body of the article, or taking a direction markedly different from what we'd agreed on 15 hours earlier. This would lead to quick questions from the late night senior reviewer. Is the article salvageable now, when we have maybe an hour or so to work on it? How time-sensitive is it—does it have to be in the PDB book tomorrow morning? Is someone expecting it? Does it reflect a breaking event about which we will be expected to comment in the morning, an issue that will be stale if we wait a day? If it wasn't especially time sensitive, the obvious answer would be to scuttle it until morning. Frequently, though, we did two hours' worth of triage between roughly 11 p.m. and 1 a.m., on a secure phone, with an analyst or editor sitting at Langley and one of us on the other end of the line, trying to figure out whether investment banking would be a better career option. The night editors were old pros, though, and we succeeded on these wayward articles more often than not.

Almost as frequent as these nightly debacles were weekend calls from those watching global events from the CIA's 24-hour watch centers. A bomb would go off in some far-flung part of the world, and immediately the Operations Center—we had one for the CIA generally and a separate one within the Counterterrorist Center, dedicated only to counterterrorism operations and analysis—would light up phone lines all over Washington. So the news would go down the chain, to an analyst or group of analysts who would come in, research, write the story, and prepare something for CIA officials and downtown policymakers. Weekend phone calls to analysts, often people with kids and weekend responsibilities, were among the most unpleasant parts of the job, especially as the years passed and the pace remained high. But it is a tribute to a dedicated workforce that there weren't any complaints, at least that I remember. The echoes of 9/11 resounded for years. The people staffing the Counterterrorist Center didn't forget, not always because they wouldn't, but maybe because they couldn't. There is no more compelling motivator than memories of lost lives.

~

THANKFULLY, OUR mission for the matrix was more straightforward than all the additional analytic work that went into studying Al Qaeda. The matrix offered a synopsis of the threats that had rolled in that day, or significant threats from previous days or weeks that required steady follow-up, but it did not require the kind of accompanying analysis that chewed up so much time. The matrix fueled the multiple daily interagency conversations about what follow-up was underway: everything from when we might meet a source again to ask for further information to whether we had coordinated with foreign security services, other Washington agencies, or other entities across the United States. If there was a threat to Los Angeles, for example, the director would routinely ask us, with the FBI representative in the room, how we should pass the threat information. The exchanges we had were infused with Director Tenet's energetic, colorful, often agitated personality: he pressed us on how quickly we could share information, and he bristled when he sensed that the answers were clouded by bureaucratic barriers. If we had some issue related to sharing sensitive information, he had a standard response I still remember: "Get it done." So we did.

We had a small team of people who dedicated themselves only to staffing the matrix. Adding items frequently during the day, following up to ensure that raw information was properly disseminated among Washington agencies, outside the Washington beltway, and overseas. Tracking progress in resolving threats and trying to figure out a better way to do the matrix business. At that time, for example, we tried to be careful about prioritizing threats: if we weighed one threat too heavily over another, the argument went, would that mean that threats judged lower priority would fall off the table? Over time, with the experience we built on looking at individual threats, these analysts also became more proficient at writing about trends in threat information. This meant not just processing individual threat reports, but studying the ebbs and flows, the types of threats that were emerging, and other interesting commentaries to help educate what was a new threat industry in Washington.

Though this sounds illogical years later—after all, with the number of threats flowing in, we had to prioritize attention and resources—it made sense then. If you had told someone on the street the day before 9/11 that planes would crash into the World Trade Center towers, taking them down, you'd have been viewed as a bit crazed, at the least. Later, this inability to piece together Al Qaeda's grandiose plot was characterized by outside critics as a "failure of imagination." So we wanted to be careful about the assumptions we made, about too quickly assigning a low priority to a threat before we could adequately understand it. Our concern was, in the wake of the 9/11 surprise, downgrading threats just because we thought they might be too far-fetched. The matrix has come a long way since then—it is simply a fact of life that, even with significant resources dedicated to hunting down threats, some receive higher priority than others—and interagency processes today are much smoother and the matrix more sophisticated. But the early days were messy.

The challenge of dealing with threat information was complicated by the high-level attention it received, including from the president. Washington has many predictable elements, one of which is that if the president is interested in something, the number and range of people who then themselves become interested expands rapidly. And so the senior-level focus on the matrix intensified, to levels we had not anticipated. After all, this wasn't simply a compilation of the best information we had; it was simply meant to be a rough tracking document to help those who met by secure videoconference every day keep track of what was flowing in, what hadn't been tracked down, and what we could strike off the list.

To that end, included on the spreadsheet was everything from unvetted walk-ins around the world—people who simply walked into an Embassy, for example, and volunteered information—to nuts who wrote into U.S. government websites to second-rate sources who made up tales to earn a paycheck. All this was read by the president, in a document intended initially to serve as a working-level draft. What was initially a simple, almost inevitable way of tracking threats—it had to be done somewhere—became a means by which senior policymakers reviewed raw material that many of us, myself included, thought was "below threshold" for them, or "BT." BT, in our world, wasn't meant to suggest that these policymakers were too unsophisticated for the arcane world of intelligence. It was simply a judgment that much of the material in the matrix was trash, and the people who had started reading it were looking at material not worth their time. But they saw it differently, and the matrix took on a life and legend of its own, a profile we never ceased to find either amusing or downright irritating, depending on the day.

This threshold was far more art than science. The science was pretty straightforward: if there's a major breaking event, or trend, where intelligence brings value, write about it. And, generally, don't shy away from putting stories in front of a senior policymaker that are sometimes either irritating or fringe, but focus largely on the core areas of what that policymaker needs to know.

The art, though, was much harder to get at. Retelling an audience with years of experience reading PDBs—and with many independent sources of information outside what we knew—the current trends in the world of terror financing was tough. It wasn't the challenge of writing the story; it was the art of finding angles that both served the policymaker well and offered a different angle, something new, and sometimes, because of a manager's good idea or an analyst's sudden insight, just coming up with an interesting story that hadn't been told before. Many observers compared what we did to editing a city newspaper: you might have to write, for the hundredth time, the story of city council corruption, but figure out how to write it well, with attention to detail and a line of march that matches the facts as you know them. And, meanwhile, tell it differently.

I often thought during those days that the deluge of daily threats, and the relentless counterterror campaign itself, would blunt the edge of the Center. Reflecting back, it now seems that the immediacy of the attacks, and the daily reminders of how many had been murdered, drove the staff. So did the clear sense that the different components in the Center—operators in Afghanistan, CIA offices overseas dealing with foreign security services, and analysts trying to piece together mountains of data—all had a clear and significant role in this new war. The agility of the Agency, the lack of space and time between planning or analysis and action, also motivated employees. A decision one day could easily lead to a field operation the next. Rather than writing long, drawn out strategic reports, an analyst following a particular terrorist might be able to sort through a lead and cable the field a day later, requesting action against the target that might take place immediately. If you want a motivated workforce, you can make up for an office with a slowly developing support structure as long as you can add this level of immediate satisfaction on highly critical counterterrorism operations.

As we grew on the analytic side of the Center, I often asked analysts about morale, how they were doing, what they thought of life in the Center, their work, their management. Hoping that the answer would be "I love it here because the quality of management is so strong," the answer instead, every single time, was uniform: "I feel close to the core mission of the Agency, and I feel I can make a difference." I am still smiling today, waiting for the word that perhaps one analyst stayed on because of the quality of the work environment. It never happened (and I mean never), but maybe it's for the better. Managers come and go. Morale driven by a fast-moving mission against a lethal adversary stays. To this day, the Center has an edge that should have dulled years ago but never did. Some of the people involved in chasing down bin Laden, and in collecting and collating the intelligence that is helping dismantle the Al Qaeda leadership in the tribal areas of Pakistan, are the same as those who were in the hunt when I left for the FBI, in 2005.

⤶

PERHAPS ONE reason the focus remained so sharp is that the threat was so real and persistent. Despite our unwillingness to quickly downgrade what would initially appear to be a low-grade threat, anyone in the business for any amount of time could quickly discern those that would immediately raise alarm bells. Looking back, a few of the threat streams we handled stand out, in terms of the quality and credibility of the information and, occasionally, the specificity. The two characteristics, quality and specificity, often do not go hand-in-hand: a proven human source who has episodic contact with Al Qaeda members might be able to listen to a vague conversation that lacks enough clarity for U.S. agencies to take specific action. But his position might not allow him to probe. The quality of the information, and its credibility, is high; the specificity is frustratingly lacking, limiting the ability of operators and analysts to take action.

We often knew something was brewing in Al Qaeda circles, but equally often we didn't know exactly what. And we had to be wary of quality information that was nonetheless purposefully misleading: senior or mid-level Al Qaeda members talking broadly about impending operations might seem ominous, but these comments might also simply reflect the idle boasts of operatives who might want to persuade nervous subordinates that the organization was thriving when it wasn't. A longtime quality source reports that serious Al Qaeda members, above his pay grade, are talking about the next big one, coming soon. The source is credible, and he is reporting accurately what he heard. But is it right? No, he's just reporting what he's been told, by superiors who don't want his morale to flag. The world of threat analysis became as much art as science.

Some of the most significant threat information, that first year after 9/11, came from the first major takedown of the Al Qaeda leadership, Abu Zubaydah. This was our first opportunity to talk face-to-face with an Al Qaeda player, after the attacks, about what operational planners in the organization might be conspiring to do. As with many of the plots we later deal with, working on threat streams then was like peeling back an onion, or, in this case, multiple onions at once.

We had known of Zubaydah's prominence for some time. So did leaders at the most senior levels of government in Washington. It's not every day that the town can hold a secret, but the steadily increasing drumbeat of the hunt for Zubaydah was a secret that held, allowing the net around him to slowly close. Little did he know how much briefing time he took up, as his days of freedom came to an end. Because he had been the subject of so much microscopic scrutiny at senior levels, the first night after his takedown, we knew we had to think through what to write for the president's morning book, and how to balance a major success with the knowledge that this was only one brick in the Al Qaeda wall that would take years to bring down.

We also knew we would have a testy customer in the form of Tenet, who was every bit an analyst himself and who read closely what we wrote. Like other senior policymakers in Washington, he had his own CIA briefer, who was in the SUV every morning with a pile of material, from press clips to secret phone intercepts, when Tenet was picked up from his home for the drive into Langley. And it was not uncommon for the briefer to return from his morning session with our mercurial boss and report a highly negative reaction to a piece we'd labored over, sometimes for days. Oh well—it's all part of the business. We were paid to put out thoughtful material on a wide range of issues, every day. The occasional irritability from a Mediterranean boss who didn't think the analysis was right wasn't a good enough reason to lose composure. It wasn't uncommon. And it came with the turf. If you only received positive feedback, you'd start to believe that you weren't getting the truth. He had an aggressive mind, he followed the substance carefully, and he liked to engage with analysts. Furthermore, he had been in the seat so long that he had the capability to offer perspectives on how a storyline might work best with the senior audiences reading our material. And he knew some of the foreign players well enough to offer views on how to understand them.

Our first struggles to offer clear analysis of the impact of Zubaydah's takedown were not entirely successful, and what we wrote for the next morning turned into one of those times when the director was extremely unhappy.

He wasn't always right—sometimes, it seemed, he just got up on the wrong side of the bed—but he was probably on the mark this time. We were clear in saying who we thought Zubaydah was, what he might know, and which directions he might take us in. But we were not experienced, at the time of this first takedown, in trying to explain what the loss of a single senior individual in a serious, deeply committed organization might mean. I will never forget huddling that evening with analysts, after Zubaydah went down and we received the first draft of a PDB piece that was fuzzy, knowing that it would be a long one. One of the core questions any analyst faces, in the midst of mounds of data, speculation, gaps—and customers who are intensely interested—is how to make sense of an event or trend so that those who have to deal with the problem have a better understanding of what they face, and a better chance of making a good decision. Proliferation. Political stability. Terrorism. All, at their core, raise the same questions for analysts: When something happens, what does it mean? What do we know about what's happening? What do we not know? What do we think? After a lot of time telling the downtown audience we were closing in, we now couldn't figure out how to offer the right balance in the next chapter of the story. He's gone. What does his exit from the scene mean for the group? Characterizing who he was simply wasn't good enough; everyone knew already.

What we were struggling with, in retrospect, was the satisfaction of watching the first in a series of operational successes that would heavily damage Al Qaeda's leadership ranks over years. A few single leaders were so significant that their takedown alone meant a significant step back for Al Qaeda. Khalid Shaykh Mohammed, architect of 9/11, was one. It was hard to replace those earlier operational leaders of Al Qaeda, those who had long experience, great respect in the organization, and, sometimes, rare and highly valued experience living in the West. But aside from those unique cases, what damaged the group most was not the takedown of one or another but the steady erosion of the entire leadership cadre, over years and at a pace Al Qaeda couldn't match. No organization could weather that kind of succession crisis.

We did not know then that we would see such steady takedowns of senior Al Qaeda players, and we could not characterize the first tactical success as either insignificant or as a strategic breakthrough—Zubaydah was just one player, though a big one. In the end, no one was happy with what we put together that night; it was either too optimistic in portraying Zubaydah's role or too pessimistic in downplaying his takedown. As it turned out, the real story did come later, in the steady erosion of Al Qaeda's leadership ranks. There were no leaders with the experience in terrorism and history with the group to follow the terrorists who were captured or died in the first years after 9/11. Those who did follow were killed or captured themselves—the constant news drumbeat of "another Al Qaeda number three gone"—at a pace too rapid for the group to compensate. The strategic plotting against Western targets remained an Al Qaeda priority, but repeated leadership losses disrupted plotting. We couldn't think of Al Qaeda as a simple, Western-style hierarchical organization with top leadership and lower-level commanders. Instead, it was more like an interwoven fabric. Most of the takedowns were unnoticed by the press or the American public. But taken together, each of these seemingly slim threads frayed the organization, and it is now tearing apart, steadily. Al Qaeda leaders could not prepare for the rapid exit of so many of their long-time members, and the decimation by drone strikes of their cadre today, along with that of associated fighters in Pakistan, is destroying the organization.

In addition to the degradation of Al Qaeda's leadership ranks, the capture of key Al Qaeda figures became an invaluable source of knowledge about the group. Many observers, viewing these captures from the outside, may suspect that what we learned related to grandiose plots, or well-advanced plans to take down more major targets. And we did learn about threats. Zubaydah talked in 2002, for example, about threats to U.S. banks. But despite the explosiveness of threat information in a world where we still anticipated another strike any day, threat reporting was not always the most important thing detainees discussed—helping us understand key players, both organizers and foot soldiers we had not yet identified, was a critical facet of debriefings. Clearly, one of the first lines of questioning would always center on imminent threat: whether there was attack plotting that would reach fruition soon. But it was the nitty gritty details, below threshold for the media, that made these detainees into intelligence treasure troves.

Senior detainees like Zubaydah routinely engaged in general conversations about what they knew, information lacking names, dates, or other specific detail. And we had a responsibility to send the information out to

other agencies, inside and outside Washington, so that others who had defensive responsibilities in the United States, or who might be able to match
Zubaydah's comments with other information, could analyze and potentially
act. We might have learned bits and pieces of information from other sources,
snippets we could not fully understand. Zubaydah, and detainees afterward,
might be able to offer other pieces. We could view no single source or bit of
information, especially with the mountains of data we were absorbing, in
isolation.

In this sense, questions about the criticality of any single detainee, telephone intercept, or foreign security report lost relevance. We didn't look at
single reports: we looked at the universe of what we knew and matched it
with what else we knew. We built beaches out of bits of sand; typically, no
source would or could provide the entire beach. For example, senior detainees involved in training might reveal bits and pieces of seemingly innocuous
background about Westerners they had trained, even years before, at Al Qaeda
training camps in Afghanistan. The art of tactical intelligence, in those cases,
might be to take this additional intelligence—possibly even the fragment of
a name—and match it with other bits and pieces. Over time, the value we
found was not in the grand plotting revealed; it was in the tactical details
that might help put together a painstakingly assembled puzzle that could lead
to the identification of plotters. The first debriefings might inevitably result
in overdramatic, embellished threat reporting that we felt obligated to disseminate, but it was the tiny details later that brought the most value. Some
of this I came to know as a new specialty that grew partly from the explosion of data and sophisticated network analysis software in the intelligence
world: identity intelligence. The art of starting with a fragment of a name
or an identity—"Larry the American"—and arraying vast amounts of data
to piece together who this might be. In an intelligence game where hunting
people is a primary responsibility, the age of data is allowing this art form
to explode, and the evolution of identity intelligence has become one of the
most critical side-effects of the counterterror campaign.

The Zubaydah debriefings also drove home, for the thousandth time, the
impossibility of keeping a lid on sensitive reporting. In most intelligence, a
security service validates the source before disseminating the intelligence to
the broader intelligence and policy communities. In understanding the prob-

lem of how a foreign government is selling nuclear technology, for example, human and technical sources go through layers of validation, possibly over years. Terrorism source reporting is different: because threats might be imminent, the mantra in disseminating intelligence reporting about terrorism is that threat information should be sent to other agencies immediately, with the view that those who have the responsibility to provide security might not have time to wait for full validation of the source. The same held true for Zubaydah's information: we couldn't wait to piece together everything we knew, and to continue exploring down every alley of inquiry, before we let people know that we had received pieces of threat information.

Almost as quickly as we published this information, the reports would leak, leading to myriad challenges for us. Before we had a clear picture, the public, for good reason, wanted clarity. And the media had great headlines that might affect public safety. How could they hold a story that was so consequential? For us, every leak led to a flood of media inquiries we had to handle, balancing the need to protect intelligence we thought was sensitive— the identity of an individual we might be hunting down, for example—with the fact that the information had already leaked, that the public had a right to know, and that we did not want bad information floating around, feeding a cycle of rumors that might eventually reach other branches of government, especially Capitol Hill. We knew that releasing reports immediately, and without context, would lead to completely uninformed commentary, but we also knew that holding back would lead to some unsanctioned leak somewhere that would still find us answering questions. And with the focus on the threat matrix, when we had information that might affect whether we escalated from "yellow" to "orange," how to explain the escalation to an American public glued to the screen of 24/7 news coverage without saying something about why the level was shifted?

For us, though, over time, detainee reporting became one of the most critical tools we had. Classic intelligence collection includes human source reporting, intercepted communications, reports from foreign sources, open-source information (newspapers, journals), technical information (data emanations from missiles, for example), and photographs from orbiting satellites. There was little question for us that the information provided by detainees grew in importance to take a place among the top sources we had. As the group of detainees expanded, we could take information from one and match it with information from another. And as our databanks from other sources grew, we could cross-compare this information with a rich database of additional material.

On the surface and in isolation, some of the information we collected might be viewed as minutiae, bits of data collected for their own sake. This judgment misses the crux of the intelligence work we did: the fragment of a name from a training camp years ago, matched with other data, might yield the beginnings of an identification of that individual. In the world of intelligence, this is gold. And in the world of counterterrorism, where the identification and location of individuals is the coin of the realm, detainees provided gold we could not get elsewhere. Plots are sexy; they grab headlines. But stopping plots without stopping plotters eventually will lead to failure: the plotters are persistent, and they have proved they will never go home. Stopping plots is a good mitigating measure in counterterrorism work. Stopping plotters is the gold standard.

The threat information we received also fed into the regular raising and lowering of threat levels we witnessed after the Department of Homeland Security went to the color-coded system of grading threats. From the inside, it was easy to see why the system existed and why the threat levels fluctuated. The government needed to find a simple way to advise people who were worried about terrorism but lacked the knowledge and experience we had to put in context the seriousness of what we saw. And the general jumpiness of the nation after 2001 forced us to act even we had information that was not fully developed.

Almost by definition, this new threat warning system required us to take action at times when we had only limited insights into plotting, sometimes frustratingly fuzzy. This even as the general public, perhaps because the simple step of moving up on the color code suggested clarity, got the sense that what we knew was much greater. We could not reveal what we knew or didn't know, though, because much of what we received might be single-source—that is, from only one reporting source. So revealing the nuances of our knowledge to help the public understand would also, in some cases, have pointed almost directly to how we had acquired the information. Today, with hindsight, if you were to go back and assess the science behind raising and lowering plots, you would quickly be overcome by the frustration of seeing gray information quickly become perceived as black-and-white. This was a new world, without clear rules.

One of our first priorities in dealing with detainees and working with the threat matrix involved chasing WMD threat reporting. Many worried, and still do, particularly about the threat of weapons of mass destruction falling into the hands of Al Qaeda. We had received reports of this, including a number suggesting that scam artists were trying to sell materials such as a fictitious "red mercury" substance. None of us had doubts that Al Qaeda would use such a weapon; they had said as much. But the question was whether they had acquired a weapon or dispersed WMD material. Whether they were still attempting to acquire material, perhaps through contacts in the former Soviet Union with access to nuclear material that could be used in a dirty bomb. Or whether specialists who had once worked on the program might be able to reconstitute it someplace else, developing either a panic device or something more deadly, such as the Aum Shinrikyo plot in Japan.

The picture that slowly emerged in the years after 9/11 showed a group that had been bent on acquiring WMD capability, especially in the biological area but also in nuclear and chemical arenas, before Al Qaeda expulsion from Afghanistan in 2001–2002. For those who regard this type of plotting as more in the realm of fiction than fact, what we saw would have convinced any skeptic that Al Qaeda, had it maintained the room to experiment in an Afghan safehaven, would have moved inexorably toward WMD capability. Rudimentary, perhaps, but the kind of capability that would have transfixed the West in a way that conventional attacks could not.

The biggest concern was anthrax, and the work Al Qaeda had done at facilities in Afghanistan. There was no question that anthrax-related research had occurred at Al Qaeda facilities, along with research on other poisons. On-the-ground site exploitation of those facilities by experts showed evidence of the research program, another of the examples of Al Qaeda infrastructure that did not survive Al Qaeda's strategic blunder of 9/11. The intelligence work, over time, focused on whether samples of that material had survived and where fleeing scientists had ended up.

The disruption of WMD plotting was one of the most significant, and immediate, aftereffects of the invasion of Afghanistan and subsequent efforts against key Al Qaeda players in the Afghanistan-Pakistan border region. Key revelations after the invasion, particularly the anthrax program, confirmed the group's commitment to WMD. And the loose threads in these threats remained troubling for years, particularly questions about whether loose samples had been smuggled out of labs before the invasion, or whether scientists or technicians who had worked on Al Qaeda's WMD effort had found other locations, and other labs, at which to continue their work. The invasion of Afghanistan, in addition to severely damaging Al Qaeda's ability to plan and stage another mass-casualty conventional attack on the order of 9/11—another strike at a transit hub, for example—eliminated the relative freedom Al Qaeda had there to conduct the basic research and development that might eventually have resulted in an anthrax attack. To this day, I believe that this lack of safehaven, the loss of time and space to work on WMD, has been among the most significant factors in keeping America safe from terrorist WMD.

Worth noting is the difference, or lack thereof, of the development of a catastrophic capability that could be dispersed via aircraft and a more rudimentary dispersal option that would require far less technology and expertise without sacrificing much in terms of effect. Much of the plotting we discussed, as time went on, focused on less sophisticated devices, such as a basic dispersal device that could have released a lethal chemical cocktail in a small, enclosed space, such as a subway car. We knew Al Qaeda was interested in these kinds of devices—we had picked up the basics of one, known as the "Mubtakar"—and we saw limited efforts to use unconventional materials, such as videos of testing on dogs.

The reasons for the focus on these less sophisticated devices were simple. Obviously, more research-driven, complicated plots would require time and operational space to piece together, and Al Qaeda plotters no longer had the luxury of the relative peace of pre-9/11 Afghanistan to conduct research for any extended period of time without worrying about military raids. Second, and as significant, Al Qaeda would need recruits with some rudimentary technical skills to carry out such attacks, and the group simply did not have an influx of people who were easy fits for a complicated WMD plot. Time and again, from failed backpack bombs in London in July 2005 to the problems potential New York City bomber Najibullah Zazi encountered trying to construct a bomb to the unexploded vehicle in New York's Times Square, would-be terrorists, even those who received training in Pakistan by bomb-making specialists, have constructed faulty devices. Part of the reason, one former Al Qaeda trainer told us when he was detained after 9/11, was that the quality of recruits, at least during his time, was often not high: some of them, simply put, just weren't that smart. Good for the trenches of Afghanistan, but not for working on nuclear dispersal devices in Manhattan.

The group also had clear nuclear ambitions, evidenced by its efforts to reach out to nuclear scientists and scammers alike. While there always have been stories about terrorists' acquisition of "suitcase" nuclear devices, sourced to the former Soviet Union and rumored to be available through mafia contacts in former Soviet states, of far more concern were contacts with sympathetic scientists across the border in Pakistan. Partly fueled by the rise in Islamic radicalism in Pakistan during recent decades, the country's scientific cadre and lower-ranking officers included people who supported Al Qaeda's goals and tactics, and the group was fully prepared to try to acquire their knowledge. Again, absent disruption of the Al Qaeda infrastructure in Afghanistan, we might have witnessed the first terrorist acquisition of a nuclear capability. A functioning device would have been highly unlikely—more movie script than reality—but the ability to disperse nuclear material in a panic scenario is entirely within the realm of the probable.

Despite these higher-end efforts by Al Qaeda to acquire a WMD capability, I came to believe that that the most significant, and probable, WMD threat we might face in the future would be a relatively unsophisticated weapon designed to cause panic, not mass casualties. Not to say that these concerns are insignificant—the economic and social damage of even a panic WMD device or material in a major urban center would be massive. But compared to acquisition of, for example, a large-scale capability to disperse anthrax across a broad area, panic attacks would result in far fewer casualties.

The reasons for the panic attack scenario are simple. First, the group lost its freedom to experiment in relative safety when it lost its Afghan safehaven, and many of its leading technical experts were either captured or killed in the years following Al Qaeda's post-9/11 flight. Unlike conventional attacks, the planning and execution of a WMD strike involves not only the training and placement of operatives into the target country with access to explosive material, but also expertise, experimentation time, weaponization, and transport of volatile materials. In other words, a technically unsophisticated high-school graduate might be able to execute a horrific backpack bomb in a crowded area; operating alone, though, he wouldn't be able to get close to a high-end WMD strike. Design, development, dispersal—all these require a level of expertise, along with the time and secure space to conduct the WMD program without constant disruptions, that everyday Al Qaeda recruits lack, and they have proved their limitations time and again with failures to properly prepare and detonate conventional devices.

The same does not hold true for simpler panic weapons, and we have seen modest efforts by Al Qaeda to focus on them. For example, simple chemical devices—an emptied, modified paint can with a simple feature that would allow combining two chemicals into a deadly mix—would require less than sophisticated operatives, and placement of one or a few such devices on a transit system during morning rush hour might not lead to mass casualties. But it would lead to mass panic, and possibly economic damage that would far outstrip the actual impact of the attack itself. Similarly, dispersal of low-grade nuclear material from medical waste might also have limited impact in terms of casualties. Nonetheless, the economic impact, if such material were spread around high-profile economic targets, would be substantial.

The almost forgotten attack by the Japanese extremists Aum Shinrikyo offers an example of the potential damage from lower-grade WMD strikes, and remembering this attack underscores the prospect that we could, and almost certainly will, see such a strike again. The ease with which a group could develop and deploy such a simple device, and the proliferation of groups that have an interest in creating mayhem, combine to explain why many experts would agree that this kind of attack is likely, and certainly far higher up the chain of probability than a sophisticated nuclear or biological event.

Because of the potentially devastating impact of a WMD event, the approach counterterrorism specialists took to attack this problem looked different from what an intelligence professional would take to other difficult challenges. We applied the 1 percent rule: if information has even a small, even tiny, prospect of credibility, it had to be pursued, leading to a dedication of resources that was, on the surface, disproportionate. Typically, chasing intelligence that has such significant credibility gaps would not be pursued with as much vigor, and manpower, as low-credibility WMD threats. Pursuing every angle of every problem with that low standard of credibility would require manpower resources that no security service—no government—would or could dedicate. But WMD was different; other intelligence disciplines might limit themselves to the pursuit of small fires, but WMD pursued wisps of smoke. And WMD specialists, themselves a breed apart, relished the pursuit.

The differences between traditional counterterrorism work and WMD work often caused friction in the Counterterrorist Center. Managers working more conventional problems sometimes saw the WMD managers and analysts as crying wolf too often and writing analysis that hyped reports based on information of questionable credibility. The operational side suffered from the same problem, with personnel who had rotated in from field offices overseas, or other headquarters units, viewing the WMD operational component in the Counterterrorist Center as an overwrought group of scaremongers who practiced looser "tradecraft"—that is, lower standards of professionalism or attention to the basics of intelligence operations and analysis—than more traditional intelligence collectors and analysts.

Our good fortune was to have an energized group of WMD pursuers who did just what they were criticized for: applying the 1 percent rule, they chased leads that would otherwise have been left on the cutting room floor. They knew full well that their jobs depended on applying different principles, more aggressive pursuit of seemingly weak leads despite operating in a Center where some would have argued that they could have used the personnel chasing those leads to work on much higher credibility threats. But we couldn't afford to fail on WMD, something Director Tenet pressed us on constantly, and the dedication of resources then still makes sense ten years later, despite the lack of a significant WMD attack.

Furthermore, the leadership of the WMD effort, and the analysts and operators who worked under them, relished their pursuit, perhaps partly because of the sense that they were a breed apart. And they had some of the best talent in the business running the program, both analysts and operators, who maintained the spirit of the chase and the morale of the unit. Chief among them was Rolf Mowatt-Larssen, who helped build the WMD operational capability we had and who never shied away from a battle with others in the

Agency who saw the battle he and others were waging as wildly overdone. Rolf was occasionally difficult to deal with—he was unpredictable, and he regularly dropped surprises in the nightly 5 o'clock meetings with Director Tenet that had us all scratching our heads. But he built the program beautifully, with just the right "us vs. the world" sense that we needed on a pursuit that was so often fruitless that it needed passionate leadership. Similarly driven were the leaders of the counterpart analytic program on WMD, seemingly unfazed by either the pursuit of endless ghost leads or the derision from other groups focused on clearer leads. Without this kind of leadership, the program would have floundered. Instead, it flourished.

These analytic managers Rolf worked with, side-by-side, were highly talented as well, some of the best we had. They worked as long as anyone, early in the campaign, pursuing stories—some of them, in retrospect, not only credible but representing real threats—without missing a beat for months and then years on end. I cannot remember how many times they walked into the office, even after an already long day, and announced that we had some disaster or another on our hands. And then went and worked on it, through a night or a weekend. Testimony to what they built was the commitment of highly qualified analysts, many with advanced scientific degrees, who grew attached to a program that was so often frustrating.

CHAPTER 3

THE SPREADING THREAT: MOVING BEYOND
THE CORE OF AL QAEDA

SITTING ON the inside, these were difficult years, trying to grapple with where this onslaught of violence would end. Years later, looking back, it is easy to see that this adversary could not win. The senseless violence, the nihilistic ideology, the murder of local innocents would almost inevitably turn the tide of Muslim public opinion. These all conspired against Al Qaeda, to the point where few pay attention to leadership pronouncements today, in contrast to the global attention to the bin Laden and Zawahiri statements featured on al-Jazeera in the first years after 9/11.

The seeds of this self-destruction were sown in the rise of violent Islamists during the early and mid-1990s. Today, men seeking to join the jihadist fight travel to South Asia—and, until a few years ago, Iraq—from the Al Qaeda heartlands of Egypt and North Africa. A generation earlier, these jihadists' predecessors traveled from these same areas to fight the Soviet soldiers who had invaded Afghanistan. These Arab brigades, including those under the Al Qaeda banner, did not have a significant role in the brutal battle that bled Soviet forces until they withdrew. But the men who fought gained experience, and their commitment to the fight, to changing the world by overthrowing what they saw as corrupt and un-Islamic regimes in their home countries, led them to organize and mount violent opposition movements during the 1990s, particularly in Algeria and Egypt.

In both cases, they were working on fertile ground. Algeria had canceled elections in 1992 as Islamists were poised to surge to victory. In the absence of a political outlet for their frustrations, more extreme Algerians turned to violence and revolution. As lethal as they were, the government response was brutal, and the terror and counterterror that characterized Algeria during those years left, by many estimates, more than 150,000 dead. Some of those at the heart of the revolution were returnees from Afghanistan, using their credentials as seasoned commanders and their experience on a battlefield with a conventionally superior foe to organize. They failed, however, murdering so many fellow Algerians that they lost credibility.

In Egypt, too, returnees from the war against the Soviets in Afghanistan helped spark an Islamist revolt that left many civilians dead and resulted in an attack in 1997 on tourists in the ancient city of Luxor, an event that captured global attention and spurred a security response that eventually devastated the Islamist movement. The violent extremists at the heart of this movement—including Ayman al-Zawahiri, who merged his Egyptian group with Al Qaeda and eventually became Osama bin Laden's number two—had their roots in the Islamists who had been imprisoned and tortured by Egyptian security forces after the assassination of president Anwar Sadat in 1981. This time around, in the mid-1990s, they made the same mistake as their ideological colleagues in Algeria: they killed too many Egyptian civilians, and alienated the pool from which they needed support and recruits.

These earlier miscalculations of violent extremists presaged what was to happen after the Al Qaeda bow wave of 2001, but it didn't look that way to me in the first years after the 9/11 attacks. Instead, the picture, as I saw it, was a striking and broad spread of revolutionary activity, from North Africa and Europe through the Middle East and South Asia and into Southeast Asia and the Philippines—all representing the geographic spread of a national caliphate, the golden age that represented the spread of Islam at its height, centuries ago. It was a past that Al Qaeda openly talked about reclaiming.

We were gaining against the Al Qaeda base in Pakistan and Afghanistan, evidenced by the success in ousting the group from Afghanistan and taking out leaders from Pakistan. But in parallel to this steady, intense fight that was taking place as Al Qaeda's core membership began to put down roots in the tribal belt along the Afghanistan-Pakistan border, terrorist attacks in this other areas, states that are part of the vision of a restored caliphate, gained momentum in the years after 9/11. The pace of attacks by these affiliates in those early years led me to feel, for years, that we were facing a phenomenon that might come from any direction, at any time. Attacks and attempts against synagogues, aircraft, oil facilities, diplomatic and military installations, transportation hubs, ships—it seemed as if not a month went by without another attempt. Meanwhile, the geographic spread of these attacks meant that our operational and analytic efforts had to be correspondingly diverse, with serious terrorist activity spreading through North Africa and Europe through East Africa and Turkey and into the Middle East, South Asia, and Southeast Asia. And, finally, the diversity of attacks meant that no single defense mechanism would be even close to effective, as Al Qaeda and its partners tried car bombs, backpack bombs, small weapons assaults, shoulder-fired missiles, ship-borne explosives, and a return to aircraft take-downs. The breadth and diversity of attacks and plots underscored the point that the move into Afghanistan had come late in the revolution of violent Islamists: we didn't have just an Al Qaeda adversary to deal with, we had a metastasized collection of different local and regional groups that had already been infected with the Al Qaeda ideology.

These groups had connections with Al Qaeda that were closer then than they are now. The isolation of the core organization has limited its interaction with its followers; bin Laden and Ayman al-Zawahiri can make occasional video and audio statements, but the kind of operational linkages with their followers that developed after 9/11 is not possible in an environment where they fear that every exposure risks their lives. So these groups have taken more operational initiative on their own. In a sense, it was a success for Al Qaeda: the revolution that Al Qaeda leaders always designed the group to spark, a vast movement of likeminded believers who would conduct attacks on their own, had begun. The believers, in contrast to the 9/11 hijackers or the Al Qaeda cells that menaced the Arabian Peninsula in the early 2000s, took their ideological inspiration from Al Qaeda, but they had limited guidance from its leaders and operational commanders. Today, the most significant Al Qaeda affiliate, in Yemen, has even less contact with the core. The operational complications of communicating across long distances, when the Pakistan-based leadership is so embattled, has left the affiliates to interpret the ideology on their own, to plot attacks that they think match Al Qaeda goals without necessarily coordinating, or even consulting, with those who are at the heart of the organization.

The early impact of Al Qaeda on these regional and local affiliates was not a simple transmission of training, money, or operational sophistication. As military and intelligence operations degraded Al Qaeda's core leadership and the group grew more isolated from its followers, these groups nonetheless applied the ideological lessons they had learned from Al Qaeda. In the past, these groups might have hit local targets, as they did in the Egyptian and Algerian violence of the 1990s. The calculation was simple: the ruling regimes were viewed as corrupt and un-Islamic, and striking them would, in the eyes of the new generation of militants, lead to the inevitable decline and downfall of decadent rulers.

Meanwhile, Al Qaeda and its affiliates were changing, and the core Al Qaeda elements in Pakistan were not, by a long shot, the only terrorist adversary in the game. Watching the nightly 5 o'clock briefings with Director Tenet, talking to analysts in the office, and watching the worldwide attacks in the early part of the decade clearly indicated that the Al Qaeda organization we faced had won support from likeminded groups and individuals around the globe. We now see Al Qaeda crop up periodically in American news media as a terrorist group and a collection of planners and suicide bombers below bin Laden and Zawahiri who are bent on attacking airplanes, subways, oil facilities, military locations. We also see the group—or we used to—when one of its leading figures appears in an audio or video file, exhorting followers to attack, or advising them of Al Qaeda's views on global issues as diverse as Palestine, Darfur, or global warming.

These Al Qaeda attacks and the vague statements are not the real story. Revolutionary ideology is. Al Qaeda's intent behind these attacks is to spark a wave of affiliated organizations, or likeminded individuals who have never met an Al Qaeda member, to see that Western targets are vulnerable—that the United States and its allies are not supermen. The core of the revolution is straightforward: the world of Islam should be returned to a time when the only guide for law, culture, politics—civilization at large—stems from Islamic law, Islamic values. From this perspective, governments across the Islamic world are apostate regimes; they reject this simple view of Islamic order, and their leaders must be overthrown for Al Qaeda ideology to succeed. And for these governments to fall to a mass army of those who follow this ideology, the pillar of Western military, economic, and politic support must fall. Once we go, in this line of thinking, corrupt Middle Eastern regimes will follow. Attacks are a means to spark a revolution, not an end in themselves.

⟿

SOME OF the most significant manifestations of this nascent post-9/11 revolution boiled over in Southeast Asia, centered on the Jemaah Islamiyah (JI) organization in Indonesia, and in the heartland of the Al Qaeda ideology, the Arabian peninsula, where heightened Al Qaeda activity not only energized the global movement but also threatened oil markets. Indonesia has a long history of Islamic activism, going back decades. The violent inheritors of that history, JI, organized in the early 2000s the most organized, effective vanguard of the Al Qaeda revolution outside the Pakistan/Afghanistan region. The impact of Al Qaeda was not operational; instead, JI's absorption of the ideology of revolution, that attacks on the West could make local regimes more vulnerable to overthrow, took hold. And Western targets began to be hit—nightclubs in the tourist center of Bali, the Australian Embassy in Jakarta. Both represented Western influence that had to be expelled, like the attacks by distant affiliates against diplomatic targets in Saudi Arabia, or Iraq, or Algeria.

The strength of this movement in Southeast Asia lies partly in its long-standing ideological leadership, along with local political dynamics that made leaders wary of confronting JI and its strong organizational backbone head on. The group had spread roots into Malaysia, Singapore, and the Philippines, and its leaders were contacting Al Qaeda's top players in South Asia, drinking at the well of Al Qaeda ideology and, more tactically, talking about specific operations and sharing operatives. We are witnessing this even today, over the past few years, with the contacts between Al Qaeda-ists in North Africa and the new wave of Islamists in the Sahel, and the repeated trials of the ideological leader of Indonesian extremists, Abu Bakr Bashir. Most in the United States probably have forgotten the strikes that devastated Jakarta early in the 2000s, but Bashir was the inspiration behind those attacks. Years later, he was convicted and sentenced for helping to run a terrorist training camp in southern Indonesia. This example, of a deeply rooted ideology resulting in an eruption of violence that appears to subside but then emerges again, captures the gravity of the counterterror campaign. The ideology runs deep, particularly in cultures with Islamist roots, and a hiatus in attacks over five or ten years does not mean the death of the messengers of violence, or of the message.

Al Qaeda adherents on the Arabian peninsula also erupted early in the decade. The bombing in Aden harbor of the USS *Cole* in 2000 was a harbinger of what was to come. As other global elements of the Al Qaeda movement—as far west as Morocco and east to the southern Philippines—took on the spark of the revolution, the heartland exploded in Saudi Arabia, with deadly attacks convulsing the city in spring 2003. I remember these attacks, stretching over months in the heartland of Al Qaeda ideology. After 9/11, the events in Bali and Saudi Arabia, evidence that Al Qaeda affiliates were moving into the southern Philippines, plots broken in Morocco, the knowledge that 9/11 had been spawned in the intense Islamist atmosphere of Western Europe—it was easy to get the sense that the global post-9/11 campaign had started too late. With fingers in the dike one day, we'd find plotters or an explosion the next day, someplace else. I never remember a sense of panic. But there certainly wasn't a sense that we were winning, at that time, and the impact of the twin prongs of Al Qaeda's steady degradation in Pakistan and the negative response to the group's killings of Muslims elsewhere was not at all clear. There did not appear to be a light at the end of the tunnel in those years, not yet.

As these key affiliated groups attacked, other adherents, farther afield, also staged attacks: commuter trains in London and Madrid; synagogues and diplomatic sites in Turkey, Tunisia, the Netherlands, Jordan, Syria. The sense of the unknown in those early years was pervasive: Al Qaeda adherents would stage an attack in some part of the globe, revealing new cells, individuals, or contacts with the central Al Qaeda organization. And new questions, such as where the next attack would occur, or whether we had missed something related to what had just happened. There are far fewer surprises now, in a global terror campaign that has become a heavyweight grind, day in and day out, but with less of the sense of surprise and unknowing that characterized early rounds.

We were quickly expanding our analytic capability to understand the evolving Al Qaeda-ist movement—not the group itself, but the revolutionary movement of adherents who were appearing in cells worldwide—by dedicating analysts not only to the core Al Qaeda problem but to emerging trends from East and Southeast Asia through Europe and into North America. These hotbeds of activity not only proved to be increasingly important as years passed—the series of attacks and broken plots in Europe during the past few years alone, in countries that have visa-waiver policies that allow their citizens easy access to the United States—is a testament to this growing threat. But these centers of jihadist activity also proved to be one of the most heartening areas where more junior analysts could shine. The relatively small cadre of analysts looking at Jemaah Islamiyah, for example, was superb, able to follow detail and offer broader perspective that are the hallmarks of good analysis. And, during the early post-9/11 years, they were working on the group that posed the most serious Sunni terrorist threat to Western interests outside Al Qaeda, at least until security services decimated JI in a long series of take-downs that continues to this day.

These more junior analysts marked one of the more significant transitions in the management of the rapidly expanding counterterrorism program at CIA: from a small core of analysts prior to 9/11, the analytic workforce had grown to several hundred. Their experience on the problem was obviously limited when the surge came after the attacks, but working the terrorist threat all day, every day, quickly matured the analytic product we could provide. The bureaucratic backbone to support them slowly developed. In one of the most telling examples of both CIA's commitment to invest in growing quality analysts and the evolution of analysis from mostly deskbound officers to savvier, more field-experienced analysts who could deal with both Washington policymakers and CIA field officers, we expanded overseas, including in locations that were emerging but not yet core to the terrorism problem. These were investments, designed not just to further the day-to-day work of the Agency in the field, including work with security service partners worldwide, but also to give analysts experience with terrorist adversaries up close and personal, and to give them an on-the-ground understanding of how intelligence was developed and what its strengths and weaknesses were. We started investing for the long term, in an analytic workforce, not just a group of loaned analysts from across the Agency who would one day leave counterterrorism and return to their home offices.

In particular, the sense that another catastrophic attack—a 9/11-style event that could result in the deaths of thousands—has, for many of us who watched this problem for years, become significantly less likely, or even improbable, compared to what we saw a decade ago. Even a few years after 9/11, we still had questions about whether the central core of the group could mount a follow-on spectacular, and they attempted to do just that, with plotting in Europe and North America. It was useful to remember what is known as the "Bojinka" plot, the effort to take down airliners in Asia several years before 9/11. That plot, which included some of the architects of 9/11 as planners, was disrupted, but the group resuscitated the identical concept years later in New York, Washington, and Pennsylvania, and the leadership's patience and perseverance led us to understand that a few years between attacks didn't mean that another spectacular event was out of the question. It was useful to remember, in the domestic sphere, the Oklahoma City bomber, Timothy McVeigh, who with limited resources and no infrastructure to speak of brought about the tragedy that was the federal building bombing. For all the criticism that some of the broken plots post-9/11 have been terrorist wannabes—low-level unsophisticated amateurs who don't merit the time and attention they are getting—one moment remembering the background of McVeigh is enough of a lesson: they're only amateur wannabes until they hatch a plot that results in mass murder. Then they're the murderous plotters who were missed.

Interestingly, I do not remember bin Laden and his deputy Ayman al-Zawahiri dominating our thoughts as the terrorist threat spread. They slipped into and out of our terrorism reporting and our counterterrorism consciousness, and we always had a dedicated program looking for them. But there was always a difference between the core mission of the post-9/11 CIA and the hunt for the two key leaders: those most involved in the immediate plots directed at U.S. shores were operational commanders, such as Khalid Shaykh Mohammed, just one step below bin Laden. It is clear from the data collected at bin Laden's compound in Abbottabad that he had, and retained, a key role in leading the organization ideologically and pressing for specific plots, including those directed at the United States. But the more critical cogs in the effort to stop another catastrophic event were closer to the plotters and the tactical training, logistics, and planning that went into the threats we saw. This is not to say that bin Laden's downfall will not feature as a major chapter in years to come of the downfall of the Al Qaeda-ist movement. It is, though, to draw a clear distinction between leadership and execution: he did not execute the training and tactical planning that went into attacks, as far as I could tell. We went after those who did, with successes starting in 2001 that gutted the group's leadership.

Simple in concept, the execution of this grand plan failed when attempted. Brutal regime responses gutted the new Islamists, who had lost popular support as a result of civilian massacres that even now tarnish the movement. But Al Qaeda's strategy of attacking the far enemy—striking the United States and its allies—took hold. Following the 9/11 attacks, global jihadists across North America and Europe and into North Africa, the Middle East, and South and Southeast Asia added Western targets to their earlier, more local target sets. Algerians targeted not just police but UN offices and oil companies, Indonesians attacked the Australian Embassy and nightclubs in Bali, and, more recently, the Yemeni offshoot of Al Qaeda targeted cargo aircraft and a civilian airliner over Detroit.

The setbacks of the central Al Qaeda leadership in the Pakistan-Afghanistan border region in no way eliminated the threat it posed, and still poses, to the West, including Western Europe, the United States, and Canada. The first years of the morning threat briefings included regular hints that the organization would take any opportunity to send trainees back into Europe or North America; only the combination of eliminating their safehaven in Afghanistan, pursuing them relentlessly in Pakistan, working with partners to disrupt or dismantle them in affiliated cells worldwide, hardening borders, and chasing every threat lead in the United States prevented more deaths here. Often, the question of how we avoided another attack comes up when commentators, the media, and government officials review the years since 9/11. The answer is not easily packaged in a simple sentence or two. The multilayered responses developed post-9/11, inefficient and expensive as they are, combined to keep an aggressive, persistent, and smart adversary away from our shores. Not forever, most likely, but the relatively limited problems we have had, in contrast to expectations in the immediate aftermath of the 2001 attacks, is not attributable to any single solution.

These threats from the central organization appeared most consistently in those early years, and more often than plots from affiliates or the newer phenomenon, likeminded youth in America who believe the Al Qaeda message. Not to say that the threat matrix is less challenging now; the threats simply have devolved to more local cells or individuals, with fewer plots showing a direct line back to Al Qaeda trainers, facilitators, and leaders in the tribal areas along the Pakistan-Afghanistan border. Clearly, the main reasons for this change center on the painful intelligence, military, diplomatic, law enforcement, and local efforts to push Al Qaeda out of Afghanistan—its fighters are still there, but not the kinds of training camps we saw pre-9/11—and to eliminate Al Qaeda leadership in Pakistan's tribal belt, particularly North and South Waziristan.

Reflecting back on the years of the matrix, though, the evolution of threat, from a central organization to dispersed cells or individuals espousing an Al Qaeda-ist ideology, was clearly represented in matrix entries. Information suggesting a plot organized by Al Qaeda central was a regular feature in intelligence briefings, and such plotting took up substantial amounts of time, even when we received bits and pieces of information that, to an untrained eye, might be useless or untraceable. But more and more frequent were the one-off plotters, less capable of strategic threats but harder to track, who simply got the idea in their heads that they believed the Al Qaeda message and wanted to act on it. These plots were easier to dismantle once we found them. But the sheer frequency of uncovered plots illustrated the breadth of the problem. No oddsmaker would take the bet that plotters will never get through, perhaps with more devastating consequences than what we witnessed at the deadliest attack since 9/11, the Fort Hood shootings.

As key leadership figures filtered east into Pakistan—bin Laden, Zawahiri, 9/11 planner Khalid Shaykh Mohammed—others went west into Iran. What ensued was one of the more curious, but perhaps predictable stories of international political and intelligence hardball of the entire counterterror campaign. The Shia theocracy of Iran has long been harassed by Sunni oppositionists, some violent, and no doubt views Al Qaeda with suspicion. After all, Al Qaeda leadership has vilified the Shia, and the house arrest of the key leadership members in Iran in 2003 caused great friction between Tehran and Al Qaeda leaders, who could not draw on some of their most experienced, valued members as their leadership ranks in Pakistan were devastated by arrests and UAV operations. This has now changed: the rise of Sayf al-Adl to one of the top positions in the organization illustrates the seniority—and importance—of the detainees from Iran. Al-Adl has been a key player in Al Qaeda for years, and he was detained in Iran between 2003 and 2010.

⌁

THE SIMPLE fact was that the writings of some Al Qaeda strategists—some of whom advocated the rise of independent cells that could operate without a direct chain of command to Al Qaeda small core leadership—seemed to be playing out as cells globally appeared to attack without much interaction with the core. In these attacks, though, were the seeds of failure for a group that has no convincing explanation for why so many innocents have to die for a cause that is not clearly defined and certainly not close to reaching fruition. American commentators on national security have for years lamented the inability of the United States to execute a clear, long-term public diplomacy strategy on terrorism. We coordinate responses to threats and overt and covert military, intelligence, and law enforcement efforts overseas, but we cannot seem to get our arms around how to coordinate a coherent message that talks to the problem of those who use terrorism to further their aims.

The battle over how to handle messaging in the West is partly symptomatic of how democratic societies operate: the free flow of speech and ideas mean that corralling the disparate elements of government into one coherent narrative is difficult, perhaps even suspect. And unlike military operations, covert activities, more traditional diplomacy, and law enforcement, this type of public diplomacy lacks both the same history in government—with the possible exception of anti-Communist efforts decades ago—and a focal point in the bureaucracy who has stature at the National Security Council table. We often discussed this issue of "countermessaging"—how to answer the Al Qaeda ideological wave—at the same time we talked about going after Al Qaeda members, but no one ever successfully got their arms around this problem. It seems to me today that this was not, and is not, a critical problem, because Al Qaeda's actions have already undermined its message, irretrievably. But the challenge of fighting a war of messaging does underscore the challenges of the West in moving beyond what we know, how to fight people and groups, to a war that is so much subtler, the war for the minds of those who might be seduced by Al Qaeda's ideology.

To be clear, policing a coherent narrative would be difficult, if not nearly impossible: which entity could or would tell the legislative, executive, and judicial branches what they could or could not say? And what reaction would we face if, in the land of the First Amendment, we tried to muzzle the written views or speech of those who chose not to toe the line? Madison Avenue messaging, it seems, does not translate well to the government sphere. But opening up a clearer conversation about the direction of our message on terrorism makes eminent good sense. Short of charting a formal path on what we should say, I always thought that we should at the least have an understanding of what might be appropriate—and why—that is based on reasoned analysis and underpins what speechwriters and policymakers think about before they speak. Something between enforced uniformity and random responses seems a reasonable goal.

We might start with one premise: we should use language that shows respect for the tragedy of lives lost and avoids commentary that aids the adversary. Try to do good while doing no harm, in other words. Our goal, after all, is not simply to present what we believe; it is to do so in an environment where we face an adversary with a magnetic ideological message designed to recruit impressionable young minds and twist them into an acceptance of suicide bombings and indiscriminate murder. Far from castigating ourselves for performing poorly in this arena, we can accept two critical positives from the outset. First, that the adversary believes we are potent public diplomats and that our messages resonate, and they worry about what we say. And second, that the young minds we seek to speak to are wavering; we have an opportunity.

After years as an analyst, it seemed to me that this messaging campaign need not stem from our own ideology, that of democracy, choice, freedom, and the rule of law. Instead, we could simply look at the opportunities the adversary offers, because they have certainly, in their voluminous public communications, given us enough clues about what they fear. Given the vulnerabilities Al Qaeda and its sympathizers feel on the messaging front, coupled with the fact that what they fear matches our values, we should consider using their words as our starting point.

The result of those early fights that preceded Al Qaeda's rise, during the decade of the 1990s, was a jihadist legacy of increasingly bloody operations that left more than a hundred thousand dead in Algeria during the decade; a discredited movement in the Egyptian heartland of the ideology; a disaffected population that rejected the groups that sponsored the violence; and security forces motivated to crush the movement. In Egypt today, even once-violent groups reject the attacks they once sponsored, along with the Al Qaeda organization—and Ayman al-Zawahiri, Al Qaeda's second-in-command and once a key player among Egyptian extremists—that followed.

Indiscriminate violence—attacks that killed more Muslims than non-Muslims—followed the spread of Al Qaeda and its message during the past decade. The attacks of 9/11 revealed a reservoir of anti-U.S. sentiment across the Islamic world. It also revealed a mirroring crest in support for the group that captured this sentiment and stood up to the world's only superpower. But the years that followed left the same poisoned legacy for the group as the killings of the 1990s, including among the Muslim followers it needs as a recruitment pool and source of financing.

This unbroken history of killings spans virtually every country that serves as a potential Al Qaeda breeding ground. Extremists debated the advisability of the killings in Saudi Arabia, starting in May 2003, that resulted in local security forces gutting the cells in Al Qaeda's heartland within a few years, after a difficult fight. They were right to debate: the group resurrected itself in neighboring Yemen, which is now the self-declared "Al Qaeda of the Arabian Peninsula," or AQAP, partly because maintaining operational cells in Saudi Arabia became too difficult.

Similarly, Jordanians turned against Zarqawi's brand of Al Qaeda after hotel bombings in 2005 killed many local Muslims. Iraqi local councils stilled foreign fighter cells in neighboring Iraq after Zarqawi and his followers attempted to drive a national Islamist movement by massacring opponents. In Pakistan, as Al Qaeda and its Pakistani Taliban affiliates turned from a focus of attacks on Afghanistan, the Pakistani tribal areas, and the West to strikes inside Pakistan, security forces and politicians backed far more aggressive, lethal, and long-term operations to clear out militants.

Limited data from polling supports the contention that these attacks have undercut support for a group whose revolutionary message depends on public support among the same public now alienated by two decades of murder by militants. In Jordan, for example, Pew Research polling shows that support for suicide bombing as a tactic declined from 57 percent in 2005 (the year of the hotel bombings) to 20 percent in 2010. Confidence in Osama bin Laden also dropped precipitously, from 61 percent in 2005 to 14 percent in 2010. This is not to say that favorable opinions of the United States are high: in two key areas, Jordan and Egypt, respondents with a favorable opinion of the United States hovered around 20 percent, abysmally low and an indicator of why Al Qaeda had a potent recruitment message a decade ago.

Later, as Al Qaeda- and Taliban-linked suicide bombings hit Pakistani locations outside the tribal belt along the border with Afghanistan, public ratings of the groups dropped dramatically. In 2008–2009, those with favorable views of Al Qaeda dropped from 25 to 9 percent of respondents; those with favorable views of the Taliban from 27 to 10 percent. Unfavorable views rose even more markedly: from 34 to 61 percent regarding Al Qaeda, 33 to 70 percent regarding the Taliban. Perhaps not by coincidence, Pakistani army operations in the tribal areas stepped up, despite public perceptions that these operations reflected a bow toward American interests (and dollars).

It is not only broad popular opinion that has reacted against the spate of killings and the lack of solid justification for the loss of life among innocents. Two traditional centers of Islamic thought, Saudi Arabia and Egypt, have seen prominent Islamic experts, including clergy, speak out against Al Qaeda's tactics. In May 2010, the Saudi Council of Senior Ulema (clergy) issued a formal judgment condemning attacks and funding of terrorism as contrary to Islamic law, defining terrorism as "crime aimed at destabilizing security."

Earlier, in 2008, one of the key founders of the Egyptian Islamic Jihad, a group at the center of atrocities in Egypt during the 1990s, called armed operations wrong and counterproductive, and condemned attacks based on nationality or race. Sayyid Imam al-Sharif, often known as Dr. Fadl, also excoriated Al Qaeda for killing women and children. In the midst of supporting operations in Palestine and Afghanistan, he also referred to the 9/11 attacks as a catastrophe, denying justification for killings in the United States, Britain, and Spain. Notably, Dr. Fadl had once been at the heart of the same group that helped launch Zawahiri; the two are now ideological enemies, divided by Al Qaeda's specious arguments about the appropriateness of murder. This is no superficial quarrel: the Islamic Jihad in Egypt's most prominent attack came in 1997, when its murder of 62 people in the tourist center of Luxor sparked the kind of revulsion that is at the heart of Al Qaeda rejectionists, including Dr. Fadl. This debate about Al Qaeda tactics has been brewing for years.

Internally, members of the Al Qaeda group and the broader violent movement understand the vulnerability of their defending killing of innocents. Al Qaeda's fatwa in 1998 against the United States and other jihadi writings talk of a battle waged against invaders of Muslim lands; attacks against the "far enemy," civilians in distant countries, are not as legitimate a target. Nor are Muslims in the Islamic world, though Al Qaeda has created a theological argument for explaining away their deaths as well. The 1998 fatwa explicitly mentions the invasion of Muslim lands by Westerners, specifically mentioning forces in Saudi Arabia, for example. More than a decade later, and after the departure of U.S. forces from the kingdom, few among potential Al Qaeda adherents would dispute the righteousness of killing invaders on Muslim soil, as the fatwa argues. Many more would question taking the battle to distant locations.

Among the clearest indications that Al Qaeda's central leadership is concerned about this slip in support has come from the two top leaders themselves. Ayman al-Zawahiri, in an exchange posted by Al Qaeda on the Internet in 2008, took questions from an Internet audience and later posted replies. Notably, the first question he took, in the only Internet interview he has given, relates to civilian casualties among Muslims. In what he calls an "open meeting," Zawahiri opened the conversation with a question-and-answer concerning the "killing of innocents." The questioner, a geography teacher from Algeria, asks who is killing innocents in Baghdad, Morocco, and Algeria, and whether the killings of women and children can be considered jihad. Zawahiri denies that Al Qaeda has murdered innocents, claiming that such deaths are either "unintentional errors" or necessary when the enemy uses Muslims as "human shields."

Zawahiri returns to the theme in the second part of the published interview. The interview refers again to Algeria to argue that Al Qaeda cares about the "lives, property, and honor" of Algerians. He was reacting not only to the Internet questioner but to the earlier announcement that North African extremists, with the main Algerian militant group at the core, had taken the Al Qaeda banner and now called themselves "Al Qaeda of the Islamic Maghreb" (AQIM). Their absorption into the Al Qaeda global jihadist movement brought back bitter memories of the militants' killings of Algerians during the uprising of the early 1990s, a frenzy of violence that even militants viewed as having stained their movement. The leadership of Al Qaeda might have wanted the merger to cement their presence in North Africa, but the slowness of AQIM's accession suggests debates about the wisdom of affiliating with groups that would inevitably reopen old wounds about extremists alienating the very populations they need to recruit by murdering too many local civilians.

Zawahiri had earlier made clear his concerns about Al Qaeda killing Muslims to extremist leader Abu Musab al-Zarqawi during Zarqawi's leadership of the foreign Islamist violence in Iraq. In July 2005, in a letter that is now public, Zawahiri talked of the movement's goals in Iraq—expulsion of Americans and the creation of an Islamic emirate—but then counsels Zarqawi against actions that the "masses do not understand or approve," referring to attacks against Iraqi Shia, the majority of Iraq's population. And he later, and publicly, responded quickly to Dr. Fadl's allegations in 2007, another indicator of the seriousness with which Zawahiri takes these ideological attacks.

These perspectives on attitudes about Al Qaeda and its affiliates, along with suicide bombings, reflect opinion that might seem distant from the spate of plots uncovered in the United States since the late 2000s. But some reporting surrounding the U.S. plots in recent years suggests that this debate overseas has an impact on opinions in the United States. New Mexico-born Al Qaeda ideologue Anwar Awlaki, the cleric who inspired the Fort Hood attack, the December 25 airline bombing attempt, and the Times Square plotter, made significantly different statements after the Fort Hood and December 25 incidents. Within the movement, he is on solid ground after Fort Hood, which he justifies as an attack on a military target by a Muslim military officer. Military personnel, in this argument, are fair game because they are destined for deployment in Muslim lands.

Awlaki's statement after the December 25 airplot over Detroit—the attempted strike by the "underwear" bomber who had earlier met with Awlaki in Yemen—lacks this clarity. In an interview published by al-Jazeera in February 2010, Awlaki responds to a question about the difference between the Fort

Hood target and the December airliner attempt: "It would have been better if the plane was a military one or if it was a U.S. military target," he says, echoing other statements he made that attempt to justify attacks on American civilians by saying they are participants in the "crimes" of the U.S. government.

Faisal Shahzad, the Times Square plotter, was an Awlaki sympathizer who watched the preacher over the Internet. In a little-noticed quote, Shahzad suggested that he, too, was aware of this debate about the killing of innocents. After his arrest, he cited an "excuse that Islam does not allow innocent killings" as one of the concepts that might have argued against his attempt. He ultimately indicated that he saw no alternative to violence, but the fact that a plotter in Connecticut, connected to an ideologue in Yemen, was aware of this internal ideological debate suggests its prevalence in jihadist circles.

Other plotters have subtly underscored the difference between the legitimacy of the "near enemy," foreign forces fighting in Muslim lands, and the "far enemy," civilians in non-Muslim countries. As the homegrown phenomenon grew, five educated youths from Northern Virginia, conspiring without the knowledge of their friends, family, and community, traveled to Pakistan for training in 2009, claiming they intended to fight in Afghanistan, not return to the United States. Similarly, many Western European jihadists have been caught up and killed in battles with the "near enemy" in Iraq and Afghanistan, far more than have been captured returning to plots in Western Europe and North America.

Some of these internal debates in the jihadist community center on arcane religious points that do not lend themselves to commentary or intervention by Western governments. We in the West lack the legitimacy, knowledge, and nuance to enter these religious debates, and we should not waste our time and resources attempting to participate in theological disputes that are not ours and where we might do more harm than good. Commentary on twenty years of terrorist violence, though, is less fraught with peril: when we speak of the killing of innocents, we reflect not only values that are cross-cultural, we also play into the Achilles' heel of an adversary that has signaled this issue as a core concern. This campaign against terror has many years to run, and we will see more bloodshed, and more brutal moments when we are called on to comment publicly about what we think. After years of stewing about our response, one option is simple: we should, every time we speak, talk of the unacceptable tactic of murdering innocents. After the next attack, we should point to the loss of life among women and children, and the devastation families will suffer. Al Qaeda will respond, but with arguments that are stilted and increasingly disputed.

Analyzing Al Qaeda's messages also has given us clues about what we should avoid. For example, language that elevates this adversary to the level at which they wish to engage us, the level of military foes, is a mistake. They want to be timeless warriors, carrying on centuries of battle against a mighty adversary they believe they can vanquish. We should not offer them the luxury of calling them jihadists, or even terrorists. They commit murders for which they have no clear justification; we should simply call them murderers.

In addition to using straightforward language attacking a group whose ideology extols killings, we should consider enabling other countries that are themselves victims to do the same. In the wake of future attacks, messages that drive home the point that the indiscriminate nature of terrorism, which leaves children without parents, parents without children, is never defensible, and an ideology based on this concept is bound to failure. Not just because we say so, but because those who seek to further this idea feel vulnerability, and in their vulnerability is a key to public messaging. Enabling other countries to use public media to talk about loss of life, and destruction of families, should be one of our tactics, even when we support statements by individuals who are opposed to U.S. policies.

This simple approach has more far-reaching and debatable implications, however. This is no easy solution. First, we should consider that the families of suicide killers are themselves victims. In most cases, the parents of those families have lost a son, typically one who has gone down a path of extremism that the parents themselves were unaware of. We might consider reaching out to these families, expressing sympathy for parents who, along with us, often are repelled by the ideology that gripped a son to take his own life. We should offer them sympathy and share their revulsion. This approach is not foreign: citizens across America watched after a murderer killed young students at an Amish schoolhouse in 2006. The local Amish community's opening to the family of the killer attracted national attention. A member of a community living in Pennsylvania's Lancaster County commented: "I don't think there's anybody here that wants to do anything but forgive and not only reach out to those who have suffered a loss in that way but to reach out to the family of the man who committed these acts." This may sound soft, but my experience watching Al Qaeda taught me that they have no response to this type of approach. Their answers are long, difficult to follow, and defensive. They're telling us, in other words, that they have no answer.

There will no doubt be countless more commentaries on how to engage the vast capabilities of the United States in this war, relating to both the battlefields of terrorism and the battles for potential terrorists' minds. One starting point for the future might be consideration not just of what we think, but of what the adversary fears. Their fear is our opportunity. We will, in this long, painful campaign, have ample opportunity to turn that fear against them. And, perhaps, over the long term, accelerate their decline, and the decline of an ideology that depends on glorifying murder as an appropriate tool in war. It is not, and most among their potential followers know it.

Al Qaeda, because of its ideological underpinnings, will have difficulty escaping its legacy of attacks overseas that kill innocents. The group's strategists have written about the importance of focusing on the "far enemy," Western countries they see as the power behind the throne of Arab rulers. Focus on the far enemy, the strategy goes. And, sometimes consciously taking a page out of the writings of Sun Tzu, recruit the local populace. Swimming with the fish is the analogy: if you drain the water of local support, the fish—the Al Qaeda sympathizers—will be unable to survive. Al Qaeda's leadership, in now-public communications with Zarqawi, even warned of the dangers of alienating the local populace.

Zarqawi, always his own man, ignored the warnings. In Amman, Jordan, for example, suicide bombers sent by his organization galvanized public opinion against him overnight by staging the hotel bombings. Zarqawi's foreign fighter apparatus witnessed the water of local support in Iraq draining away. The foreign fighter problem in the country, once the biggest reservoir of suicide bombers in Iraq, suffered from a loss of local support as Iraqi militias weeded them out. We often worried, early in the Iraq war, that the foreign fighter phenomenon in Iraq would eventually fuel the same kind of "bleedout" we had seen in Afghanistan in the 1990s: fighters would return home from the crucible of Iraq better trained, more operationally secure, more committed to the fight Al Qaeda wanted to spread. It didn't happen. Most of those fighters died in Iraq. And, as local hostility rose, the foreign fighter pipeline slowed. Once again, Al Qaeda overreached: the lessons of alienating local populations in Algeria and Egypt during the 1990s, and the admonitions from Al Qaeda in Pakistan, weren't enough to stop another group of foreign fighters from killing too many opponents among the local population.

THE SECOND WAR: THE INTELLIGENCE PROBLEM OF IRAQ

AS TIME passed, the Al Qaeda battle was coupled with questions about this other, unexpected battlefield that would soon emerge as one of the biggest challenges we faced: Iraq. Consumed as we were with the immediacy of Al Qaeda threats and how we were faring in that campaign, the Iraq problem came to us out of our peripheral vision, off the horizon and then slowly looming into view directly in front of us. We should have recognized sooner the keen interest the policy community had in Iraq and adjusted our analytic resources accordingly. We did not, and we suffered for it.

Early on, and as the Iraq crisis progressed in Washington and at the United Nations into 2003, we had a fuzzy picture of the Sunni extremist situation in Iraq, and this picture did not clarify much over time as war drew closer. Saddam was a committed opponent of Sunni radicals—they might, after all, pose a potent threat to his secular regime and his iron grip on security in the country, especially as the rise in Islamic militancy swept through the Middle East. He could only have looked around to see Palestinian Islamists gaining prominence in refugee camps, or Al Qaeda-linked extremists' growing prevalence on the Arabian Peninsula. A similar strain of extremists in Iraq could mobilize people to threaten a regime that valued, first and foremost, its capability to stamp out any threats. Why would a despotic thug want to allow such a potential threat in his midst?

At the same time, Saddam must have known that this Sunni extremist threat was one of the biggest challenges the United States had faced in years. The 9/11 attacks had galvanized the attention of America, exposing weakness at home and drawing American armed forces ten thousand miles from home into Afghanistan, a country that had already proved, through the failure of the Soviet experiment, fully capable of sapping the resources of a superpower. Saddam, meanwhile, had shown a willingness to work with Islamist radicals when it suited his purposes, paying stipends to families of suicide bombers in Palestine when he wanted to portray himself as a champion at the forefront of popular Arab causes. Why wouldn't he find a marriage of convenience to use the most potent tool around, Al Qaeda, to threaten us? The answer to this question was never straightforward, and the intelligence was mixed, at best: did Sunni radicals make Saddam so uncomfortable that he would never work with them, or did the old phrase "the enemy of my enemy is my friend" apply, particularly in light of his regime's openly acknowledged willingness to pay Palestinian suicide bombers' families?

Because of the combination of limited intelligence and the intense policy, Congressional, public, and international scrutiny of the intelligence we had, the Iraq-Al Qaeda problem tested some of the fundamentals of intelligence work. The first principle is clear articulation of the difference between what analysts know; what they don't know; and what they think. The second is the distinction, often muddled, between an adversary's intentions and capabilities. Saddam clearly had the capability to maintain some sort of contact with Al Qaeda elements, but his intentions were less clear. He was a man consumed with internal security; we had to try to judge whether this paramount concern, which would clearly lead him to distance Iraq from groups that might foment Islamist opposition to his dictatorship, trumped his interest in working with groups that were fighting his mortal enemy, America.

The policy consumers of intelligence we dealt with every day wanted to know a lot about Saddam's capabilities and intentions in great detail; we knew very little, and our knowledge did not grow substantially over time. These policy consumers wanted clarity; we could not provide it. And they wanted an understanding of what we thought about Al Qaeda's actions and intentions; we had limited knowledge of the former and even less of the latter. What we did have was sometimes contradictory.

Bits of what we did know were captured and summarized in Secretary Powell's speech to the United Nations in February 2003. We knew Al Qaeda-linked individuals were in Iraq. We knew Saddam had aided other radicals; ideological purity was not his strong suit, and he might be willing to pull a lever that was seemingly at odds with some of his other actions if he thought that lever could hurt us. Maybe. We also had since debated reporting from a high-level Al Qaeda captive about contacts between Baghdad and Al Qaeda. In the background were snippets of information over the years about contacts, both in and outside Iraq, but these were hazy. And, as time went on, we also had a key detainee who provided reporting on linkages, with some describing contacts and others denying any links and instead talking about an ideological divide they would never bridge with Saddam's Iraq. What we didn't know vastly eclipsed what we did.

Into this vacuum almost inevitably grew analytic differences in the Agency and across the intelligence community. Given the paucity of information, analysts were forced to look at the limited bits we had from countless angles, examining our information from many different perspectives to answer endless probing, and often repetitive, questions from policy consumers. The lack of information left us spending far more time on the third pillar of analysis—writing about what we thought—than on the first, what we knew. Whenever analysis focuses on the soft subject of judgments rather than facts, you can be assured that analytic differences will emerge quickly. And they did in this case, persisting throughout the entire prewar period. At one point, we had to bring in an outside arbiter to take a formal look at the analytic differences and the relationship between the two camps. He came to the conclusion, I think accurately, that the analytic processes on both sides of the issue weren't the primary problem; festering personality conflicts, and the analysts' inability to overcome them, were at the core.

⮌

THERE WERE competing views in the analytic arm of the Agency, divided unsurprisingly between those who believed Saddam had some sort of links to Al Qaeda elements and those who judged otherwise. As analytic rifts are wont to do, these differences hardened, and the conversations grew rancorous and personal. The battle lines were drawn early and never faded. Eventually, we produced two lines of analysis, clearly differentiating between them and characterizing one as a more aggressive interpretation of pre-war intelligence. We knew Al Qaeda members were operating in Baghdad, and we knew they seemed to operate with relative impunity. We also had asked the Iraqi regime to locate these people; no response ever came, suggesting to some that either Saddam didn't want to dignify the request with an answer or, maybe, that he didn't want to do anything about the issue. As an optimist, I suppose some of these differences had a silver lining: analysts working this problem, like those on other issues across the Agency, didn't just come to work each day. They had a passion for the business, and for their subject areas, and they weren't willing to back down just to calm ruffled feathers. Fighting over analysis could be tough, but it was not all bad. The people all cared enough to argue for their views.

The policy questions, meanwhile, were heating up. We probably fielded many hundreds of them over time, maybe thousands. They were not general questions about a broad analysis of possible links. More often we received very specific questions, again and again responding to "taskings" posed by senior executives at agencies across Washington and from Congress—on issues such as the contentious reporting on a reported meeting in Prague between 9/11 leader Mohammed Atta and Iraqi intelligence. The senior executive time we spent on that one issue alone, whether Atta had Iraqi contacts in Prague, probably numbered in the dozens of hours, offering a sense of how much time the Iraq-Al Qaeda linkages generally took up. Many hundreds of hours were consumed, including time spent with Director Tenet, the Congress, and the White House. We eventually came to judge that such a meeting never took place, though even today, a decade later, there are those who are convinced that it did.

This controversy was punctuated by a rarity in the intelligence business: analysts affiliated with the policy side of the Department of Defense began producing their own independent analytic studies. The divide in the intelligence business between policy and intelligence is clear, and analysts are taught about the golden rule behind this divide from Day One: analysis is supposed to help a policy consumer understand a problem better, to enable more informed action. Intelligence analysts are supposed to be policy neutral so as not to skew what they say to favor any particular choice. Conversely, analysts are taught not to be swayed by policymakers, who by definition have made policy choices that could lead them to want to highlight pieces of analysis that support their particular position, while undercutting those that don't. Analysts analyze; policymakers use that analysis in decision making. The two are supposed to be oil and water—they don't mix.

So the combination of an analytic cell with a Defense Department policy office raised questions immediately among analysts about what is termed "politicization," or the coloring of analysis to support a policy objective. These questions were resolved with a simple approach from Tenet. The Pentagon analysts had an analytic viewpoint they wanted to present; they thought CIA analysis was too reluctant to portray linkages between Saddam's regime and Al Qaeda elements. So Tenet invited them to a conference room adjoining his office to hear them out.

The meeting was short and strained. I don't remember how many people were in the room—maybe a dozen, between CIA and Pentagon personnel. All these years later, I also don't remember how long the meeting lasted— maybe 20 or 30 minutes. The Pentagon presenter moved quickly into a formal presentation about analysis of the limited data we had. The analysis, to me, appeared almost immediately to weigh heavily in favor of the fragments we had suggesting a relationship between Al Qaeda radicals and Saddam. The gaps in our knowledge were not highlighted, and the analytic tradecraft appeared to be questionable. This was analysis crafted to support policy, the equivalent in analytic terms of a mortal sin. Nor did it seem subtle.

It did not much matter that day. Not long after we started, Tenet stopped the meeting, saying that the detailed analytic issues being raised were better suited for a discussion among expert analysts who had command of the intricacies of the data, rather than senior executives who couldn't go toe-to-toe on detail. I did not attend those follow-up discussions among experts, but they took place shortly thereafter. They caused a fluttering of commentary among CIA analysts working on Iraq-Al Qaeda issues, but no more. My only recollection of long-term follow-up from these discussions centers on congressional and media questions about what happened.

Too much was later made of both the meeting and the impact of the Pentagon cell on the broader debates within CIA. I remember the meeting because of the odd juxtaposition of policy and analysis, because Tenet chaired an initial meeting, and because the media and Congress later picked up on the issue of conducting analysis in a policy office. We also received congressional and media queries about the meetings, and we probably spent more time answering these queries than we did responding to the Pentagon analyses themselves. Even at the time, though, the issue did not appear to me more than a blip on the screen: interesting and sometimes irritating, definitely unusual, but not highly consequential for our work inside CIA. The influence of this analytic cell on Pentagon intelligence consumers and others in Washington was a question we asked among ourselves, but the analysis itself did not have a significant effect on what we wrote. We were insulated from it, though we knew policymakers in town were reading it.

This interaction was one of the frequent, almost everyday indicators of the level of policy focus on the question of murky linkages between Iraq and Al Qaeda. Obviously, one of the most voracious consumers of the intelligence, both the raw reports coming in directly from the field and the "finished" analysis produced by Langley analysts in the Counterterrorist Center, was Vice President Cheney and his staff. We probably handled thousands of questions from them during the prewar period, many of them extremely tactical requests for analysis of everything from the contentious debate on whether one of the 9/11 hijackers had met an Iraqi intelligence operative in Prague to potential WMD linkages to hazy reports about contacts between senior Al Qaeda members and Saddam's security services. We received the lion's share of our taskings from the morning briefers who fanned out every day to share intelligence with the vice president, and most of our responses were contained in written memos that responded to his questions. But a number of us also spoke with him and his staff directly, including in highly publicized trips he took to CIA headquarters at the main, campus-like compound in the Washington suburb of Langley, Virginia. CIA leadership also had regular interaction with the vice president and his staff. As Cheney once said during a speech at that time in the CIA auditorium, Tenet was spending as much or more time with him as he was with his own family. And, Cheney added, "that's as it should be." For a man not known for humor, he brought down the house for at least a few minutes.

Then and now, I find the coverage of these exchanges overwrought. This is not to say that these sessions were at all easy and unimportant: the back-and-forth could be difficult during the tense prewar days when the political debate was so heated, and Cheney and his staff were so immersed in the intelligence that they could conduct their own tactical analyses of the relatively limited amount of material we had. But critics who say this was undue influence on intelligence, or undue pressure on analysts to draw analytic conclusions that meet a policymaker need, are missing part of the point. I thought engaging with policymakers was what we were paid for, and I also believed it was better to feel the heat than to work on analysis at the other end of the spectrum, on issues that no one cared enough to ask about. Intelligence isn't simply a compilation of what the U.S. government knows; it is arraying that information so that it helps answer a policy question. And if the policy guys are asking tough questions because they are facing tough questions, it's a pretty good indicator that you're working on something where intelligence and analysis are making a difference. Better to be in the kitchen feeling the heat than outside, looking in.

Also present for these conversations was Cheney's chief of staff and legal adviser, Scooter Libby. Libby later became known for his conviction in a lengthy prosecution related to the leaking of the name of CIA officer Valerie Plame, whose husband, ambassador Joseph Wilson, was involved in what became a controversy about Iraqi efforts to acquire nuclear material in Africa. But when we interacted, he was running point for the vice president on prewar Iraq intelligence. In particular, he was a voracious reader of raw intelligence about Iraq-Al Qaeda linkages and a tough critic, to say the least, of what we wrote about Iraq and terrorism. We spent countless hours answering his questions on what in retrospect was a very small Iraq analytic team at CIA that worked as hard as any I have ever seen. Libby was a relentless questioner, prosecutorial in his efforts to check the rigor of our analysis, and how we reached our conclusions. In my limited dealings with him, I found that there was no way not to respect him, though he could be extremely difficult to work with: among a lot of smart people in Washington, and in senior circles of government, he was easily one of the sharpest I ever saw. He had an extremely acute intelligence, coupled with a drive that was almost unequaled. If you want to check the quality of your analytic thinking, spend time with a high-end prosecutor. And that he was.

There were times, especially early in my career, when intelligence was far more insulated from policy, when it was unclear to me whether intelligence was serving its core purpose at all, whether what we were writing was more for internal consumption than to help a client understand a security problem to make better choices. Certainly, in the months before the Iraq war, we were not naive, and we understood fully the dimensions of the political debate underway and how different sides of the debate were using, and sometimes abusing, information about Iraq-Al Qaeda linkages. And it was clear that the vice president and his staff were looking for aggressive interpretation of those linkages. If the purpose of intelligence analysis is to engage a client on key questions of U.S. national security interest, then be prepared for engagements that aren't always fun—a simplistic perspective, maybe, but real world. I didn't like the interactions, and I didn't like the second-guessing, the occasionally ugly debates, and the constant pressure. But at least we knew what we were writing was important, that it made a difference. And for those who say we bent over backward to support policy before the war, I would beg to differ; they never sat in those tense rooms and witnessed the heat of the conversations, and the views of those on the policy side that CIA was somehow opposed to them.

꩜

FAR MORE significant for me than the issue of Pentagon analysis on Iraq before the war was the preparation for Secretary of State Colin Powell's speech to the United Nations. I do not remember when it was first suggested that a senior U.S. official should make such a speech. I do remember that the framework of the presentation was under discussion for some time. Tenet asked that I participate in the planning sessions, representing the CIA for the segment of the speech that would outline our intelligence about Iraq-Al Qaeda linkages. Initially, it was not clear who in the administration would make the speech. And there were some suggestions that the speech itself might stretch over two days, to offer a detailed briefing about Saddam's weapons of mass destruction programs, his efforts to evade UN inspectors, his human rights abuses, and, of course, his contacts with terrorists.

When Powell stepped in as the designee to give the speech, he quickly added critical structure to these conversations. He knew where he wanted to go, and he shaped the discussions and drafting over the next few weeks in very clear directions. If he were to give the speech, he would have a strong hand in how he presented it. Furthermore, he was obviously a gifted public speaker, and beyond shaping the substance, he looked to what would work from a presentational perspective.

There were many experts involved on the WMD side. This made sense: as Powell pointed out, this was the United Nations. Sanctions imposed by the UN on Iraq didn't relate to human rights or terrorism, but they did stem directly from concerns about WMD, and the years of frustrating UN wrangling with Iraq were the result of Saddam's failure to come clean during the WMD inspections process. Powell wanted to talk about what the UN might listen to—violations of sanctions UN member states had enacted. And we at CIA had a lot of analysts who looked at this problem; we'd been at it for years, before the first Gulf war and afterward. Given the questions through two presidential administrations about Saddam's sidestepping UN sanctions, there was a long history of looking at both installations where Iraq had held WMD—old chemical sites, for example, and dual-use facilities such as chlorine plants—and at deception programs designed to outfox UN inspectors. What we knew about WMD, and the number of analysts dedicated to the WMD problem, easily dwarfed our knowledge of and analytic effort against Iraq and terrorism. For obvious reasons: until the early 2000s, nobody asked about Iraq and terrorism; everybody asked about Saddam and WMD, and CIA also had a significant and labor-intensive mission of supporting UN inspections.

As Powell dug into the problem during the weeks of preparation for the speech, he spent long hours at CIA headquarters, in the director's conference room, talking about what experts had proposed he say, what intelligence we had, and what gaps we faced. It seemed to me then, watching him question WMD analysts, that his challenge was almost insurmountable: we had the expertise, some of it highly technical and built on years of knowledge about Saddam's pre-war programs and how he had reacted to roving UN inspections teams. Powell's credibility was on the line; he had to depend not on expertise but on his sense of smell about what seemed like it would make sense to present to a global audience. And he had to work out what to say with analysts who had spent years on the problem, when he had only weeks to prepare.

Shortly after Powell became the choice to make the speech, Tenet brought me to a conversation with the secretary at his residence in suburban Virginia.

We went to see him early in the process because we needed to get a sense of how he wanted to shape the speech. He hadn't been designated for long, though, and the conversation at his kitchen table was about broad outlines, not details. That would come later. Condoleezza Rice, then national security adviser, also was there. On a casual Saturday, with most of us in jeans, Powell answered the door, and we walked in to a greeting punctuated by two small dogs running around energetically. It seemed such a contrast: the secretary of state, former national security adviser, former chairman of the joint chiefs of staff, one of the most respected public officials in the United States, living with two small dogs that would have been lunchmeat for my brother's hundred-pound golden retriever.

Powell took us on a quick tour of his basement office, full of family photos and memorabilia. He spent a bit of private time with Tenet, while I marveled at the history in the many living room photos. All of us then went back up to the kitchen. While I sipped a Diet Coke, the five of us sat at the kitchen table, talking through which intelligence themes deserved consideration for inclusion and which didn't. In the ensuing weeks, there were differences about what the speech should contain, with some arguing that it should include a laundry list of information that would take many hours to present. But it was Powell, who knew that this speech was as much about presentation and credibility as it was about mounds of data, who set the tone from the outset.

The terrorism section of the speech was a sideshow compared with the core WMD sections, but the question about how much extensive detail and data should be included in the speech cropped up early about what terrorism material should be included, and the debate proved to be persistent. An early draft was tabled by the White House. It was voluminous, amounting to an encyclopedic recitation of all the intelligence—from all variety of sources and going back years—we had that suggested a link between Saddam's regime and Al Qaeda. Included, for example, was the story of the alleged contact between the Iraqi Embassy in Prague and Mohammed Atta, a story that we had slowly, steadily judged was lacking in credibility, after a mountain of analysis to try to determine its veracity.

This mammoth draft did not get much traction. With WMD at center stage and many questions about both the credibility of much of the Iraq-Al Qaeda intelligence and the advisability of dwelling on the subject in front of a skeptical and uninterested UN audience, few thought it advisable that the speech become a telephone book of allegations. This early draft of terrorism information, though, had some support. And there was no counter-draft. So after a few days of playing around with options, adding and subtracting intelligence from the draft, Tenet looked at me one day with a simple directive: write the terrorism section.

This was not a conversation; it was a directive. Over the course of days and in frequent conversation with the line analysts conducting the assessments, I worked on a draft from scratch. It seemed like an honor, the boss having enough faith to ask us for a fresh draft. And the group around me supporting the drafting were superb: they knew every detail, they could provide the background material for every statement or claim we made, and they were endlessly willing to help. That initial version was relatively short, focusing on material in which we had the most confidence and trying to present intelligence coherently, without heading down alleys that would have little or no impact on the audience Powell was trying to reach.

Powell, in a crowded conference room, took the original draft one day and read it start to finish to an assembled room of probably two dozen people. I remember being on edge, sort of like the oral exam for my master's degree English literature twenty years earlier, though that had been on the nineteenth-century English novel, and this was on allegations about Iraq that would be released to hundreds of millions. It was not at all clear to me whether the work would score or fall far short of the mark. But it read smoothly, and that draft quickly became the text on terrorism from which we worked in the coming weeks. As with the WMD portion of the presentation, the weeks of work between that draft and the presentation of the speech were intense, focusing on a few broad issues: substantive conversations about what merited inclusion in the text; stylistic questions about how the language flowed and should be presented; and internal scrambling to check, re-check, and check once again not only what made the cut for inclusion but whether the language we were using precisely reflected what the intelligence said. Speeches aren't written in traditional intelligence style: we wanted to ensure that there wasn't a gap between what we had said in intelligence documents and how the speech, which didn't afford much space for explanation or nuance, came across as a public statement and document of record. We also knew we would be picked apart, and we wanted to be on solid ground when the questions started coming in. Every sentence in that document had some piece of intelligence behind it, which we held in a large, well-organized binder.

Working with Powell and a few members of his staff, we added nothing but weeded out quite a bit, slowly but steadily slimming down the Al Qaeda section day by day. Powell spent a remarkable amount of time in that conference room, many hours, going through the speech again and again and again, asking questions of analysts, trying to get a feel for how to deal with the bits of intelligence information he had to weave together into a clear story for an audience that was global and decidedly nonexpert. The information that we excised from the Al Qaeda section fell into each of the three categories. We (often Powell) took out stuff that seemed substantively thin as well as material that distracted from the clean line of march in the speech. And we altered material, time and time again, to try to ensure that it matched as closely as we could how the same material was characterized in classified documents, which do not make smooth reading.

As the speech approached and public attention grew, Tenet asked me to join the group going to New York for Powell's UN presentation. This wasn't a nicety: we continued to work on the speech in New York, staying in a hotel across the street from United Nations headquarters, with a room at the end of the hallway for the director and an adjoining communications suite. The refining process continued at the U.S. mission to the UN, nearby. We didn't close out the final text until late the night before the speech. Powell wanted one more read-through that evening, which he held in a large room in the U.S. mission. A number of us sat there—State Department personnel, a few CIA people, and others—while he went through the speech. His attention to detail was striking and instructive: this was not only a final substantive check, he was also marking in pencil areas for voice inflection.

We finished the final run-through with the secretary the night before the speech, maybe nine or ten p.m. We were tired: the UN audience and global TV audience saw the next morning's speech as an exclamation point, and we had worked nonstop on the language for weeks. For those of us in the process, it was the end of dizzying weeks of preparation, a full-time job and then some during that time. Even in the midst of Powell's late run-through, I remember placing a phone call to a CIA analyst, checking a key fact yet again.

It had been an exhausting process. But there was no mistaking that we were in the midst of something history would remember. For a career CIA analyst, hired in 1985 at an entry-level GS-9 salary, it did not take much reflection to know that this was an experience that few, if any, analysts would ever live through, another seat to watch history in the making.

It wasn't done yet, though: there were a few areas in the Al Qaeda section that we needed to alter slightly as a result of Powell's last practice session. At the conclusion, Powell's staff writers went back to their hotel to work on the changes, and I walked over at about midnight in midtown Manhattan to review, once again, whether what was in the speech was substantively solid. I brought a late dinner for the few people there, and we stepped through the newest changes.

They were few, but I had lost track, in the intensity of those days, about how far we had come from the original text, how many changes we'd made in recent days, and whether the new, last-minute changes were significant. When I returned from that final editing session, Tenet was waiting at the hotel, dead tired. In the early hours of the morning, I told him I was concerned that the text had lost too much, that its coherence was slipping. He was always a committed intelligence professional, never one to say "heck, let's just go to bed," so his response was predictable. He wanted to see the new draft. This was past midnight. The speech was in hours. So we asked for the reworked version via fax. And then, from the communications suite rigged in the adjacent hotel room, we got word that the fax wasn't working. This was not my finest hour as an analyst. We sat and waited.

Even then, I knew that the ensuing hours would not be a career highlight. Quite the contrary. Tenet was in old gym shorts and a ragged t-shirt. I was fatigued. We were both too tired to say much, surrounded by technical gear and wondering when a fax would be up and running. It was surreal, even then. Sometime after two a.m., or maybe three, the communications links were back online and we received the final draft. Almost immediately, comparing this final version to a copy of the speech from the evening before, it was clear that I was wrong—the speech had not changed substantially. With the fatigue and constant textual changes, I'd just lost track of where we were, and how little had actually been altered. The director turned to me, in a room filled with communications equipment past two in the morning, when we had an early wakeup call. "Phil," he said, "is this it?" after we had compared the new draft with the earlier version. After a mumbled apology, we walked off to our rooms. And he forgave me. I think. To his credit, he never gave me a hard time for that evening, but he has directed a few pointed barbs over the years about it.

The photos of Tenet sitting behind Powell at the speech the following morning show a tired man. I suspect most observers would assume he had simply lost sleep over the speech, never guessing that a skittish fax machine and a jumpy analyst were partly to blame. I do remember looking at him on the TV screen and feeling guilty. Anyone who glanced at him that morning would have seen shadows under his eyes. The backstory is that he worked hard, for years, and was often tired when I saw him, during the workday and on that trip to New York. But it wasn't the work that night. The fax did us in.

A few of us gathered in a room at our hotel across the street from the UN that morning to watch the speech live. I remember sitting there as the auditorium came on screen and Powell started into the speech. Like a student who can't bear to review a term paper after it's returned from a professor, I just couldn't watch. After just a couple of minutes staring at the screen, I walked out into Manhattan and headed to a Dunkin' Donuts to wait out the speech with a cup of coffee and a cinnamon donut. I couldn't wait for it to be over. So much work, and I knew that if I'd stayed to watch the speech, I'd spend the entire time picking over every excruciating detail, yet again, but this time without a chance to change a word. Waiting for the inevitable questions to come in, picking apart what we'd done.

It was one of the most memorable few weeks of my career, but quickly over. I have seen Powell a couple of times since then. Despite his frustrations about the speech as the WMD hunt in Iraq turned up nothing, he was always unfailingly polite to me. Another lesson in leadership.

A NEW VIEW AT CIA: DEPUTY DIRECTOR
OF THE COUNTERTERRORIST CENTER

THE IRAQ-AL QAEDA story crept into our work occasionally after secretary of state Colin Powell's speech to the United Nations in February 2003, but never with the same intensity. As war loomed and then the initial Shock and Awe strikes hit Baghdad in March, media coverage and public interest shifted quickly to the invasion, to the emerging shock at the lack of WMD, to the hunt for Saddam, to the infusion of foreign fighters heading to Iraq as suicide bombers, and to the bloodshed in the middle of the decade as Iraq descended into chaos. The prewar intelligence issue was focused on WMD; the post-invasion after-action work, including the endless studies about what had happened with the faulty WMD analysis, consumed Iraq watchers, partly because of the massive intelligence effort— in both resources and high-level attention—involved in supporting the series of officials who went to Baghdad to lead the hunt for WMD. Over time, too, attention shifted, as the violence grew and inter-ethnic clashes left countless Iraqis dead, to what had happened with postwar planning. The issue of possible Iraqi links to Al Qaeda, never a focus for the UN anyway, slipped into the background.

Meanwhile, I had gotten a promotion, a couple of steps up. As second-in-charge of analysis in the Counterterrorist Center, I had worked for Pattie overseeing a group of analysts and managers that numbered in the low hundreds, and we had made progress with the transition from a chaotic post-9/11 mode to a vaguely more organized, professional office. But one morning, I got word to appear in the office of the Agency's head of analysis—the deputy director for intelligence, as the position was titled on CIA's wiring diagram. CIA has an internal classified instant messaging system on employees' computers, and many of us used it heavily. That morning, senior managers across the analytic arm of the Agency traded instant messages: "Did you get called upstairs? What's up?" None of us knew, but it was clear some sort of major shakeup among the analytic leadership was underway. The meetings we were called to were stacked so tightly that there wasn't time for much speculation: all the dust of who would sit where was settled within a day.

The conversation later that morning was a surprise for me. Over the course of just a few minutes, the head of analysis, Jami Miscik, told me I'd been slotted to become the deputy director of the entire Counterterrorist Center, one of the best analytic jobs in the Agency and, post-9/11, one of the most challenging. In contrast to the position I had held as deputy for terrorism analysis, the role of deputy for the entire Center included oversight of not only analysis but also all overseas operational elements, which were far larger than the analytic components. In addition, the new role required expanded representational duties at the White House, Congress, and on the CIA's 7th floor executive suite. There was no need to hesitate; it was an honor, and the opportunity of a lifetime. I came to believe, and still do, that it is the best analytic position at the Agency, a fusion of analysis and operations that is at the center of the counterterrorism fight. Furthermore, though CIA is not nearly as hierarchical as the Pentagon or other military organizations, there is at least a vague sense of command: I didn't receive an order to take the position, but the answer of "no, I don't want to do that" would not have seemed appropriate, especially in what was still a wartime environment.

My first boss in the new position was Jose Rodriguez, a highly experienced field operator at the Agency, mostly in Latin America, with a penchant for fieldwork and a disdain for anything that smelled like Washington bureaucracy. Among the first directions he gave me was his expectation that I would handle all the "downtown" work—the representational duties in bureaucratic Washington that were of no interest to him. My predecessor, Bruce Pease, one of the most respected managers in the analytic ranks, also had performed these duties. And before him, there had been a long line of some of the Agency's best, who set the standard for what the deputy was supposed to do.

Pease talked me through other responsibilities in the Center as well. The Center is strong on the operational and analytic fronts, he told me. Both are the heart and soul of what CIA does for a living, and has done for decades. But the Center's weakness lay in problems and processes that were outside these traditional lanes, areas where no single element had a clear responsibility, or where the responsibility was shared. How we honed the large effort to create a watchlist of potential terrorists coming to the United States, for example, was a management task that turned out to be one of the most significant problems on the plate of the Center's deputy. But we also worked on a range of issues, such as exploiting the growing mountain of digital data captured in terrorist raids and the relationship with the military, which had a seasoned civilian representative in our front office.

Jose was true to his word during the entire time I worked for him and shared a wall with him. Though I'm sure he went downtown occasionally, I can't remember a single time. At every media, congressional, or policy request, the answer was always the same: "Mudd," he'd say, "I'm not going. You're the man for this." Easily one of the funniest bosses I ever had, his direction would be followed by a laugh. We became very close over time, and he was always candid and supportive. "I hate that shit," he'd say. "You do it. You talk pretty." Having grown up in Miami, I spoke maybe 200 words of Spanish, a lot of it Cuban slang that Jose found funny himself, and he would regularly correct what he regarded as my erroneous Cuban words and replace them with Puerto Rican equivalents that were unknown to me. He would then poke humor at his own Puerto Rican accent and claim that he wasn't capable of speaking publicly anyway. These were all lies, of course, to get out of what he hated to do, along with the endless claims that he would jeopardize his "cover"—his ability to operate overseas without people knowing he was a CIA officer—if he became known through too much public exposure. This was complete nonsense, and we both knew it: the chief of CIA's Counterterrorist Center is well known in Washington counterterrorism circles, and Jose's name wasn't a secret. But the excuse of protecting his covert status was convenient, if humorous, and he used it regularly. Today, all these years later, he still laughs about it in one of the countless examples of friendships growing across the Agency's analytic and operational divides.

The beauty of the arrangement we had, though, was that he remained supportive under every circumstance we faced during that time. His guidance was often light-hearted, which I took as a compliment: he thought those of us involved in representing the Agency downtown in what was by far the biggest intelligence game in town would be able to handle ourselves without his intervention. And he didn't micromanage us or provide much guidance. As he typically would say, "Just tell them all to go to hell," after which we'd spend a few more serious minutes discussing the issues and how we should talk about them. It was broad enough guidance that I felt comfortable executing it however I saw fit. He later mentioned that, in one of his rare appearances before Congress, he had been talking about some issue I had earlier discussed with the same congressional committee. "They told me that Mudd said something different," he related back to me, laughing. "So I told them you must be right." A classic Jose line.

He was also supportive as we tried to build relationships with other major U.S. government entities involved in the counterterror campaign. I thought, in particular, that the partnership with the Pentagon was important: as the war expanded globally, the Pentagon had authorities, responsibilities, and resources that complemented ours. Among our Pentagon counterparts, though, CIA often was seen as an opaque organization, a place that wasn't always keen on sharing information. So one mechanism we worked on, to build trust over time, was to communicate with the Pentagon's chief military officer for intelligence on the Joint Chiefs of Staff—the Joint Chiefs' J-2, in other words. In this case, we were working with general Ron Burgess, who turned out to be a great partner and who remains a friend.

General Burgess was responsible for participating in the morning briefing for the chairman of the Joint Chiefs, and a lot of what we were working on at CIA involved overseas operations, and terrorists, which would regularly crop up in the chairman's morning briefs. To avoid surprise, and to prevent the J-2 from providing erroneous or dated information to the chairman, I would occasionally call General Burgess on the secure phone and tell him, for example, that a particularly prominent terrorist who was featured in threat reporting had been captured or killed, news that might not otherwise appear for a few days or might be misreported, unknowingly, by people who did not have access to our operations.

The rationale for developing this relationship was straightforward. I would not have wanted to be in the J-2's shoes, reporting on what a particular terrorist was up to, only to find out later that the individual at the center of the plot was already dead or captured. This would not only be embarrassing in front of the chairman, it would create mistrust between our organizations. So when we had sensitive breaking news, I would simply ask General Burgess not to reveal the information during the morning briefing but instead approach the chairman afterward to let him know privately that the terrorist they had just discussed was already off the radar. I remember one occasion when I was watching a remote live video feed of a significant operation we were running, one that I was certain would feature in the Pentagon's briefing, but the nature of the operation was such that what had happened might be misreported by the media, clouding the briefing in erroneous information before we had a chance to provide the behind-the-scenes story. So while the operation was unfolding live on the screen, piped via the magic of twenty-first-century technology into CIA headquarters, I called General Burgess and reported to him what was happening, live. This was one of the few examples I remember where what happened in real life matched what the public might expect to see in the movies. And all with Jose's unwavering support. Every time I advised him that we should notify the general, he concurred, without hesitation, and the general never let us down.

This kind of support proved immensely valuable in building trust, and in opening up lines of communication at times that might otherwise have been tense. When we had to work through problems, for example, the trust built by sharing this kind of information ensured that we went to the table with some of the walls already down.

These linkages proved valuable, again and again. One reason is not self-evident: when I joined CIA, in 1985, the organization seemed like a huge entity that was beyond the ability of any junior officer to understand. And this even though the Agency's workforce is one of the smallest in the constellation of national security agencies. As I slowly moved up the chain, though, I learned what all officers have learned in large bureaucracies since the beginning of time: organizations that look huge when you're looking up from an entry-level position really aren't that large. The number of people who can make serious decisions is relatively small, and making enemies of those people only ensures that when you cross paths with them years down the road—and you will—you've already built a wall of mistrust. In the case of building bridges with the Pentagon, General Burgess and I continued to work together, even after I moved onto the Bureau and he moved to become head of the Defense Intelligence Agency, one of the main players in the intelligence community. Washington appears to be a huge, unwieldy beast from the outside, but the number of core counterterrorism players on the inside, even as the campaign mushroomed, is smaller than I would ever have imagined earlier in my career. Furthermore, the sense among analysts, when senior executives across the intelligence community met, was that these were scripted, formal sessions among the giants of intelligence. "Elephants," we called them, though I later came to find that those same people were as human as the rest of us. Building personal relationships and trust at senior levels turned out to be no different from the need to build these types of relationships among GS-9, entry-level analysts.

⌐

THIS TRANSITION to the deputy position in the Counterterrorist Center's front office came in 2003 and lasted two years, one of the most significant periods in the counterterror campaign and in my career. The big ticket issues we handled seem overwhelming, in retrospect: ramping up as the post-invasion battles in Iraq raged, assessing the series of takedowns of Al Qaeda's operational commanders, trying to mature the Center from a vast organization that mushroomed in a hundred different ways after 9/11 but did not have management processes or structure to match the expansion. And watching the seemingly constant back-and-forth about how the Agency would deal, over the longer term, with the now-publicized group of detainees held at CIA "black," or covert, sites, an issue we all knew would have a ripple effect on us and on the Agency as a whole for years to come.

Those years now seem a blur. The Agency's operations chief, Jose's boss in the Agency's 7th floor executive suite, held a tactical update meeting every morning attended by the senior operational managers across the Agency, including the manager/coordinator for the Counterterrorist Center, and we then had a daily staff meeting within the Center where senior managers discussed operational, analytic, and administrative issues. Given that I had grown up on the analytic side of the Agency, this operational focus in the Center led me to decide, quickly, that the first step for any new deputy would be to develop an effective working relationship with the managers on the operational side of the Center. Traditionally, the two core business areas of the Agency—operations (the collection of intelligence by field officers who run human sources) and analysis (the synthesis of information by mostly headquarters-based professionals)—have different management chains, different career paths, and different personality types, perhaps something like R&D and sales in the same company. Introverts and extroverts. People comfortable dealing with documents, data, and research, and field personnel more comfortable recruiting and running spies. Even a different ethos in each. The Center was almost unique, housing operators and analysts side-by-side, with analysts often heavily involved in operational work. Learning the other side of the business more deeply than I had before was therefore something new, and fascinating.

The organizational structure in the Center also was almost unique in the Agency. In size alone, the Center dwarfed other management components at Langley. And the joint operational/analytic management team at the top was rare, though not unheard of. Oddly, though the arrangement worked remarkably well in the Center, other components of the Agency were loath to adopt it, and though the Agency is far more integrated than it was when I joined in 1985, operations and analysis of the same issues are still managed separately. We sometimes joked about it in the Center—managers of highly sensitive Eastern European operations, for example, would be assigned to the Center and quickly realize the power of joining operations and analysis without walls of separation. But culture changes slowly: despite the fact that many returned to their home areas of expertise elsewhere at CIA after their tours in the counterterrorism world, the rest of the Agency maintained a traditional divide between operational and analytic disciplines.

Almost the first move I remember, within a day or two of taking over as deputy, was a conversation with the chief of operations for the Center, historically an extremely powerful position given the number of people and the amount of money we were dedicating to counterterrorism. The fact that, operationally, CIA operations officers around the world, regardless where they worked, were seized with the counterterrorism mission after 9/11, increased the clout of the Center's chief of operations. He was a player, not only on operations but on personnel assignments, promotions, and the other pieces of management that make big organizations run and make employees take notice. Examining a wiring diagram of the Center's managers, you would come to believe that this position was subordinate to the Center's overall deputy, my new role. Like every organization, though, paper often doesn't match reality: traditionally in the Counterterrorist Center, the operational component has far more power and resources than the analytic component. And, in this case, the chief of operations, a long-time field operator who once served as the Agency's chief in Moscow, wouldn't be likely to assume that the analytic deputy called the shots.

Those first conversations with him proved to be some of the most signifi-cant I ever had at CIA. I told the chief of operations, Rob, whom I did not know well at the time, that I would never make an operational suggestion without acting side-by-side with him. I would never be out in front, not just out of deference to his position but because operations was not my specialty. We should be partners with complementary skills and responsibilities. He agreed. And, it turned out, he kept his word. We forged a partnership—and, over time, a friendship—that was remarkably enduring. I have rarely met a more talented professional, and one from whom I could learn not only les-sons of management but lessons of leadership and humility.

We also shared humor, a critical asset in the midst of days that often featured tense moments. Often, we would both go to the 5 o'clock with Te-net, after co-chairing a quick preparatory meeting among managers, only to find that some officer from the Center would raise an issue we hadn't coordinated beforehand that would lead to a free-for-all at the table. We'd come back, sit in the office, and laugh. "What the hell was that?" was a frequent comment after someone dropped an unannounced bombshell on Tenet. We'd then figure out whether the hiccup was worth pursuing, devise a quick fix, and move on.

The days had little predictability, beyond the morning staff meetings and the regular evening 5 o'clocks with the director. After I moved up, one of the first agenda items was overseeing the Center's effort, largely staffed by contract personnel, to review vast streams of incoming intelligence information and determine which individuals should be nominated for placement on U.S. travel watchlists. Mundane as it sounds, this was and is a critical task, partly stemming from the missed watchlisting opportunity that had led to some of the 9/11 hijackers entering the United States years earlier. No one let us forget this, especially the 9/11 Commission report that was the official assessment of the U.S. government's performance before that attacks. Tenet had looked at me, shortly after I took the job as the Center's deputy, and told me to be "all over" the watchlisting issue. Later, he would periodically ask me about watchlisting, always showing little patience for bureaucratic blocks that might stand in the way of further streamlining the process. My predecessor, Bruce Pease, also highlighted the watchlisting process as a particularly tricky issue, partly because it was one of those classic problem areas that fell between the cracks of the core Agency responsibilities of analysis and operations.

Pease offered a piece of advice that I will never forget, so elegant in how he captured a problem and, as it turned out, so remarkably true. He commented that we had done operations, intelligence reporting, and analysis for years. Not only were these the core of the intelligence business, but many people felt responsible for them personally. There were specific job descriptions, obviously, for operators, collection managers and reports officers, and analysts. But those job descriptions didn't cover the critical missions that fell through the cracks, not because they weren't important but because they weren't part of the traditional core mission and weren't things any individual might see as falling within his or her job description. Watch out for those, he said. Don't get trapped into simply focusing on managing what a hundred other people are watching over. He was right, though I remember puzzling over exactly what he meant when this came up during my initial conversations with him about what the new job required, and where he had found pitfalls and risks. "What the heck is he talking about," I remember asking myself, only to find the answer was self-evident after a few watchlisting meetings.

Watchlisting sounds more straightforward than it is, as I quickly discovered during the many regular meetings we had solely dedicated to this issue. Simple enough, it seems, to take a known terrorist, when we had enough biographic information to identify him, and place him on a list so he'd be screened out before ever getting on a plane. But in diving into the problem, the complexity proved to be vexing, and it never got easier. Which screening criteria should you use? How do you ensure that you look at all data, including highly sensitive data that few people have access to? How about the balance between reviewing current material—a huge task, given the quantity of data we were absorbing every day—and sorting through old data that predated 9/11? How far back should you go, if the historical work is taking personnel off reviewing current information?

We also looked at error rates. How high were they? We obviously wanted to be near zero. How could we get there, efficiently, without mistaken "hits" that would keep innocent people off airplanes and out of the United States? Despite the seeming simplicity of the watchlisting task, and the maturity of the watchlisting program Pease had helped developed before I arrived, this problem of keeping undesirables offshore turned out to be a knotty issue for the entire two years of my tenure as deputy. Watching the case of the almost-bomber on December 25, 2009, brought it all back. The millions of records out there, from many different agencies, are hard to match up. Watching the debate about how the government missed matching up records that might have identified the Nigerian "underwear bomber" who attempted to down an airplane over Detroit that Christmas Day immediately reminded me of the challenges of pulling together disparate data sets from different agencies when names are entered differently and millions of records pile up, day after day. It always appears, in retrospect, that the job is ridiculously easy: why didn't anyone see that the warnings of the father talking to a U.S. government official in Nigeria matched records of a Nigerian youth in Yemen? But it was a smart group of people sitting around the table regularly to iron out details such as how to ensure that data acquired from our most sensitive sources could be included in a broadly disseminated watchlist database. And even then, we missed occasionally.

These kinds of twenty-first-century problems in a large bureaucracy took substantial amounts of time. Another challenge was how to develop a centralized program to process the data we collected in counterterror raids and share that data with the rest of the intelligence community. Yet another was transitioning to a new appraisal and bonus program for senior Agency managers, a process I participated in during my tenure. Accompanying the challenges of how to manage the data, in a large, complex interagency bureaucracy, came the inevitable personnel battles. Every resource manager, particularly in a time of war, wants more people. In the intelligence business, more people automatically mean you can do more. Hire more contractors and you can review older intelligence files for possible candidates to add to the no-fly watchlist, for example. Or add more analysts and you might be able to develop deeper insights into second-tier terrorists who might grow into the first tier months or years down the road.

The personnel battles I remember were difficult; even in wartime, internal battles over people were tough. Everyone wanted more, and the offices from which we could get new positions had already been heavily raided in the years after 9/11. There was, added to this, a persistent question of how efficient we were with staff and contractors, raising the question of how many people we should have as the Counterterrorist Center mushroomed, and what percentage of that workforce should be contractors versus full-time staff.

Occasionally, we battled not just over adding more positions but also over shifting specific individuals. "Poaching," as we called it, was supposed to be off-limits. No senior manager, not by written policy but by standards of professional courtesy, was supposed to approach an especially talented junior analyst and dangle a better opportunity to encourage the analyst to jump to a new office. On the other hand, hiring analysts who applied through the standard open application process internal to the Agency was fair game.

Unsurprisingly, in a business that depends fundamentally on human talent, the distinction between "poaching" and simply taking recruits who applied through the internal jobs database was honored in the breach. Incidents of managers hunting for talent in the hallways were fairly common. And probably, I'm guessing, little different than what you would find in corporate America. After all, this wasn't a peripheral issue: the quality of the analysts defined the quality of the analysis. Every manager knows this, and every manager will press hard to recruit the best. We all did. Harder to stomach, though, especially in wartime, was the constant harping from managers in other offices who would speak to their former analysts, newly transferred to the Center after 9/11 to positions for which they had little or no background, and list the complaints of those analysts as they settled into a stressful, sometimes poorly managed environment.

⌐

THESE WERE internal issues, though, germane to getting the daily business done but not as demanding as working on issues such as what to tell the
president every day, day in and day out, for years. The external duties outside
the building were more time-consuming and no less significant. First among
them were representational responsibilities to other Washington agencies, to
the Congress, and, less frequently, to the U.S. media.

The counterterrorism staff at the White House National Security Council,
for example, hosted a weekly interagency session, called a "Steering Group,"
that dealt with everything from threat issues to relationships with foreign
countries to preparations for potential attacks. Around a table in the old
Eisenhower Executive Office Building across from the West Wing of the
White House, representatives from the Pentagon, State Department, Treasury,
National Counterterrorist Center, CIA, and White House gathered to discuss
these issues, all in an effort to try to ensure that we moved in a coordinated
fashion and had a venue to keep each other abreast of what we were up to.

These were also the sessions where we would coordinate briefing papers
for "Principals" and "Deputies," the heads and deputy heads of agencies who
would meet to discuss policy at the NSC. If they were considering a policy
initiative on a particular issue, they might farm out questions to the Steering Group for ideas. We gathered every week to look at issues ranging from
tactical to strategic. At the low end of the spectrum might be how to handle
a problem that had emerged in recent threat reporting, such as information
highlighting a potential lower-level vulnerability that we needed to fix and
might be particularly vexing. At the high end, the discussions might shift to
countries that were important to the global counterterrorism campaign but
were proving complicated partners. We might talk about what our collective capabilities were, where we could bring pressure, what we could offer a
recalcitrant partner, and what steps we might recommend to our superiors
when they needed to engage.

These regular meetings, held in the ornate rooms of the old office building
with its checkerboard marble floors and intricate wood paneling that would
never appear in today's beige federal buildings, also offered the chance to
catch up with colleagues in hallway conversations. Most of us knew each

other well—the Washington counterterrorism community, despite the massive growth during the past decade, still has at its center a fair number of experts who haven't changed dramatically over the years. Some rotate in and out, but many are still familiar. So we'd discuss, in the hallways, everything from personnel changes across government to how we were faring with whatever was on the front pages of the newspapers.

Congressional interaction was as frequent, and sometimes more so, as some of these policy exchanges, especially during the early years after 9/11. Soon after I had returned to the Center in January 2002, we were fielding too many complaints from members of Congress and their staffs who thought the Center was not providing a good enough understanding of the war in the regular briefings Congressional committees were receiving. Interest in counterterrorism issues then remained intense: the members, who are pulled in so many directions that it is often difficult for them to focus on any one issue extensively, spent lots of time on terrorism issues both because counterterrorism was by far the most significant policy priority and because their constituents were focused on the war. Interest was obviously especially intense among members and staff of the CIA's "oversight" committees—those congressional committees in both the House and Senate specifically charged with overseeing the activities of CIA and other intelligence agencies.

One of my early duties was to fix these problem briefings. So I went down to classified hearings on Capitol Hill, after preparing with our congressional support staff, for an initial briefing in a Senate conference room, to provide a top secret briefing on what we were doing at CIA and, more broadly, to explain what the complex global war looked like from a CIA perspective. I didn't know what to expect early on, but I had great help from an enterprising analyst on the Center's support staff who helped me pull together a large binder of background detail on all the issues we thought might come up. We went through everything, from what general line of analysis would be helpful, to what specific operations worldwide might merit mention, to what was appearing in the media and therefore might spark a question from a senator. They all were inundated with questions about the counterterror campaign when they returned to their home districts, and it wasn't hard to understand why, when their constituents read stories in the newspapers or saw reports on TV about CIA activities, they would want to understand what we thought about the questions they were fielding at home.

My view going in was that this should be more of a conversation than a formal briefing. The stories of the counterterrorism world were of such intense interest, and the elements of the story were so broad—from the hunt for "high-value" Al Qaeda targets in Pakistan to the emergence of threats in the Arabian Gulf, Southeast Asia, and elsewhere, to questions about how we were conducting the campaign and how we might do better. We could discuss detail, and we did, but it would be understandably difficult for a legislator, even one on the Senate or House Intelligence Oversight Committees, to digest and remember any of that detail unless there was context around it. So I tried to come up with a unifying narrative, a sense of where we were in the war, and weave the details into the narrative. A story more than a formal presentation. We had talented senior analysts discussing these kinds of issues every morning when we talked about types of strategic analysis should appear in the president's morning briefing; why not take some of these same lines of analysis and weave them together into an informal narrative?

All this is in no way to suggest that these were highly scripted events, with a huge effort to prepare a conversational narrative. In later years, on more contentious issues, I have had to prepare formal "statements for the record" to submit to committees in advance of hearings. But back then, with events changing so quickly and our interaction with the committees so frequent, there were no written statements. Nor did I prepare a script for myself. Instead, after combing through analysis and operations, a few of us would sit down and pull out a pen and paper, old style. After jotting down a few notes about themes, and a few reminders about details that seemed particularly relevant to anchor each theme, we were ready to roll. After all, we were living and breathing this stuff all day, every day: it wasn't as if we needed help remembering trends and details. A script would have undercut the effort to engage in a conversation. I didn't want to look down at a piece of paper while I was trying to make eye contact with an audience of senators.

I still remember clearly walking into that closed hearing room for the first of those briefings, knowing that this was an unhappy crowd. It was packed with senators and staffers alike. Hearings, open (that is, accessible to the public) or closed, often get mixed attendance from senators and representatives who suffer from overbooked schedules. Such was not the case at this briefing. The U-shaped table for senators was full, and every single seat behind them, for Committee staff and some of the senators' personal staff, was taken. Sitting to the left, as was customary, was a Committee employee who spoke into a plastic cone, orally recording every word clearly for the record by repeating what I said into a recording device. I knew the senators were hungry for more than what they read in the newspapers, and I knew they weren't happy with what they were getting. We had to change this.

The conversational approach seemed to work, and the briefing rolled far more smoothly than I had anticipated. We talked about how we were doing in the fight against Al Qaeda's operational leaders, who were slowly settling into a few cities and throughout the lawless tribal area straddling the Afghan-Pakistan border. We talked about how affiliated cells and groups were doing, in places like Indonesia and Yemen, and how our partners in the campaign were faring. All these corners of the globe settled into a single line of analysis, capturing the ups and downs of an expanding global campaign by using what our analysts were writing as a backdrop and peppering the briefing with anecdote and detail to provide color and explain how our work was proceeding in practice. The back-and-forth that ensued was productive, rich, lengthy, and more varied than I could have handled earlier in my career. And, in retrospect, it turned out to be among the more interesting, rewarding, and even enjoyable tasks in my career, though admitting that engagement with Congress is "enjoyable" is not something any executive branch official is likely to do while in the service. It was sharing an unfolding panorama of war, albeit grim, with the elected members of the highest legislative body in the land. Following my inauspicious start of driving up to CIA headquarters with a resume in hand in 1984, this seemed like the kind of career any aspiring analyst could hope to witness.

Over the next few years, into the time when I began my tour as the Center deputy, the congressional briefings were frequent. I grew more comfortable in the role, knowing that the committees with whom I spoke had to answer more and more difficult questions from their constituents and the media about issues such as threats in Europe, especially after the July 7, 2005, attacks in London, and the location of senior Al Qaeda leaders. They had a role in educating the American public. And, whether we liked it or not, they had a role in overseeing our activities, crafting laws related to the increasingly complicated counterterrorism battle, and budgeting us for what was becoming a long campaign. Even then, many of us thought that the groundwork we were laying would be part of a fight that would last for a generation of Americans, and that children of those years would have to fight this same battle as they grew up. It wasn't, and still isn't, just a fight against terrorists. It is a war of wills against individuals who have spent years developing an ideology, an idea, that has resonance among youth across a broad swath of the Islamic world. Operators can come and go, but ideologies persist when they have core believers who are as ardent as they are misguided.

⟿

THE CONGRESSIONAL exchanges were among the most interesting experiences I had, both at CIA and at the FBI. Soon after my return to the Agency in January 2002, the Counterterrorist Center had a need to send one of its staff to provide frequent briefings to the Senate Select Committee on Intelligence (SSCI), the committee that oversees the activities of the Agency and other intelligence entities. The oversight committee—both members and staff—of the House of Representatives also requested frequent briefings, and the exchanges were similar: a narrative followed by a back-and-forth series of questions and conversation, rather than a formal, extended briefing. At one point, I went to see assembled senators and staff as often as once every two or three weeks, offering updates on what the early war against Al Qaeda looked liked from Langley's perspective. And since the Agency, along with U.S. special forces, Afghan elements, and then more conventional U.S. military units, was at the heart of the war in Afghanistan, we knew a great deal, both about the fight in Afghanistan and the expanding battle around in the world, from the Persian Gulf through South and Southeast Asia.

There was much less public information about how we were conducting the war then, and the thirst for knowledge during those briefings was high. Not only did there remain the sense that we could face another catastrophic attack any day—the sense that the unknown loomed large, and that more likely than not we would see another major event—but the senators and representatives to whom I spoke regularly wanted to know more about a war they had to explain at home and pay for in Washington. And we provided answers to questions about how we were doing, what the level of threat was, how other governments were aiding in the fight.

Almost all the senators and congressmen treated me courteously. There is a great deal of comment among my colleagues about the pain of congressional oversight, the ritualistic grilling by members who can play for the cameras during public testimony. Testimony is a critical part of the balance of powers in our country, and it is critical to ensuring proper allocation of funds, adherence to the law, and reflection on how the execution of policy in a place like CIA reflects the will of the people, as represented in Congress. That said, testimony is often the cod liver oil of government work: a daily dose goes a long way to good health, but that doesn't mean the dose tastes good.

I confess that I actually enjoyed the interaction. In those early days, the challenge of combining all we knew from a wide range of sources into a relatively short briefing that captured intelligence for an audience not trained in technical intelligence issues was a high bar. The audience, meanwhile, was not partisan in those days, so the briefings didn't come with the sense that whatever one said would be looked at through two different lenses. It was genuine engagement, with an intensely interested, courteous audience that had to answer questions among voters every time they went home to their constituencies. And the members themselves wanted to know: they had to budget the money, pass the laws, provide the oversight mandated in the Constitutional provision of three pillars of government.

As time went on, of course, these engagements became more difficult, and sometimes nasty. They were still interesting, however: I never tired of the give-and-take, always viewing it as a challenge and a responsibility. The philosophy of engagement was simple. These are the representatives of the people, and they are supposed to know what we're doing. And even if I don't like it, we're going to have to take this medicine anyway; it's not an option. So why not view it as an opportunity to engage, to learn, to keep a pulse on what those outside our closed world of intelligence are hearing? To educate and be educated, through questions that showed me how perceptions were evolving.

The most difficult of all the engagements I witnessed came before the Iraq war. The core justification for the war, of course, was the question of Saddam's development of a WMD capability. As the previous chapter describes, secondary to this case was sketchy intelligence about whether Saddam had linkages with Al Qaeda or its members. In the analytic component of CIA's Counterterrorist Center, we put a significant number of analysts on this problem, though the group of analysts following mainstream Al Qaeda issues dwarfed our Iraq unit. Both ends of the political spectrum requested clearance to use some of this intelligence publicly, either to argue that there was a significant connection and that we had gathered outlines of it or that other intelligence showed the two were enemies of a common enemy, but never friends, or even close. One side could cite the presence of Al Qaeda-linked individuals in Baghdad who appeared to be operating in relative comfort; the other could cite senior Al Qaeda detainees who denied a relationship.

We probably should simply have prepared a short precis of what we knew, declassified it to avoid revealing sensitive sources, and released it to Congress and others. Instead, we accepted their requests for clearance, which typically cited accurately the intelligence we had. And, because those citations were accurate, we cleared them. These citations, though, were misleading; they were cherry-picked from the clearest intelligence that would support one argument or another. So if a requester wanted to throw cold water on any intelligence about linkages, citations about Al Qaeda detainees denying the relationship would be featured. On both sides, these citations lacked context, and we fell into the game of allowing the trees to be presented without any analysis of the forest.

We were quizzed, again and again and again, by the policy side and the Congress on this analysis. Congressional hearings were skeptical and often rough, with members judging that the aggressive analysis pointing to a possible linkage was politicized—that is, shaded to favor a White House position. Ironically, the White House position was just the opposite. From senior White House and Pentagon officials, we fielded incessant, insistent questions, every day, about Iraq-Al Qaeda linkages and every shred of information we had about any such ties. In contrast to the heat we took on the Hill about being too aggressive and politicized, the pressing we took from the White House and Pentagon implied that we were too soft, especially in the post-9/11 era, and that our vision was too limited, that we looked at data too narrowly. A crisis of crippled creativity, I suppose, in an environment where many might ask "didn't you learn anything by missing the creative leap of understanding they'd use aircraft as weapons?"

Not all our congressional briefings, though, were formal, or even close to contentious. Quite the contrary. The formal briefings occasionally led to more informal engagements, outside the regular briefing rooms. A few of us would go down to the Hill to talk over sandwiches at lunch, when members or staff didn't want the formality of a hearing. I found these exchanges, if anything, more productive than the hearings. They were remarkably conversational, with questions and commentary flowing both ways, and limited staff taking few notes.

⌐

ALL THE congressional briefings and informal exchanges also extended to prepping some senators for media appearances, particularly Sunday morning talk shows. Media interest has shifted now to a host of other topics, but not then. Key senators appeared, weekly, on all of the most prominent Sunday morning shows, and a few of us talked to them beforehand, usually early Sunday morning, to ensure that they were aware of anything breaking. This was partly because CIA was so central to the war, and the lawmakers appearing on TV were therefore often members of the Agency's oversight committees, so they logically turned to us for briefings before their appearances. They didn't need help once they got in front of a camera, and that wasn't our role anyway. But I felt it was our job to ensure that the American public didn't get inaccurate information about intelligence from members of Congress, particularly those who were charged with overseeing our activities.

At that time, media coverage of the global campaign was a prominent daily feature, including in U.S. newspapers and broadcast and cable outlets, but also encompassing the global press that would regularly break stories about the counterterror campaign overseas. So before every one of these weekend phone calls, I would talk through updates with our operations center, which was up and running 24/7, but would also closely review news clips from around the world, looking for items that the senators would already have seen (typically in the Washington or New York papers) or buried stories that might merit a mention. These news clips would also include summaries of what major TV outlets were covering, in the event the senators would field a question that had first appeared on a network news broadcast the night before.

Surprisingly, despite the tight schedules of these senators, some of those Sunday conversations were lengthy, anywhere from two minutes to an hour or more. I would be drinking coffee in the living room of my townhouse outside Washington, picking up updates via a secure phone from CIA headquarters and then determining what to distill during the early morning conversations, filtering out classified information that wasn't suitable for a nonsecure phone or a multimillion-viewer audience. We dealt with the breaking issues, but then we occasionally shifted into context. How were we doing in the war? What was behind all this? What were the strengths and weaknesses of our various partners? I felt this dialogue was part of the basic background that intelligence analysis should provide to any policymaker: the best analysis helps a policy official—whether in the executive, legislative, or judicial branch—to understand a problem well enough to make decisions with greater confidence. Or to explain more clearly to the American public the nature of a global counterterror campaign, making order out of disorder.

This being Washington, with its insatiable appetite for news and its 24-hour news cycle, I also worked closely with our public affairs office on media relations. Bill Harlow, a former naval officer and CIA's head of public affairs at that time, came to be one of my favorite characters at the Agency. Smart, well known around town, and refreshingly succinct in his guidance to me (and, as I learned, to Tenet, with whom he was very close), Harlow and his staff were constantly fielding media questions ranging from the tactical (who had been captured that week) to the general (how we are doing in the counterterror campaign). Bill talked me through every major brief, often calling me into his office a few minutes before he put some reporter on the speakerphone for a quick chat. He would offer low-key tips afterward that helped me learn his side of the business. He combined an ability to help explain how we might best capture the story, in his inimitable brief style, with the capacity to let minor miscues roll off his back without a second thought. Even with the occasional hiccup—slipping in a soundbite that, in retrospect, was poorly spoken—he never jumped beyond simple, low-key guidance. "That line will work fine, but if you say it this way, it might work better," would be the type of background he would offer. Two minutes of prep, a 15-minute phone briefing, and two minutes of after-action commentary. He spoke; I learned. And, over time, we grew comfortable enough that even a major brief took almost no preparation. I knew what he wanted; he knew what I could deliver, and what I couldn't.

Bill never hesitated to engage the media quickly when he thought we should inform, fight back, or try to hold a story, partly because he had the unqualified support and confidence of Tenet. I will never forget sitting outside the director's office late one day, during a short respite, and listening to Bill tell the director that he, Tenet, was featured on some relatively small cable TV special. "Yes," Harlow added, "and a total of 12 people will be watching. Seven of them will be named 'Tenet.' And four of those will be sleeping." Classic Harlow dry humor, and a classic illustration of his comfort with the boss.

Again, the Agency's classified internal instant messaging network played an everyday role in this relationship. A media outlet would get word that another Al Qaeda operative had been picked up somewhere around the world. Suddenly the text messaging box on my computer would light up from Bill or one of his staff in the public affairs office. Was the capture significant? Once we determined that it would be appropriate to comment on a particular story, or to provide broad background, our role in these stories was to prevent bad information from circulating. And, in the best of circumstances, we could help the media understand the war well enough to educate the American public, as long as sensitive "sources and methods" issues—exposure of classified information, in other words—weren't involved. It seemed ironic to me then, the large number of media background interviews we gave, to both print and broadcast media, even while the Agency was castigated in the same media circles for everything from missing 9/11 to holding prisoners in undisclosed "black site" prisons overseas. Participating when we could, though, was better than the alternative, which would be to spend even more time answering questions from officials in the executive branch or Congress when bad information hit the streets. We couldn't win either way: play with the media, or pay the price of bad information skewing the knowledge of people who read the papers and watched the news.

There was a third category of media response beyond day-to-day, tactical stories and broad background interviews: dealing with information that we thought might damage national security if it was disclosed publicly. The culture of leaks in Washington means that the media, particularly investigative journalists in the print media, regularly picked up stories that detailed operations we didn't want publicized. Some might involve techniques we were using to collect intelligence, and we obviously didn't want adversaries to learn what we knew and adjust their tactics. Some might involve initiatives against a particular person or cell; we didn't want to publicize whom we were after, and how close we were.

I assumed that many of these leaks came from inside Washington, but who leaked most was unclear to me, beyond assuming that all the major players—Congress, the White House, and executive branch agencies such as the CIA—had their own official channels to speak to the press, with their own angle to highlight, their own secrets to bury. And their own unofficial channels, leakers, who had personal axes to grind, and who almost never seemed to get caught despite endless leak investigations after every major disclosure.

I remember one particular instance when a prominent reporter called Bill and recounted a story that we were close to a senior Al Qaeda operational commander. As often as not, the better-informed reporters, those with long histories in Washington and good contacts in government, had stories that were on the mark or at least close to it. We sometimes heard off-the-wall stories, or information, that bore little or no resemblance to reality, but those were in the minority. In this case, the reporter had the story, in some detail, and with a great deal of accuracy. The calculation in these cases was simple: either we bring in the reporter and talk about the sensitivity of the case, or we let a story break that might cause damage to an operational opportunity. Luckily, I didn't have the task of making the decision; I only had to tell the story, and tell it right, once the decision was made, in an effort to explain why exposure would be so damaging. There was no gilding the lily. Despite how Pollyanna-ish this sounds, we never, in my experience, purposefully misled a reporter. Not necessarily just because it was the wrong thing to do, but because Washington is a small town with long memories. Mislead once and your information is suspect for years to come.

Bill asked me to talk to the reporter with him and one of our senior operations managers, confirming that the reporter had the story and letting the reporter know, in some detail, what we were up to and why it was important that the story not run at that time. I knew then, and remember today, that any citizen looking over our shoulders would have been surprised during that briefing, at multiple levels, especially at the amount of excruciating detail someone had already leaked to the media (to this day, I still don't know who did it). At the amount of information we corroborated and provided in response, knowing that if were weren't straight up, our prospects of being persuasive were nil. And that the reporter would find out anyway. Finally, and perhaps most important, at seeing the quality of intelligence we had against a target who was participating in high-level Al Qaeda operations. We were close to the target, tightening the circle so steadily that we thought we would soon close in on him. And we didn't want him spooked. Publicity would have sent him to ground, and we needed to buy time. Whoever leaked had forced our hand.

Frequently and unsurprisingly, in these instances we had different perceptions of what was sensitive from the media who dealt with our press office. Occasionally, we even had differences with the media office itself, though I do not recollect many. We might want to protect a sensitive method of intelligence collection that reporters thought the American public should know about. Typically, we had to show a clear line between exposure of the story a reporter had and endangerment of human life. If we could make that link clearly, we would stand a good chance of having the story spiked, or at least delayed. If our case was weak, we would lose, even if the information was highly sensitive. Mostly, we lost, simply because we could not clearly enough link disclosure of the information with potential loss of life. But it always seemed worthwhile to try to make the case, and I never regretted those failures.

In this instance, we could and did make the case. We were dealing with an Al Qaeda operative who was directly implicated in plotting against the United States. Sending him to ground by letting him know how important he was to us would unquestionably give him more time to advance those plots. The reporter agreed; the story was delayed. Not long afterward, that same terrorist went down. And as was often the case, there was a quid pro quo, which I thought made sense: when it was time to tell the story—in other words, when the operation went down—the reporter got the first call and a chance to break the story.

These interviews seemed a long way from my first days as a junior analyst, but it was easy to understand the import of what we were up to. Without these interventions, we'd see even more exposure of classified information. It seemed like we had no option but to play in this Washington game, and I don't recollect any internal debates about the wisdom of sharing what we knew in an effort to slow the hemorrhaging of leaks.

The broader background interviews were more fun. I came to believe that they were part of a secondary mission we had during the war, that of helping the people who were paying for it, American taxpayers, understand how we were doing, and where we were vulnerable in ways that could affect their safety. Our role in these stories was simple: we had a daily, tactical window on how this war was going that no one in the public sphere could come close to replicating, and Americans who were deeply affected by how the campaign was progressing had no way of putting what they heard and read into context. We had great analytic experience putting all this tactical information together in a clear narrative that would make sense to nonexperts, so journalists often came in with basic questions that didn't test our willingness to reveal what we shouldn't and weren't driven by an insane news cycle. Questions such as whether we were better off than we had been; whether Al Qaeda was suffering; and where we were in making progress against the adversary. Strategic questions, far different from the tactical problem of dealing with reporters who had a leak to run with.

It wasn't that we were free to talk to the media anytime, about anything. Far from it. We were required to work on any media contacts through the press office, and it was virtually unheard of for any officer to do otherwise. Among my peers, talking to the media outside authorized channels would be seen as a violation not only of regulations but a of the unwritten laws of the service. It was seen as completely inappropriate. But after so many media interviews, over years, I gained a comfort level with Bill. He obviously didn't know the substance as well as we did, but he knew what they were interested in. So we'd meet a few minutes before an interview, and share notes. He'd run through what the storylines were; I'd run through what we knew, and how I thought we should march through the material with the press. He never corrected substance, which was not his area. But he might offer comments on what angles would make most sense, where problems might arise, which questions we'd want to avoid, and how to deal with difficult questions when they came up.

One of the more memorable backgrounders I remember was a lengthy session to prepare for an NBC special hosted by commentator Tom Brokaw. My job, arranged by the press office, was to sit with Brokaw for a while one morning—it turned out to be an hour or two—and talk him through what the war looked like strategically through our Langley lens, and how we thought we were doing. We were then to go on camera to tape a few questions-and-answers that might capture the essence of the lengthy backgrounder.

I had done more such interviews than I could remember, but I didn't know what to expect from this one. As it turned out, Brokaw couldn't have been easier to deal with. We talked easily during the background. He asked good questions, knew the subject, and turned out to be a good listener. The on-camera work was smooth as well. I had found that some interviewers would ask provocative questions designed to see how far the interviewee would go. Brokaw simply asked questions that helped elucidate the story. Not to say that going on-camera was a simple task: in contrast to interviews with print journalists, being in front of a camera always meant that a few wayward words would be lost forever, captured on film before you could say "let me work on that answer a bit."

In this case, too, there was the added surprise of the then-director of the agency, Porter Goss, walking into the operations center in the Agency, where we were taping the interview, to watch the progress. I saw him out of the corner of my eye during Brokaw's questioning. But it went fine. No slips that I could notice, and Brokaw didn't pop any questions designed to put me off-balance. Goss, who had a rocky tenure as CIA director but who was always courteous to me, poked fun about this for years afterwards, often asking me about a future life in the media.

As I guess is the case in all these sorts of events, the memories are those that never make the camera. Dealing with an American news icon and finding that kind of courtesy, proving once again that no matter how high you rise, you can still treat people, even those who pass by in a day or two, with that kind of touch. And, more humorously, finding a fellow fly fisherman who talked as much, when we were first introduced, about chasing fish with a flyrod as he did about the objectives for the day. I remember the fishing stories most, not the interview.

THROUGH ALL those years, one of the other consistent realities of the war we dealt with, both inside government and with the general public, were the ups and downs in the threat levels that led to so many media flurries. There was no easy way to capture what we were seeing from Al Qaeda plotting, but people across the country had a thirst, a demand, to have threat information boiled down in such a way that it was quickly comprehensible. This was understandable: many people, from airline operators to governors to everyday Americans planning vacations, wanted to know whether we saw sufficient intelligence information to believe some plot might be afoot.

This requirement for a readily digestible way to portray threat led to the now discarded, and almost forgotten, color-coding system, whereby the government would set threat levels corresponding to colors and adjust the level, and the color, based on an interagency assessment of incoming threat reporting from all sources—human, technical, foreign government, everything. Some of the most intense congressional briefing sessions I participated in occurred when the country was still faced with a barrage of reports and analyses about when and why the system would go from yellow to the more alarming orange. The concept behind the coding was laudable: give people a clear, simple way to understand when we receive information that suggests we may face a higher threat of attack, and don't assume that the complexities of intelligence are transparent. Going from yellow to orange, as a way to indicate broad concern among specialists looking at intelligence, made sense as a communication tool for the American people.

The warning system evolved, over years, to become more sector specific. That is, when intelligence information suggests plotting against transit hubs such as airports or trains, those sectors should be under higher alert. A dam in a western state might not require a step up in security. The initial system proved too broad, too inclusive, but it did offer a solution to the question of how to inform people of government concerns without complicated nuance.

The raised and lowered threat levels we experienced after the color-coded system went into effect might have looked systematic from the outside. It was hard for me to tell how the public perceived them, aside from the constant stories on cable news outlets. From the inside, these threat variations, when the levels moved up or down on the scale, were not clearly defined because the threat information was so varied. We did not, in other words, have a clearcut system that stepped through when we might shift up, to orange, kicking off another feverish round of briefings, media speculation—and also, quickly, matching speculation about when the level would drop again, and why. I have since seen allegations that some of these shifts were motivated by politics. Although it never appeared to me that the process was politicized—there was always some serious bit of intelligence that drove the debates—I was not privy, obviously, to the high-level White House discussions that led to the announcements. The murkiness was instead a result of the wide variety and credibility of the intelligence reporting we received, which often lacked specificity and didn't fall into neatly defined categories of urgency.

We in Washington knew we needed to give the public some sense of what we were seeing, without overly nuancing the information or offering long narratives that would be difficult to act on for people unaccustomed to understanding intelligence data. But characterizing one week, or one month, or one threat in such stark terms created a sense, I thought, that threat information and color coding was far more clearcut than what we saw. The reality was a mass of information that showed that Al Qaeda and its affiliated were always plotting against us, with multiple operatives in South and Southeast Asia, Europe, and the United States. The image we projected distilled this chaotic mass of data into two words: yellow or orange? The later shift to a more sectoral approach—raising threats to air transport specifically, for example—was a critical refinement of threat warning, but we had the far more blunt instrument of simple and general threat warnings when we first went down this road.

Congressional and media briefings always resulted from the shifts in threat level. Lawmakers heading home to see constituents had to answer for what cropped up in the news—people wanted to know whether we were going to be hit again with a terrorist strike, and the newly created terror threat levels were almost tailormade for never-ending news cycles. There were threats one week, more threats the next week, all hard to sort through and make sense of, until the federal government says "pay attention, this one is serious." Early on, people paid attention, before the drumbeat of constant threats, the lack of devastating attacks in the United States, and the crowding in of other national problems, from health care to the economy to global warming—eased terrorism off the front pages.

Especially at this early stage, there was tremendous unity of effort, as the news still carried daily reports on many aspects of the war on terror, so obviously shifts in threat levels were front-page stories. I remember going to Congress repeatedly with Tom Ridge, secretary of the new Department of Homeland Security, to explain in closed briefings to members why the level had jumped, to try to make sense of the morass of threat information we received so that a shift up to orange made sense, and to ensure that the intelligence information was captured in some sort of context that the members of Congress could translate to their constituents.

These briefings were some of the most memorable of my career, both because of the import of the briefings and because some of the moments were unique enough that they are unforgettable. The interest was so high that we had dozens of senators in the room on multiple occasions, asking questions often related to how they could explain intelligence to constituents. At one point, I remember receiving a request to brief several hundred members of Congress one evening, during one or another of the threat spikes. I went downtown, with CIA and White House congressional liaison staff, to find a packed room, including many dozens of members who had little or no experience handling classified intelligence information.

After an initial briefing from a podium, I fielded questions, all the while trying to balance the need to offer enough to provide context while not delving into classified material that wasn't suited for the general threat background we were supposed to discuss. Even so, a senior member of Congress approached me afterward, clearly uncomfortable. I thought the balance between informing so many members and protecting classified information was fine; he, by contrast, was deeply concerned that the briefing had been too detailed, and that members who were not steeped in national security matters might reveal sensitive elements of what they'd heard without purposely doing so. I was so struck by the irony I almost had to laugh: the intelligence guy, supposed to be the protector of the secrets, approached by the politician, the interlocutor with the American people. And the latter, the one counseling caution in revealing information! He was extremely polite, though, and probably right, as I reflected on his comments. This was one of many moments when politicians in Washington treated me with courtesy, despite the disparity between their rank and mine.

Many of the questions centered on broad issues, such as how we were faring, whether the threat was rising or falling, and how various governments' cooperation measured up. They were highly engaging, with lots of back-and-forth focused not on partisan politics or on disputes about what we presented but simply on how the war was being fought, how they could understand and explain it, and how the Congress might play a role. Only later, as the drumbeat of the Iraq war grew louder, did the briefings decline in frequency and in increase in pain. Questions about estimates of Iraqi WMD, and Saddam's relationship with Al Qaeda, because of their political salience and the open debates about them across America, came to color everything, over time.

We also had frequent engagements with staff, but in the first year or two, member interest was so high that many or most of my interactions were with members themselves. This, too, changed as interest slowly waned and Iraq took over. Staff always wanted more detail, and they often had perspectives on how CIA and other agencies were working that they wanted to ask us about. Questions about information sharing among agencies perceived as rivals were common, especially after this issue grew in the wake of the 9/11 Report and the emergence of the National Counterterrorism Center. The staff had a profound impact on what members thought and said, and engagement with key staff members always seemed worth the effort. As time went on, though, it was clear that political issues were moving to the fore, and staff engagement became more difficult, resulting on more than one occasion for requests from staff on one side of the aisle to be briefed separately from their counterparts on the other. We routinely denied these requests.

Other incidents underscored the gap between those of us who dealt almost exclusively with national security information, without a second thought, and politicians who had to handle everything from fundraising, national budgets, defense issues, taxes, local economics, jobs. . . . Their positions seemed daunting to me.

Perhaps the most memorable briefing I remember, during one of the spikes to the orange threat level, involved standing in the formal well of the Congress of the United States, two podiums arranged on the floor. Secretary Ridge took one; I took the other.

The CIA is a flat organization, far more interested in what's happening overseas that in the incongruity of how we ended up with a mid-level CIA analyst sharing the briefing floor in the well of the Congress with a Cabinet secretary. Tenet was always good about letting his subordinates spread their wings. He gave us chances to succeed, or fail.

Ridge was similar, and great to deal with. We probably went to the Hill together a handful of times. Each time, he was gracious and remarkably humorous. Immaculately tailored, with a perfect haircut, I couldn't figure out how he pulled it off every time I saw him in my wrinkled suit. Never flustered, maybe reflecting his background as a former marine. Like Tenet, he often deferred questions, not interested in showing that he knew everything when the questions became too detailed or outside his area of responsibility. Multiple times during classified briefings, he'd turn, unscripted, and say "What do you think, Phil?" I'm sure I hit a few and missed a few, but I had to restrain a smile a few times, holding back the urge to turn it around: "I don't know. What do you think, Mr. Secretary?" Just to give him a hard time, because I could tell quickly that his sense of humor would win out.

In this instance, once we gave an overview—I don't remember which of us said what—we launched into questions, with perhaps a few hundred members in attendance. Ridge deferred occasionally during the question-and-answer segment, turning the intelligence picture over to me and focusing more himself on homeland issues, such as securing American infrastructure and measures the Department of Homeland Security might take in response to emerging threats. But I will never forget one member, rising in his seat in the midst of this sea of people, asking about individuals he thought were suspicious walking out of a house of worship across the street from his apartment in Washington. What should he do, he asked? Could I do something about this?

Even two decades of analytic experience and training doesn't prepare you for a member of Congress asking what to do about suspicious people outside his apartment. I felt like pitching the question back to Ridge. Call your local police or the FBI's Joint Terrorism Task Force in Washington was the response, I think, though the details escape me now. But as a trained analyst, looking at the broad problem of Al Qaeda and its implications for the United States, it was a good reminder that all politics is local. We could provide great strategic briefs; the audience always wanted to know what it meant for them. What they should say. What they should do back home, and how they could help in Congress.

Like so many aspects of those years, though, those experiences sharpened the learning curve for someone trained in what had been the relatively isolated corridors of CIA analysis. Getting schooled by a weeks, months, and then years of Congressional and media engagement helps you learn fast. Looking back, I see that it was learning that made me into a far better officer. But maybe it was also learning that was so unique that it won't happen again, at least in my lifetime. And that, given the pain of the years of counterterrorism, is a good thing.

CHAPTER 6

THE YEARS OF THREAT

THERE WAS so much threat reporting, often from credible sources, and so many spikes in activity, over the course of years, that the threats run together. Those years are a jumble, running from one threat to another while we tried to understand the progress in the war more broadly and stand up an office that had the bureaucratic support to provide careers and a life for all the analysts who had flooded to work the terrorism problem. Even years later, though, there were a few tense periods that stand out because of threats, and the intense attention they brought to the persistent Al Qaeda threat.

One of the most chilling resulted from the arrest of Dhiren Bharot, an Al Qaeda operative in Britain who had traveled to the United States before 9/11. Bharot also had, after 9/11, traveled to the tribal areas of Pakistan, along the border with Afghanistan, presumably at least in part to report on what he knew of the United States, and to participate in planning or undertaking operations in the UK or elsewhere.

What we found on Bharot's computer were files that reaffirmed, once again, the commitment of Al Qaeda to strike a blow against a strategic U.S. target, in this case New York, New Jersey, or sites in Washington. As the information began rolling in, we understood quickly that the casing reports Bharot had amassed during his time in the United States could have been the feed material for an Al Qaeda operation. Furthermore, it wasn't just the specificity of the targets he was looking at: it was the meticulous care with which he had studied the targets. He was methodical.

The Washington threat machinery kicked into high gear immediately, as we disseminated information from the casing packages into intelligence reports sent throughout Washington and analysts and policymakers throughout the city realized the import of what Dhiren Bharot had done. What happened afterward is now a jumble to me, but elements of it were classic as examples of how serious threat information affects Washington and the country as a whole.

We had to explain to policy consumers in Washington what we had, the import of the Bharot information, and we had to do it fast. In a city of leaks, nobody who has responsibility for responding to threat information, or for explaining it to the American people, wants to hear about a major threat from the news media. We didn't want it either, both because rapid dissemination of critical intelligence is a hallmark of a good intelligence organization and because disinformation about threats like the Bharot casing rapidly fills the void if consumers don't receive the real thing very quickly. Moreover, because there was a substantial quantity of information that would take us some time to exploit, we had to ensure that we maintained this pace, and kept people informed, during the entire period when teams of analysts were reviewing his material. It was a lot. And it was important. And, finally, it was urgent.

I remember early one morning looking through the electronic messages detailing the overnight processing of some of the Bharot information and realizing that the information was so critical to understanding the case that the CIA executive going in to see the president should know before the briefing. At that point, the information was rolling in so fast that material a day old might already be stale, circulating around Washington in almost real time, so we could mitigate any imminent threat, before the formal dissemination of the material followed. No one would want to walk out of the Oval Office only to find, a half-hour later, that the briefing should have been updated. Especially given that the President himself no doubt would learn of the updates later in the day.

The material itself was dated by the time Bharot was captured—he had actually surveilled the potential targets in the United States before 9/11—but he had more recent contacts with Al Qaeda players. And, as is most often the case with these rapidly evolving threat streams, we didn't know what we didn't know. It would be easy on the outside to say that we reacted too sharply to dated information, dusty surveillance files. With this and similar cases, though, life on the inside seemed different, sometimes fundamentally so, from life on the outside. What if there was a remaining piece of the plot that we were unaware of, or a player we hadn't identified who now felt compelled to act, before we closed in on him? The answer that such a prospect was highly unlikely, or only remotely probable—an assessment many of us would agree with—wasn't reason enough to ignore the chance that we would be surprised.

We acted quickly on this and other similar information, especially during those years, information that was dated or too fragmentary to put together well-calculated responses. I placed a phone call to our operations center and asked them to find John McLaughlin, deputy director of the CIA and, on that day, the senior CIA executive accompanying the daily presidential briefer into the Oval Office. The operations center reached the CIA officers as they were preparing to head in to see the president. Just in time.

We had similar responsibilities to keep our FBI and Homeland Security counterparts informed. The CIA process for sending out intelligence reports is a core business area for the Agency, and it is a well-oiled machine. Raw intelligence from sources comes in and undergoes review by various experts to ensure that it makes sense—for example, that a source who reports on one area doesn't suddenly report on an area to which he doesn't have clear access. The reports are then sent out to the universe of analysts who specialize in particular subject areas. A report from a source on terrorism in an African country, for example, will be received by analysts across Washington and around the world who specialize in African terrorism and might be reviewed for passage to a foreign intelligence service that is affected by the information.

But in times of fast-breaking events, even the quickest, most efficient dissemination process is not fast enough. Senior FBI executives, for example— my counterparts across the river at the J. Edgar Hoover building—had to speak with FBI director Robert Mueller every morning and throughout the day; they needed to understand, for example, what the information showed about Bharot's activities in the United States. And they needed to respond to the breaking threat picture by investigating whether pieces of the plot were still in play. We didn't know whether Al Qaeda would act on the information Bharot provided and, if so, when. So, as with the McLaughlin phone call, we lit up the secure phone lines to the Bureau, making sure that Mueller and others knew what we knew in advance of the dissemination of formal reports. Those reports might take a day or less to disseminate. Not fast enough.

Homeland Security and the New York City Police Department also had responsibilities, not only for securing streets, but for understanding the plot and which facilities might be under threat. I remember receiving a call one day, in the midst of the wave of Bharot information, from a senior Department of Homeland Security official. Bharot's information showed that he had studied individual buildings and their vulnerabilities in great detail. The official asked the kind of question that crops up frequently in terrorism intelligence but is almost unheard of elsewhere. It captures, in a nutshell, the linkages between operations and intelligence ten thousand miles away and a U.S. citizen in Manhattan. Can we share the information, the official asked, with people responsible for guarding the safety of the buildings Bharot studied? And can we share it now?

This is not the type of situation a CIA analyst is typically trained to handle. Analysis of the evolution of missile programs in rogue states doesn't require on-the-spot judgments about sharing data with managers of apartment buildings. But the world is growing smaller. Events on the other side of the globe have direct, immediate implications for U.S. cities. The intelligence community is responding, slowly, to these implications of globalization. The answer that day was easy: share it. And share it before you get the paperwork authorizing disclosure to apartment managers. The paper will follow. Don't wait.

The broad cultural shift, across the CIA and other agencies in Washington, was a rare case of bureaucracies quickly absorbing the lesson that we should take risks sharing threat information and let the consequences of releasing classified information follow later. I do not recollect any backlash to sharing even sensitive data, whether to another agency, such as DHS talking to building managers, or to the media when we tried to prevent a leak or attempted to help the public understand the threat environment during heightened periods of risk. As Director Tenet had said, on other matters, there ain't no learning in the second kick of the mule. Washington was rife with stories, some true and many not, of unwillingness to share before 9/11. This was no time to relive those stories. Not to say problems didn't persist—they did, particularly on issues such as how to share information that would expose our most sensitive sources, particularly if the information we obtained was so tied to a single source that a leak would reveal the source, halting the information flow and potentially risking the source's life.

⌒

THE GENESIS of the airline plot during the summer of 2006, looking back, also easily broke into the ranks of the deadliest plots of the past decade. It involved more conspirators than most plots we saw, trained by Al Qaeda in Pakistan and attempting an ingenious method of smuggling explosive material onto planes by drilling out the bottoms of plastic drink bottles so that the tops would appear sealed. The plot, in other words, that led to the requirement that every passenger limit the amount of liquid materials in carry-on baggage. Many close followers of the world of terrorism would agree that it represents the most significant strategic plot we have witnessed post-9/11. Every day's morning threat briefs brought new plots, from wannabes to unhinged lunatics to serious plotters from known terror groups. The significance of the 2006 plot hinges on the number of factors we witnessed in that cell. There were connections to, and training from, serious players in the Al Qaeda heartland of the Pakistan-Afghanistan border. The plotters were devising a device in Britain, and they had acquired the materials for it. Their approach, in comparison with many of the plots that crop up daily, was highly sophisticated: they had a plan that might have worked, had the British not performed so well against them. Their network was broad, and their operational security was good. Cells might hit on one or two of these characteristics, but it is uncommon to find cells that combine all these features that contributed to the seriousness of this threat.

Two factors always play into threat: capability—the ability of a foreign entity to hit inside the United States—and intent, the interest of the adversary in pursuing targets in America in furtherance of some ideological goal. This group had those traits, but also so many others: security, overseas contacts, seriousness, a broad network. Some cells have a combination of these, but few I have seen, including these potential bombers and those who succeeded against London transport nodes on July 7, 2005, combine so many, even in the ten years we have had to witness the rise and fall of countless plots in Western Europe and North America.

The handling of the threat had the classic characteristics of how Washington came to operate, over time, after 9/11. Multiple agencies were involved, from CIA working on the overseas pieces of the plot to Homeland Security worrying about domestic elements, including airline safety. All were coordinating among themselves, as well as under the umbrella of an intensely interested, and focused, White House.

When I was later sitting in the FBI, at that point finishing up my first year there, what unfolded helps clarify the complications of coordinating actions in the midst of a threat with so many core actors. Every single lead is parceled out to a field office and followed. A sample of the kinds of questions that crop up offers a narrow window on why these operations are difficult to manage, and why they consume so many resources. Multiply each question by the number of subjects involved in the investigation. Have the individuals in Britain traveled here? Do they have contacts here? Friends? Family? Do they communicate here?

In every instance, with every subject, if there is an indication of contact—phone calls, visits, etc.—there is personal follow up in a field office. In FBI parlance, every lead is "covered." And since the nature of any contact is unclear at the outset, even seemingly benign contacts, which may number in the hundreds for an investigation of this breadth, require manpower. What if a subject calls a Domino's Pizza? Is he calling because he wants a pizza? Or is he calling because he has a contact there? When a contact is identified, how quickly can we determine whether it's an unwitting friend or family member or someone who's part of a plot? Do we need to conduct physical surveillance, which is the most labor-intensive part of any investigation?

The days leading up to the takedown of that cell in 2006 were intense. The British were learning more and more, and every step of the investigation produced more data that required follow up in the United States. We found, over time, very limited links to the U.S., but we couldn't be sure then. The knowns in intelligence—having a solid lead on a potential terrorist who is in direct contact with Al Qaeda overseas—are challenging enough. It is the unknowns, questions such as whether the individual you are studying has contacts that you have not yet identified, that are the deadliest problem. Take down a plot too early and you miss people who were on the fringes of the conspiracy. Misjudge a target's intentions and he could create havoc one day when you thought the plot was in its aspirational stages.

The coordination among agencies, including agency heads, is frequent and deep during such investigations. Secure videoconferencing capabilities allow working-level professionals to talk multiple times a day. There are so many individual leads and potential dropped balls that this daily coordination is crucial in parceling out the leads, and in ensuring that the agencies following them are trading notes along the way. The most interesting lead in the morning—a direct phone call into the United States by a known conspirator—might be a dead end by the evening, confirmed as a misdialed number. In the instance of the 2006 plot, the threat was so severe that heads of Washington agencies met by video early on to ensure all understood who had which pieces.

These high-threat moments also underscored the importance of close relationships with foreign security services. Especially after 9/11, when so many European, Middle Eastern, African, and Asian services saw terrorism problems of their own, the importance of maintaining ties to services in countries that might share threat information with us was a primary focus.

On the one hand, as we grew our collection capabilities, we regularly uncovered links between terrorists we were following and their contacts in other countries, and it was standard practice to pass these contacts along with any contextual information, such as whether we knew with any specificity what they might be plotting and with whom they might be in contact. Conversely, we would regularly receive tips from other services about whether people or cells they were surveilling were in touch with individuals of interest to us. Regardless of diplomatic turbulence, these security service contacts, even between countries that might suffer bouts of difficult diplomatic weather, were a regular feature of daily business. When countries are under threat, behind-the-scenes cooperation is almost a given, except between enemies. Risking a life because of diplomatic differences, however severe, simply wasn't an option.

Many of us developed close personal ties with our foreign counterparts as well, ties that went beyond these professional links. Business during the day often became business after hours—a shared meal, meeting the family, time to cement bonds and combine business with pleasure. As with work in the office, these relationships, many cultivated over years and across continents, had their own humor, even in wartime. Among the funniest was an evening of boating on the Potomac River in Washington, hosting the head of service of a major Southeast Asian counterpart on a trip to see the lights and enjoy a meal across the river in Alexandria. As we approached the picturesque dock, though, it became clear that something was wrong. We slowly drifted in; the steering had gone out. Steady on, not quickly, but fast enough to hit the dock head-on and disable the lights. The dockmaster started scrambling, but we were now drifting back, away from the dock toward the busy shipping channel that separates the Virginia town of Alexandria from the Maryland shoreline across the river. We had to drop anchor, with amusement all around as we realized we had no way to bridge the fifty yards between the boat and dry land. I still remember wondering what the pleasure boaters who quickly realized our predicament and politely came up alongside would have thought had they known the passengers they ferried to the dock included CIA officials and the head of a major foreign service, and what that head thought when he realized his vaunted hosts had gotten him stranded in the middle of an urban river. Part of the humor was friendship: he had developed a close relationship with my boss Jose, who was not on the boat last night, and the story of this mishap quickly made its way to Jose's ears. We'd stranded his friend. On a boat. In the Potomac. Embarrassing, especially given the outlandishly courteous treatment we often received when we visited our counterparts overseas. Many of them were lavish, not necessarily in what they offered as a gift or a meal, but in the courtesy they provided, far beyond what Americans would offer in similar circumstances. And here we couldn't pull off a boat landing!

There were many such times, especially among our closest partners. The day after I had hernia surgery, during an icy stretch of another Washington winter, I was scheduled to see one the senior representatives of a Western security service. This was outpatient surgery, and as a novice in the world of medicine, I assumed that would mean a few hours of pain and a relatively quick recovery. As I learned, any time a physician messes around your internal organs, even outpatient surgery means more than a day of rest. In short, it was hard to walk for a day or two. With the streets of Old Town Alexandria, Virginia, coated in a rare sheet of winter ice, though, my colleague and his driver made it to the townhouse I shared with my brother. I will never forget feeling like a hundred-year-old relic as the two of them helped me shuffle into the car and then navigate the sidewalk for a visit to a coffee shop. I don't remember what business we had to discuss, but I do remember the courtesy of that day. And there were many such experiences, in a war that spanned almost a decade before I left.

Despite the inevitable friendships, and memorable stories that grew from close partnerships, there was serious work to do as well, and sometimes serious differences to negotiate. For example, as we developed a great deal of technical information in our databases about foreign nationals—such as information collected from seized digital material—we received questions about how we would use material that might be related to foreign nationals. This was a natural question from foreign representatives who rightly had a requirement to protect their nationals. But when foreign laws and U.S. laws differed on questions such as what information we might acquire and how we might retain and search it, the challenges could quickly become highly tricky, not to mention sensitive. Long-time friendships between long-time allies doesn't necessarily mean that every problem can be resolved over a friendly chat. Some of these problems took years to iron out. Some are still yet to be resolved, often because they are tied directly to privacy and legal questions about whether security services are comfortable revealing information about their own nationals to foreign services.

These problems grew, as information about sensitive CIA programs, especially CIA interrogation techniques, transfers of prisoners on flights through foreign airports, and U.S. government use of drones for lethal operations became more and more prominent. Human rights questions, parliamentary inquiries across Europe, and a slew of damaging press disclosures about CIA operations did not destroy intelligence cooperation, but they introduced a level of caution, and legal oversight, that mushroomed. In dealing with foreign information, for example, we might go through extensive exchanges on how the information we were given might be used. Would we use it, for example, to locate a terrorist who would be detained? Or to locate a site that might be hit by a U.S. missile?

Coupled with these current questions was a host of historical ones, ranging from what had happened to prisoners when we handed them over to foreign governments to whether flights carrying prisoners had overflown or landed in friendly countries. What had been a fast, furious, and far-flung campaign had an increasingly prominent added element: legitimate oversight, and questions, counterbalanced by excessive second-guessing and what one partner referred to as "judicial jihad," layers of scrutiny of past operations and current procedures. Security cooperation among friendly, and even not-so-friendly, services is probably broader and deeper than most outside the business would guess, but it is still a more cautious, more legal process than it was in the first years after 9/11.

In parallel with the major threat spikes of those years, there were other threat problems that were equally compelling but didn't have the same gripping sense that we were living in a high-intensity movie. Al Qaeda, for example, linked up with the Southeast Asian group Jemaah Islamiyah to recruit more pilots for suicide attacks and train them in South Asia. One of a number of plots that showed both Al Qaeda's global reach, into terrorist recruiting pools that looked different from the pool of 9/11 plotters, and its commitment to maintaining a focus on spectacular attacks, even in the face of hardened targets such as aircraft. But the plot was detected early, and it lacked the day-to-day drama of an unfolding plot directly across the Atlantic that had a broad band of dedicated plotters plotting to take down aircraft in a number of weeks. It was a reminder—more than a reminder, a sobering two-by-four for any counterterror watcher—of both how persistent Al Qaeda's Pakistani core remained. And how easily European plotters, living in countries that have visa-waiver agreements with the United States, could hop on a plane and execute the next major strike in America. World War II endured, for the United States, from 1941 to 1945; here we were, after a similar period, confronting an adversary that wasn't even close to done yet. The war seemed to last forever.

WATCHING THREATS AT HOME: THE FBI CALLS

THE YEARS after 9/11 passed quickly; the pace of change, the variety of problems we faced, and the magnitude of the challenge all combined to telescope time. Despite the complexity of the positions we occupied, though, I thought that turnover was good. CIA specializes in recruiting talent—we had plenty of it in the Counterterrorist Center—and keeping managers in management positions rotating made sense, at least to me. We had a requirement to develop a cadre of people who were expert in the counterterrorism business. But there is a parallel need, presumably the same in the private sector as it is in government, to rotate people so that new ideas can emerge, and so that old players stay fresh when they see new challenges. Only four and a half years after returning to CIA, we all had seen the expansion of the most intense CIA program of our generation, with all the ups and downs that went with it. So I was also looking for a new challenge, someplace to keep learning and to see something new. And it came. Right place, right time.

We had also seen profound changes in how Washington dealt with intelligence, as we worked through the intelligence reform legislation that followed the attacks and the endless official studies and inquiries that followed 9/11. Most immediate for us was the establishment of a center announced by President Bush in his State of the Union address in 2003 and established that May—first named the Terrorist Threat Integration Center (referred to among us by its acronym, T-tick) and growing into the National Counterterrorism

Center. The creation of this new interagency entity, which was focused on bringing all U.S. government data into one place so a mixed group of analysts would have access to everything, was easily among the toughest, bloodiest bureaucratic issues I witnessed and participated in during a quarter century of government service. The reasons were simple: the Terrorist Threat Integration Center and its successor, NCTC, took over, by statute, the responsibility for providing terrorism analysis to the U.S. government, immediately raising hackles among CIA analysts and managers who had worked on this problem, in some cases for their entire professional lives. It wasn't just the bureaucratic ignominy of this; it was the message that somehow, in the pre-9/11 days before the government made counterterrorism its top priority, CIA analysis had been somehow fundamentally flawed, so flawed that the government required an entirely new organization to fix the problem. The reaction, unsurprisingly, was human: ferocious defense of CIA turf.

There were lessons through the process of NCTC's growth that transcend infighting in government. To my mind, the question was never whether CIA analysts had erred; the better question was simply whether there was a better, or different, way to do business, especially given the criticisms of the intelligence community on the issue of information sharing among agencies. One center that received all information was almost an inevitable answer to these criticisms. In fact, I thought the post-9/11 analysis by CIA was excellent. More significant, though, was the question whether we could provide better analysis because our analysts were directly embedded in the operations, giving them a sense of the grit of the war that couldn't be replicated elsewhere. Of course, the counterpoint was equally compelling: facing the global problem of terrorism, our analysts didn't have equal focus on, or access to, other information, such as homeland security data about the border or FBI investigatory materials. Furthermore, some argued persuasively, the closeness of the Agency's analysts to operators might slant the analysis: who would want to say, from the inside, that a particular area of operational focus was failing?

In the end managers get paid to manage, and these arguments, though illuminating in understanding the tensions between centralized and federated analysis, were not entirely relevant. As I watched the problem grow, the answer was simple. Congress passed a law. The president signed it. We work for them, and they have told us to make this work. Whether we like it is not entirely relevant. In other words, get over it and move on. And if you don't like it, go run for Congress. They pass the laws; we implement them. Case closed.

These fundamental changes came to redirect my career. In 2005, Admiral Scott Redd asked to talk sometime about potentially working beside him at the still-new National Counterterrorism Center. I visited NCTC in suburban Virginia one day in the summer of that year to talk to Redd—one of the more cordial, avuncular senior leaders I'd ever met in the business—at his offices at the center. In one of those twists of fate that seem fictional in the telling, I received a phone call during the conversation with Admiral Redd, who was then the director of NCTC.

The call was from FBI headquarters, director Robert Mueller's office. I knew of Mueller—he had become close to Tenet after taking over the Bureau immediately before 9/11. And I had testified with him a few times. During a few threat briefings in Congress, Director Mueller had represented the FBI, and Tenet had told me to represent the Agency. With the square-jawed presence of a former marine and his reputation as a no-nonsense prosecutor pushing the Bureau hard in the aftermath of the attacks, I suppose I expected some sort of drill sergeant. Instead, during the limited interactions we'd had, he had always been courteous to me, never questioning why I was at the table and always poking fun at "George," as he called him. Director Tenet to me, but "George" to Director Mueller. And he had built an excellent reputation in Washington. He was tough, but direct and interested in intelligence and, potentially, willing to listen to a CIA manager entering the halls of the J. Edgar Hoover building in downtown Washington, with its clear view down the Pennsylvania Avenue corridor of power that connects the Congress with the White House.

He called to talk about the newly established National Security Branch (NSB) of the FBI, the combination of the Bureau's counterterrorism, counterintelligence, WMD, and intelligence components. This was a large portion of the Bureau's budget and manpower at that point, after the flood of agents and analysts rushed to counterterrorism. The Bureau had been under tremendous pressure from Congress, especially after the reports of the 9/11 and WMD commissions, to improve its intelligence performance, and Mueller had staved off efforts to carve out Bureau responsibilities for domestic intelligence into a new domestic security service. The Bureau would maintain those responsibilities, but it would have to change. And the most significant step, in organizational terms, was the combination of those elements and the insistence that they develop more advanced intelligence programs designed to collect information that might thwart threats before they led to attacks.

After I spoke with Director Mueller, Porter Goss, a former member of Congress and then director of the CIA, called me into his office to ask whether I wanted to go. Goss had had a turbulent tenure as director, dealing with a staff that had serious, sometimes acrimonious relationships with the senior CIA careerists who occupied positions on the executive corridor. He was unfailingly polite to me, levels below that corridor, never failing to treat me courteously. The same held true during this exchange. I had been considering trying a new assignment, outside CIA, for some time, and I had been offered another senior position earlier in his tenure. He had taken a call when I had declined the job, and he confirmed that I would not go. This time, though, it was time: the job was right, and I didn't know what else I wanted to learn at the Agency. I told him I wanted to go.

⤳

THE BUREAU is a complicated, traditional organization, and Director Mueller rightly insisted that the individual running the new NSB be a Bureau official. In any of these situations, there's also the matter of institutional development and morale: after nearly a century, would the right message be one that indicated the Bureau had not a single officer capable of running this new entity, with its span across Bureau headquarters and all 56 field offices? But the deal was that the second-in-charge should be an intelligence professional. I had worked well with the Bureau during my time as CTC deputy director. I knew the senior managers in the counterterrorism program, I knew Tenet well and Mueller a bit. And I knew Gary Bald, slated to be the new executive assistant director of the NSB, who had been my contact during the crucial days and weeks of the unfolding Dhiren Bharot threat information. We trusted each other, and he asked Mueller to call me. I'd also assumed that Mueller had asked his old friend George Tenet how this personnel arrangement might work, only to discover later, and with some humor, that this assumption was mistaken: Tenet laughingly told me he'd chided Mueller for recruiting a CIA manager without telling him.

This was a difficult career choice to ponder. It was entirely new position, with the inauspicious and, to an outsider, incomprehensible title of "Associate Executive Assistant Director," in a city where the length of the title is in inverse proportion to the influence of the job, in a bureaucracy regarded in Washington as highly traditional, resistant to change, and reluctant to absorb more of an intelligence-driven mentality, from an organization that had been a Bureau rival for decades.

The upsides were clear, however, and the decision took only a few days. It was a chance to start in a new enterprise, with a compelling mission, from its inception. Working with people I knew and respected, when it seemed time to try something new.

The timing, as it turned out, had yet a few more bits of humor sprinkled through the process. First, the director of national intelligence had to concur. Since his deputy, General Mike Hayden (later director of the CIA), had first talked to me about this opportunity weeks earlier, this was a formality. The White House also had a say—the creation of the NSB had been a mandate from a Congress that wanted to press the FBI to push harder on intelligence, and the White House knew the creation of this collection of FBI entities had a political dimension. Finally, there was a formal security vetting process: despite my history at the CIA—including financial checks and multiple polygraph tests over the years, there was still the records check that is a requirement for every such appointment. In one of the oddities of Washington, helping to oversee some of the most sensitive operations at the Agency, and undergoing CIA's regular vetting processes, didn't mean that I could sidestep a new layer of vetting before heading over to the Hoover Building. It was incredibly inefficient, but that's the way Washington works.

Hayden called my old boss at the Counterterrorist Center, Jose Rodriguez, to tell him of the impending move. Jose had moved up to become the head of operations for CIA, one of the top handful of positions at the Agency and an extremely powerful slot given the prominence of the Agency in the government's counterterror campaign. Jose, driving along a road in the northeastern U.S. at the time, took the call on his cellphone and seemingly judged that this was a consultative conversation, that Hayden wanted his opinion or sought his vote. He and I had been discussing whether I might move to a new interagency position in his operational directorate, working directly for him, an interesting potential move for a career analyst. Shortly into the call, however, he found that the call was informational, not consultative. The deal was done. He could have returned and raised hell, but he had been supportive every day I knew him, and he readily acceded to and supported the move.

The assumption that week was that the process would take a bit of time, maybe a week or so. Sort of. I received word about midweek that it would take another week or two to iron out the details before an announcement would come. That was fine by me—I could clear out my desk and say some goodbyes, in an Agency where my friends would question the move. "You've got a great future here. Why are you leaving?" would be a standard question. Or, equally likely in a world where the FBI is still perceived by many CIA officers as a law enforcement entity with limited intelligence capabilities, the question would be, "Why are you moving to the FBI?"

But this was Washington. Stories evidently were about to creep out in the Washington media once again questioning the Bureau's commitment to focusing on the intelligence mission. After anticipating a few weeks to prepare, I received a call on Friday indicating that my partnership with Bald would be announced that day. The goal was to avoid weekend media commentary, I suppose, which seems peripheral now but was more significant then, when the questions about the Bureau's future, and whether the United States needed a separate domestic intelligence service, were more pointed. Shortly afterward, I went over to the Hoover Building for a warm first meeting with Director Mueller. Warm, yes, but perhaps not quite as smooth as it should have been. "When can you start?" he asked. "Two weeks," I answered. "It's August in Washington, and I'm going hiking." In retrospect, this was one of the dumber comments I ever made in 24 years of service, but I didn't want to leave any false impressions that I'd show up the next day.

⤺

THE FIRST weeks at the Bureau lived up to some of the movie characterizations I had seen of FBI investigations. The morning briefing process started early, with an internal briefing for Director Mueller at 7:15 and a global briefing, including an intelligence briefer and the attorney general, at 7:45. The director briefings offered a crash course in high-end domestic intelligence and law enforcement investigations. I quickly learned that individuals under the spotlight of a domestic security investigation were vulnerable: if they had committed a federal violation, or if they were considering some act of violence, they were in trouble. Federal tools for looking at individuals who meet a standard for investigation—for example, people who have a relationship with known terrorists overseas—are impressive. I had known this at CIA, but only at a general level. When I first witnessed the array of methods we could use to look at a high-end suspect at the FBI, I immediately came to the conclusion that anyone who ever contemplated violating a federal statute would benefit from spending a week in the director's briefings. If you're in the federal sights and are of sufficient concern to become the subject of the range of surveillance—technical, human, and everything else in the book—then you're in a world of trouble.

The rhythm of those mornings changed little during the more than four years I spent on assignment to the Bureau. Get in early in the morning to prepare, starting with a trip to the operations center to pick up the binder of intelligence material. Sit in the morning session with the director. Go downstairs to the operations center for the broader, global intelligence brief with the attorney general. Then head back upstairs for the daily staff meeting. The first two hours-plus of every day were essentially dedicated to information gathering, about ongoing cases, global events, and the daily grind of running a huge bureaucracy. You could arrive at 6:30 a.m. and not have your first break until three hours later. This was usually a trip across Tenth Street to the Au Bon Pain coffee shop, often so busy with Bureau employees that it was referred to as Bureau office space. One of the minor disadvantages of heading downtown to the Bureau was the cafeteria quality—the Bureau's cramped cafeteria can't hold a candle to what the Agency offered. But a walk outside, and we had every variety of coffeeshop, bookstore, restaurant, and winebar you could hope for. Every organization has its lore and its prejudices, and at the Bureau coffee was one of them. I discovered after just a few days that somehow the Starbucks coffee brewed in the cafeteria was viewed as inferior. So with our central location, directly on bustling Pennsylvania Avenue between the Congress and the White House, many on the staff went to one of the several local Starbucks stores. Having tried hundreds of cups at headquarters and outside, I still can't discern a difference.

The director's prosecutorial background and his no-nonsense personality set the tone for the early morning updates on intelligence and investigations. Briefers focused on the most significant problems we were facing, typically tactical issues such as an emerging case in which a foreign partner in an overseas investigation might have turned up a contact in a U.S. city. If the subject of the partner's investigation was a serious player in terrorism—someone who showed the intention and capability to stage an attack—the antennae at the Bureau would go up instantly. Who was the U.S. person? Did he pose an imminent threat? And what was the extent of the conspiracy? We also had regular updates related to ongoing investigations, leads already developed through intelligence, tips, or foreign contacts that would slowly blossom over time into full-scale networks that might require months of effort to unravel.

The morning briefer, typically an analyst far more junior than the small group of executives around the table, would arrive in the early morning hours and wade through a broad array of intelligence information to pick and choose what the director should see, and what should be highlighted. This was more art than science, separating the wheat from the chaff, flagging issues that might require attention without accidentally stepping on toes, and knowing the director and the staff well enough to understand what briefing angles might be most productive. The briefer came armed with a looseleaf binder packed with intelligence and investigative updates. The rest of us around the table had the same book but without the masses of material prepped by the briefer, with all the documentation collated early enough in the morning that we could pick up our copy in the operations center by 6:30, review what we thought was relevant to gather our own thoughts (and anticipate questions), and walk into the 7:15 a.m. brief for the director.

Not later than 7:15, to be sure. The director was always a stickler for starting on time. Even if he didn't raise an eyebrow at a late arrival, Wanda, his assistant immediately outside the door, was dogged in protecting the boss from strays. Like every good gatekeeper, she took her job seriously, and through many directors, she became a hall legend. She and Veronica, the deputy's assistant, kept us in line along the executive corridor—"Mahogany Row," it was named (despite the government-issued veneer desks and beige carpets).

They even went so far, on my first day, as to intercept me walking down the corridor with a fresh, 20-ounce styrofoam cup of coffee, take the coffee, and announce that this wouldn't be allowed in the director's conference room. In my memory, this was the only rule I ever broke as a minor act of rebellion: every single day for four and a half years, a 20-ounce cup of coffee went with me to the staff meeting. Wanda and Veronica ruled the roost, and no lowly CIA guy would violate the sanctum. They were great.

Mueller often started with the direct, no-nonsense style that was his trademark. The briefer launched into the meat of the day's news, usually an update on the most significant threats or cases we had running. The sessions were not tense, just short and to the point. We were often out within ten or fifteen minutes, with the top handful of highlights covered. Every day was the same thing, like clockwork, even the clothes: dark suit, blue or red tie, starched white button-down shirt. Never in four-plus years did he wear anything but white, except perhaps when we were traveling. I was tempted, on many occasions, to tell him that we were charged with being creative, changing a traditional FBI organization quickly and bringing a different way of thinking to the Hoover building. Maybe a blue shirt once a year? Discretion being the better part of valor, though, we never had the conversation.

Watching Mueller operate, and learning about his commitment to the evolving Bureau intelligence mission, I was often struck by how approachable he was in smaller settings. The Bureau's hierarchical structure, where the director rules as the unimpeachable source of power, coupled with this director's marine background and prosecutorial style, cloaked the humor we as senior staff witnessed, along with the real-life integrity that never wavered. Some of the humor emerged on travel with the security detail and a small cadre of senior executives. Visiting Rome once, the entire group, including the director, had an area of one floor that allowed the security detail to limit access, a standard procedure for traveling senior security officials. With the director in his room that evening, we were all joking around the one spare room the detail always reserved for equipment, luggage, and communications gear. For some reason, during the joking, I had put a plastic hotel shower cap on my head, mostly to see if I could get the director's staff, several of whom were close friends, to laugh. Then the door opened. The boss, chiseled jaw and starched white shirt, stepped out, and laughed harder than the rest. He had a sense of humor, evident in private, that most of the workforce rarely had the chance to witness.

As advertised, he also was defined by his experience as a marine. During travels to FBI offices overseas and domestically, or during speeches to youth, he was often asked about experiences he thought had shaped him most profoundly, or what he would recommend for anyone starting out on a path that might mirror what he had experienced. His response was always the same: serving as a marine was the most important formative experience he had undergone, without question. Those overseas visits always included a stop with the marine security guard detachments.

This background was not, perhaps, always to the good. We traveled to Iraq a few times, visiting the significant FBI contingent there that helped underscore the Bureau's growing mission to assist the military in warzones, with unique Bureau capabilities. Those might include techniques such as how to gather intelligence and evidence systematically at high-interest locations— so-called "sensitive site exploitation" (SSE). Or they could include combing through anything from a terrorist safehouse to a bombed-out compound of a senior insurgent leader, along with training new investigative services that were required in countries where the United States was dedicated to fostering new, democratic governments that respected the rule of law. During one of these trips, we walked up to the roof of a building in downtown Baghdad that offered a good view of the city. As we were surveying the panorama of the city—this was at a time when bombs within city limits were still a common occurrence—some sort of rocket or mortar left a trail maybe a half-mile away. Not close enough for a duck-and-cover, but close enough for the security detail of an FBI director to determine that the rooftop tour should end, and fast. But this was their perspective, not his, the former marine. In a scene that was amusing even at that moment, he showed none of the urgency they thought was required. Quite the contrary, he appeared to think this was interesting and stimulating, and he chose to loiter on the roof for a bit. The security detail most decidedly did not find this acceptable. In the years I spent watching the detail interact with the director, it was the only time I saw them verge on getting in his face. He eventually heeded their requests to walk off the roof, but about as slowly as he could, not even close to the pace they wanted.

Traveling with Director Mueller proved to underscore the global nature of many of the threats we faced. Terrorism ranked first, and virtually every global partner with which we dealt had some piece of the campaign. But we also talked about issues such as organized crime. And, almost inevitably, we talked about training and technical assistance. Nearly every service admired the Bureau's Quantico training capabilities, and the forensic experience and technology Bureau specialists could apply to evidence collection and crime scene investigations. We visited on one trip the location of the assassination of Lebanese President Rafiq Hariri in 2005, marked by a large crater where he had been murdered by a huge bomb. It is hard to deny assistance to security services when they ask for help in circumstances that so clearly represent a need.

These trips were fast and furious, the most rapid-fire form of travel I have ever seen or will see. Memorable, for example, was the day we woke up for consultations in Amman, Jordan, flew to Beirut for lunch and afternoon meetings, flew into Baghdad after dark to avoid antiaircraft fire, and arrived at a hotel in Ankara, Turkey, at maybe two a.m., only to start again at breakfast. The director's view, fed no doubt by his marine background, was that we had a job to do—meet the local political, security, and law enforcement leadership, meet the local FBI staff, and get out to the next destination. I asked him about this once, pointing out that the cultures of the people we were meeting were based on personal relationships. Dinner, talk about the family, build a tie. "I'll leave that to you," he said, laughing.

The routines at home were, if anything, tougher, though the hours weren't necessarily longer than some of those overseas days. The early morning updates on major breaking investigations had a rhythm of their own. Within a day or so of learning of a new investigative target—a new person of interest—we would start hearing about the extent of the network around the target. The goal behind these initial investigations was never solely to understand, or simply prosecute, an individual player; instead, the focus was on the extent of his network, the breadth of the conspiracy, if there was one. The lines of inquiry, despite how complicated and slow they were to piece together in real life, were relatively consistent from investigation to investigation. Find the key players; find how they communicate; find their overseas contacts; determine their access to weapons, explosives, training; find who radicalized them, and who they'd radicalized. A 1966 book by Ori Brafman and Rod Beckstrom, *The Starfish and the Spider: The Unstoppable Power of Leaderless Organizations*, talked about the difference between the starfish and the spider. We wanted to understand the spiderweb, so that any move to dismantle a threat wouldn't happen before we could assure ourselves that the entire network would go. We wanted no stray pieces left to recreate the plot years later. Taking off the arm of a starfish might feel good in the moment—taking out a player who might be plotting the murder of innocents and put him behind bars—but starfish regrow their arms. If we moved too quickly, removing an arm before understanding the full extent of a network, we might congratulate ourselves on a successful and rapid prosecution but miss other pieces, ultimately failing to provide the kind of security that was our mission if those other players came back together to reconstitute a conspiracy.

Early in those briefings, I realized that the staff at the Bureau viewed the FBI director differently, and briefed him differently, from the way CIA staff viewed and briefed their Agency's director. Shifting between bureaucracies, in my view, is a valuable, perhaps indispensable, benefit for senior executives in government service. Without seeing how different bureaucracies operate in incredibly complex environments, it is hard for even the most talented individuals to look at problems from different perspectives. To think about management metrics, or organizational structures, or even how managers operate growing up in one organization simply cannot duplicate the perspective gained from watching how others operate. This was one of the benefits of post-9/11 reforms, through the regulations instituted by the new director of national intelligence, the overarching coordinator for U.S. intelligence established after 9/11: that successful candidates for certain senior positions in U.S. agencies had to have some experience outside their home agency. Intelligence reform remains a hotly debated topic in Washington, and many view the post-9/11 creation of a new intelligence bureaucracy as cumbersome and unnecessary. But this reform works, in my view. I learned about as much about how to view my home Agency's management style and structure by leaving as I did growing up at CIA.

Shortly after that morning brief, we moved downstairs to a small conference room adjacent to the 24-hour operations center, for a more global briefing by an analyst who traveled across the Potomac River every day to provide context and updates on worldwide events. There were maybe eight of us around the table, the FBI group joined by the attorney general and his staff, with another half-dozen sitting on the perimeter of the small room. We would start with brief updates on Department of Justice cases, followed by the internal FBI brief—a summation of what we'd dealt with upstairs (major investigations), along with occasional back-and-forth about what steps we should take in a particular case.

I found these morning briefing sessions among the most interesting parts of the day. They offered condensed insights into significant events, along with a picture of how a national security organization—professionals who typically had a quarter-century or more of experience each—dealt with complex problems at high levels. And, for the broader global briefs, they offered snapshots of global events culled from the best of what the intelligence community had to offer, from evaluations of Al Qaeda's strengths and weaknesses to brutal updates on cartel wars south of the border. These briefings underscored the impact of globalization not only on trade and finance but also on crime and counterterrorism. We had gangs from Latin America, human trafficking from Southeast Asia, drug cartels in Mexico, drugs from Afghanistan, and fraud from Africa. The most disturbing element I saw were the cases exposing the pervasive problem of child pornography, with criminal enterprises that might previously have focused more on drugs or prostitution now understanding how cheap it is to circulate images of children—or infants—for money, via virtual networks that required only electrons crossing national boundaries.

These briefings are among the few things, beyond the uniqueness and importance of the counterterrorism mission, that I miss about government. The personnel battles, organization change, resistant bureaucracies are all important and rewarding in their own way. But none of them is a draw to the service. Seeing the world unfold and having a role in trying to shape events, those are the draw. Through these morning sessions, the evolution of the counterterrorism campaign, how it was fought, whether we were winning, and how the Bureau was pursuing the slowly emerging homegrown problem were all fascinating to watch. And they are the answer to the countless questions I have heard in my limited time outside government. Do you miss anything? Yes.

⌐〜

THESE BRIEFINGS also offered a chance to sit on the other side of the table from the intelligence community, receiving the kinds of analyses that I had spent years writing and watching how senior executives, such as the FBI director and the attorney general, absorb them. Intelligence analysts consider themselves service providers, trying to take what they know, including highly classified material, and put it into context in short articles designed for busy executives. Four-plus years sitting with the director and three successive attorneys general gave me more than an education on analysts' perceptions of their role and how it matches with reality—what worked, what didn't, and what made me frustrated when I witnessed it from the consumer's perspective. Many of the rules I had learned turned out to be true. No matter how interesting the subject is to the analyst, keep the writing short, two pages or less. Get to the point immediately. Explain why it's relevant. Be timely—know what's on the decisionmaking plate of those you're trying to reach. Make sure you highlight gaps in intelligence, the unknowns. Differentiate clearly between what we know and what we think. If there are differences among analysts, explain them, but they had better be significant. All these rules are fundamental for analysts, and if anything, even more important in practice than in theory.

Early in my career, I had an impression of these sorts of discussions as formal policy deliberations with senior mandarins who were somehow different. The CIA of the 1980s was much more traditional than the twenty-first-century intelligence organization, especially given the pace of the post-9/11 world. We were always taught, as junior analysts, to guard the line between intelligence and policy as if it were sacrosanct. Intelligence officers provide counsel based on information that should be reviewed without prejudice to the policy interests of Washington agencies. Policymakers were decisionmakers, those who used what we provided to make decisions about what the U.S. government should do, how it might react to changing global circumstances. Often circumstances didn't change that quickly, so maintaining the clear divide between policy and intelligence was easier than in the fast-paced world of twenty years later.

That divide blurred after 9/11, for me. First, I had risen into positions that required daily interaction with my policy counterparts from the State Department, the Pentagon, and the White House. Second, and more significant, the counterterror campaign globally was often driven by CIA, especially in those early years. Rather than collecting intelligence to help policymakers resolve a diplomatic problem, or conducting secret activities in support of a broader policy initiative such as an effort to slow a foreign missile program or how to better design U.S. countering systems, many global counterterrorism activities were largely CIA owned and operated. Whether supporting foreign governments locating terrorists or hunting Al Qaeda members along the Pakistan-Afghanistan border, CIA often collected the intelligence, acted on it alone or in partnership with foreign services, and analyzed it at home, to add context for policymakers.

So the typically bright line between intelligence and policy, maintained to ensure that intelligence officers provided unbiased insight that was not designed to align with any particular policy initiative, blurred substantially. This turned out to be fine, as long as we remained cognizant that we were both helping design and execute policy and appraising performance by analyzing the intelligence from our operations. For example, we were dismantling terror networks, sometimes with CIA-only intelligence, but also assessing the performance of the U.S. against terror networks—a conflict of interest, potentially, and one of the infrequent instances of such clear overlap between policy and intelligence.

So often, those of us representing the Agency at meetings including other executive agencies might find ourselves in the position of advocating a certain course of action—say, pressing hard on a foreign government to provide more support against terror cells—and providing the intelligence to support this policy choice. This happened frequently in the unusual world of counterterrorism: we would often discuss a problem with Director Tenet in the nightly 5 o'clock "small group" meeting—the problem of how to handle a recalcitrant foreign leader who was soft on terrorists, for example—and then write the intelligence that would help the director explain the problem to other senior government officials, adding the policy advice that we should ratchet up the pressure on the leader.

For one who had for so long heard only about how intelligence was used in policy, and how the two pieces should remain separate, one of the most pleasant surprises during that time was the informality I saw in those FBI morning briefings of policymakers, and how much they trusted good intelligence. Watching TV shows or movies, or simply imagining, as a junior analyst, the daily meetings of people you read about in the newspapers, might lead to the impression that these briefings were always perfectly scripted, formal, buttoned up. Instead, what I saw was what you might expect if you thought about the process through a different optic: every day, year in and year out, a similar group of people gathered for 30 or 45 minutes to talk about domestic security problems and global events. We all knew each other; like any other meeting, in any other location, the jokes were common, the conversation was relatively informal, and decisions were made quickly. The issues might have been of great significance, but the people around the table all put on their pants one leg at a time. I never saw a situation in which anyone present tried to be intimidating, or created an environment that was less than collegial. Tense moments might happen in other rooms, but not in the morning briefing room. And even though some of us in the room were by far the most junior members at the table, we still had a chance to contribute to the discussion.

Attorney general Michael Mukasey, for example, who came across during his contentious confirmation hearings as the tough, no-quarter judge he was, was always prepared to engage in a serious but informal back-and-forth about the intelligence we were given in the briefings. And after months with him, I learned that intelligence was not simply a collection of secret facts or analyses provided to policy but the backdrop for a conversation with a policy customer who was less interested in the policy-intelligence divide than in having a useful conversation based on intelligence. I remember one classic example of a problem involving a senior foreign official who was giving us grief. During the intelligence briefing, Mukasey looked down the table and asked the policy question: "Should I call him?" Figuring the answer "this isn't my lane in the road" wasn't appropriate in this new environment, I said no, a phone call was premature. He listened. No call was made.

He was tough, though, just as advertised. I turned on the news one day to discover that he had suffered what turned out to be a mild fainting spell during a speech the night before. The comments on his health at the morning briefing the next day made it clear that he was doing well, and he showed up later that same day at work, across the street from FBI headquarters, at the main Department of Justice building on Pennsylvania Avenue. As the news later reported, his initial request was that we conduct the daily brief, so I walked across the street with the Top Secret briefing material—the briefer, who arrived in the small hours of the morning, was long gone—to conduct the briefing myself. He walked into the small classified conference room. At this point, we had already spent many hours around the same briefing table, and the conversations were cordial. I asked him how he was. "Fine," he answered. "What's going on today?" That was it.

Those morning meetings, however comfortable they became, put a premium on some of the foundations of analysis that are inculcated among CIA analysts but that nonetheless are anything but simple to learn, much less practice. As former secretary of state Colin Powell, always a tough critic of intelligence but a good consumer of our product, would say: "Tell me what you know. Tell me what you don't know. And then tell me what you think." And, implicitly, don't mix up the three. At the table, I always thought that any conversation about the intelligence the briefer provided every morning should clearly articulate the differences between the three, along with the even more clearly defined separation from the fourth, non-intelligence, pillar: discuss the policy question, what we should do about the problem that's just been defined.

There was also the second analytic challenge, one that even the most seasoned analysts struggle with. Many analysts are passionate about what they do; they are immersed in issues as far-reaching as how to understand foreign political intrigue, nuclear developments in the Third World, and changing dynamics in Al Qaeda leadership. As experts, they want to explain what they know. But the policymakers receiving intelligence, particularly in oral briefing situations, don't need to know what the analyst knows. They need the analyst to determine what problem the policy side is grappling with, so they can array intelligence to best help a policymaker narrow down the problem. Explaining the adjustments a potential foreign adversary is making to a ballistic missile program might involve an artful presentation of intelligence. But the better question might be to array that same intelligence to answer questions such as whether those adjustments will affect whether that missile can hit the United States or an ally, and when. What our confidence level is in those judgments, along with a candid, unvarnished appraisal of the weak points in the intelligence we've collected and the conclusions we've drawn.

⤴

NOT ALL the briefing was dedicated to analysis and investigations, though. What all of us knew implicitly, but what I always considered might surprise an outside observer, was the volume of threat information that came in every day. To be fair, much of the material was trash. This was a compilation of everything flowing into the U.S. government, from around the world, the same threat matrix we reviewed every day at CIA. And the same threat matrix agencies across the government used for a common reference point for tracking plots. It included everything from random lunatics writing to government websites to overseas contacts who reported that they'd heard some terrorist group or other had gotten access to mysterious substances. The mythic material "red mercury," for example, cropped up occasionally, apparently the leading material scammers use to dupe terrorists into believing they have the next great precursor to a bomb.

More serious threats fell into rough categories, but dividing them into neat piles—threat ABC automatically leads to threat response XYZ—is not as clearcut as it might appear. Some of the categories might include broad concerns, such as an overseas source who reports conversations about unnamed conspirators putting together plans to strike airports in Europe or the United States. Or even broader: a few youths have disappeared overseas, on one-way tickets, and families are worried. We later learn, in this notional example, that the youth were radicalized, and traveled overseas for training. Where are they? What are they doing? And the key question, of course: are they coming home to stage an attack? When? Where? How?

I have often thought that the threat issue was one problem we dealt with daily that might surprise any observer from the general public who had been given a one-day ticket to this national security show. The first surprise, especially given how many years had already passed since 9/11, would be the volume of material. There was so much to sort through, every day, often with common characteristics that made handling threat material more and more systematic but also with the unique cases that took an army of operators and analysts to make sense of. And with this high volume, a few more surprises: how much was junk, and despite the amount of junk we could weed out, how much, every day, involved real people with a real drive to acquire weapons or explosive material for a plot. I don't think I remember one single day, in nine-plus years of sitting at threat briefs at both CIA and the FBI, where there wasn't at least one significant plot cooking. Not one.

Finally, I have no doubt that a new observer at the table would be surprised about what we could uncover, and how quickly we could find it, when a real threat popped up. Between day one of a new threat and days two and three of a burgeoning investigation, the briefings presented to the FBI director, developed by agents and analysts in the field who received direction from their counterparts at headquarters, grew so complex so fast that the only way we could piece them together was by connecting the players through annotated network diagrams. If I heard it from the director once, I heard it a thousand times: "Can you put this together in a chart," he'd ask. The phone data, linkages to earlier investigations, connections to plots overseas, money flows, recruitment networks, weapons purchases—a high-level intelligence investigation would uncover links so quickly, across the United States, that none of us could follow the chain within 48 hours after the investigation was opened.

And when one individual eventually appeared at the center of a spider-web of conspiracy, forget about it, as I quickly learned. With human sources, technical coverage, even aircraft to cover extended car travel by a suspect, anyone implicated in a serious terrorism investigation would have been in shock to see the extent of the hidden blanket around him had he seen the brief. As any intelligence officer would tell you, it was never what we knew that was scary: once someone made the mistake of swimming into the net, they were in deep trouble, assuming they were involved in wrongdoing. It was always what we did not know—conspiracies that had not been unearthed by intelligence—that could bite us. The fear of the unknown. Or at least a constant respect for it, and the acknowledgment that there were always things out there, unknown conspiracies, that would surprise us, in an open society with open borders.

In the past, these types of investigations might be driven largely by the field, and largely independently, with modest input from FBI headquarters. One of the significant changes post-9/11, though, was the profound shift at the Bureau to headquarters-driven counterterrorism investigations. This occurred for a lot of reasons. Many investigations were complex, with no single field division as the sole focal point and with spokes of the investigation reaching into multiple countries overseas. Too much, in other words, for any single field office. And the complexity of these investigations, with legal approvals and oversight for phone taps and Internet coverage from a variety of skittish American communications companies, meant that even larger field offices needed both manpower and expertise to develop the intelligence and pursue the investigation.

The serious threat posed by some of the clusters of people involved in terrorism also meant that senior headquarters officials would participate in discussions about the threat, up to levels including the Oval Office. So those at headquarters who had to sort out how to respond—how, for example, to warn the American public—wanted to know. Finally, headquarters required field divisions, some of which might not have seen the full scope of the investigations with which they were involved, to prioritize intelligence over prosecution. Figure out the full extent of the conspiracy we're facing, in other words, before we move against it. Move too early and we risk leaving a piece of the conspiracy on the cutting room floor, raising the prospect that remaining conspirators will resurrect the plot at some point down the road. Collect intelligence, and when the picture clarifies, talk about how to dismantle the threat. Headquarters drove the decisions across field offices on when we knew enough, when it was time to move.

The clearest threats were those posed by clusters of people who had already started preparing for some sort of strike. There is a common perception that terrorists form well-defined cells, but this is a misperception fed by TV shows and movies. When we looked at threats, this simple cell structure was often not what we saw. Instead, to use a well-chosen NYPD term, we often saw clusters, typically of young men, who were angry, thinking about doing something, but lacking plans, weapons, or any clear way forward. They might separate from the broader community, complaining among themselves that other community members spoke angrily about events—in Iraq, or the Gaza Strip, or Afghanistan—but never took action. These clusters would become self-fulfilling, youth who might never have taken action as individuals but who, as vulnerable and malleable young men, persuaded each other that their destiny was to be the martyrs who would act where others would only show cowardice. A cluster might become a cell, but without the formality you might see in the movies. And on a schedule—maybe months or years—that could burn substantial intelligence or investigative resources.

The threat, in this case, was ensuring, first, that there was a good enough pulse on access to weapons or explosives to ensure that lives would not be lost as the intelligence investigation blossomed. Second, keeping a day-to-day watch on the intentions of a cluster was critical: was there any sign that they were going to transition unexpectedly from slowly putting together a plan to pumping each other enough to do something rash, without warning? Or might one of them peel off and go it alone?

The follow-up, then, had multiple elements. First, ensure we had an understanding of imminent threat. If we could not control the threat, there was no choice but to sacrifice intelligence collection—and the potential lead to uncover other conspirators—in favor of public safety. Second, if the threat appeared not to be imminent, uncover any elements of a conspiracy spiderweb—other participants, sources of funding, overseas training. In a slowly evolving cluster, mapping this web can take months or longer: the conspirators are not necessarily in a hurry, they don't know they are being watched, and they themselves do not know what they're going to do, beyond a thirst for attacking some perceived adversary. This concept that there are deep-rooted sleeper cells out there, well-trained, with a leader, various musclemen, a well-defined plan—this paradigm played out at 9/11, with catastrophic consequences, but it was not the character of the plots we typically faced as the decade passed. They were looser, less defined, slower to gel.

Like the misperception about neat terrorist cells, there is a common perception that these clusters operate with some knowledge of community leaders, or family members, who either knew or had a vague inkling of an emerging plot and failed to approach law enforcement, because the community was somehow broadly sympathetic to the plotters or simply lacked trust in law enforcement. This, too, I found to be inaccurate. My sense was always that disaffected youth separated themselves from their communities and families, and that those around them did not know what was going on until it was too late. Added to this was a common problem you might find in any American household, regardless whether its occupants are new immigrants: if there were vague concerns about a young man drifting off with friends, calling local law enforcement, much less the FBI, would not be a course of action a family member, friend, or community leader would consider first. Furthermore, this typical reaction might be magnified in communities that had emigrated from countries with oppressive, or even abusive, security services and a lack of respect for rule of law. Trust in security services—and the FBI would be considered one—among new émigrés might be predictably low, given the reputation of the services in these émigrés' countries of origin.

More often than not, family members and communities were, in my view, surprised and even appalled when cases broke. Families often lost sons, killed in wars overseas or arrested here at home. And community leaders, in the post-9/11 world, knew full well that a highly publicized investigation in their community would lead to extremely unwelcome scrutiny, in communities that faced unemployment, gang invasions, and the broader struggle to integrate. "See something, say something," is the New York slogan to encourage the public to report suspicious behavior. The problem I saw was that people didn't see anything, so they didn't say anything. Until it was too late.

This is not to say that community outreach, often billed—and sometimes oversold—as a key to the counterterrorism campaign is not important. It is, just not for the reasons you might think. First, tips do come in, and families do talk, not only before a conspiracy emerges, but after. Building community ties might not often lead to the first break in a case, but if a young kid is brought in by federal agents to have a conversation about recruitment for overseas training, you want the family members to be hearing from leaders in their community who already have had some kind of positive interaction with the FBI or local police. You can't build trust overnight; meeting community leaders to gain their confidence might, just might, encourage them sometime down the road to tell that family that they're talking to people they can trust. This can be invaluable.

⤶

IN ADDITION to community outreach, the agencies I saw that worked on the counterterrorism problem tried to reach out with threat information to state and local leaders, including state and local law enforcement. This proved to be more challenging than it sounds, for a number of reasons. Often, the format for the provision of intelligence to state and local partners would be a written bulletin, summarizing some new bit of data and adding context—the arrival of chlorine canisters on the scene in Iraq, as crude chemical devices, for example. The bulletin might add a bit of background to the fact that these munitions were becoming relatively common in Iraq at some point—and that a copycatter in the United States might try the same here—but any highly classified detail would be stripped out. With thousands of state, local, and tribal departments in the United States, we wanted the broadest dissemination for this kind of product, and we wanted anything we disseminated, with the Department of Homeland Security, to be useful to anyone working on the street. So, unclassified bulletins became the norm. We also faced the problem of constant, even instant leaks. As soon as one of these bulletins hit the street, it was guaranteed to be leaked.

Over time, though, the value of these relationships with state and local police grew in depth, and in value. More police received security clearances— albeit slowly—after 9/11, giving them not only access to more intelligence but also an understanding that there was often less intelligence out there than they might have thought. And police departments across the country joined in the expanding network of Joint Terrorism Task Forces (JTTFs), the interagency units in FBI offices that handle high-end terrorism investigations. Furthermore, major cities, such as New York and Los Angeles, developed highly capable units dedicated to the counterterrorism problem. And finally, as the threat from Al Qaeda ideology slowly reached homegrown individuals on America's shores, it became clear that this cooperation with state and local law enforcement would continue to grow in importance. In 2001, a terrorism lead might have grown out of information gleaned from Al Qaeda, passed from federal authorities to a terrorism task force in some city across America. With the rise of the homegrown phenomenon, these leads might more commonly move in the other direction, from a law enforcement officer in a major city who sees something odd during a raid and reports it up the chain and to federal investigators.

Like these evolving partnerships with state and local entities, the Bureau's links to other agencies in Washington were growing as well, partly as a result of the 9/11 intelligence reforms. Much of the analysis at the Bureau (as well as the CIA) was conducted in conjunction, or coordination, with the National Counterterrorism Center, where analysts and data from all agencies came together to try to offer policymakers a single, comprehensive threat picture. Established by President Bush not long after 9/11, NCTC quickly became the focal point for assessments such as those that would guide policymakers when they were considering changing the country's threat levels. Its first director, John Brennan, was a career Agency official who later became the top terrorism adviser to President Obama, and he was instrumental in pushing NCTC from concept through inception and reality: quickly, under his guidance, NCTC was recognized as an analytic center of thinking, not just a presidentially supported, congressionally mandated entity that existed on paper. Brennan was smart, tough, and an ultimate Washington infighter, pressing on all cylinders despite intense resistance from CIA, which lost both analysts and prestige when NCTC gained ground. Brennan persisted, alienating officials through all levels of the Agency where he had once served but delivering on what the law required: one-stop shopping, in a world where many still believed that agencies did not share enough information, when the policy world needed an analytic picture that combined the best of what every agency knew. Rather than have a policymaker look through analysis from Defense, CIA, State, Homeland Security, and others, NCTC analysts, on loan from all these agencies and with access to their raw data, would compile that picture themselves.

Despite some of the roughest Washington bureaucratic battling I ever witnessed during the years NCTC grew, the analysis matured well, and the product we received at the senior-level briefings while I was at the FBI was helpful. The broader analytic items were similar to what we received at the Bureau briefing table from other agencies, particularly CIA. But the threat updates—particularly the weekly product that captured intelligence on each of the major threat "threads," or plotlines, served their purpose, giving us one place that laid out what new information had come in on the threat and what every agency knew. This sometimes caught our own Bureau units off-guard, particularly when an item gave the director an angle on FBI information that he hadn't seen earlier through his internal FBI briefings, but this seemed like a good thing to me. The operators and analysts hated having the director see some aspect of their work before they could present it through their lens, but the NCTC process provided a sort of check-and-balance: if their analysts thought something was important, they would force it into the regular threat updates, whether our guys liked it or not. And, I confess, these surprises sometimes added a little humor. I don't recollect the director becoming particularly disturbed at hearing from NCTC first about something the FBI was doing, but I do remember a fair amount of squirming when he asked questions at the morning meetings that no one could answer. The words "I don't know," among the most liberating in the intelligence world, were not words any senior Bureau official liked speaking to the director.

The rise of NCTC also exposed one of the more interesting long-term analytic divides in the intelligence community. There is a longstanding view among intelligence professionals that "competitive analysis"—that is, different groups of analysts looking at the same data and writing their own independent conclusions about the data—is a good thing. The unknown is almost always a large slice of the pie in the world of intelligence; try to understand what a foreign leader might do on deploying military forces and you're judging not only capability, such as what his force structure is, but intent. Professing to understand what another human being thinks is, in my judgment, one of the more tenuous aspects of intelligence, and judging intent is inherently risky. I'd often ask myself, as we approached a major decision at FBI or CIA, whether a well-placed human source in our conference room, even with perfect access, could find out what the decision would be. Almost invariably, the answer was no, because we didn't know ourselves. So competitive analysis allowed for a healthy debate about conclusions, in a world where analysts often believe they know more than they do and present analyses that suggest far greater clarity in understanding foreign motivations, intentions, and future actions than the intelligence merits.

NCTC and CIA analysts regularly wrote about similar issues, providing a sort of competitive analysis that the law probably didn't envision—to some, this work might seem redundant or even wasteful—but the divide between the two groups of analysts proved valuable. CIA, with the echoes of criticism in the post-9/11 environment about not thinking creatively enough about the threat, was always aggressive in interpreting threat information and the terrorism problem in general. NCTC, created after the cauldron of criticism had hit CIA, was often more neutral, almost reflexively so. I am not certain which was right, but it was not uncommon, when one or the other was writing about a threat issue, for someone at our briefing table to ask what the other thought. I am certain that those doing the analysis were grinding their teeth at having a client want different, potentially competing perspectives. But, on the other side of the fence, those of us consuming the analysis found it useful to have data that was fuzzy by definition—the plans and intentions of a closed terrorist organization—viewed through different lenses.

This was one area where serving as a consumer of intelligence analysis, at the FBI, offered a different perspective from writing and managing the analysis itself. Analysts are, by nature, fully prepared, sometimes overly so, to defend their analyses in the face of interpretations of data from other analysts, or other intelligence agencies. Competitive analysis makes sense, on its face, in light of the significant issues analysts address, from foreign proliferation efforts to the plans and intentions of Al Qaeda. But in practice, analysts are human, and experts who question their interpretation of facts are, unsurprisingly, seen as anywhere from wrong to woefully ignorant. Reading the analysis, though, I came to appreciate differing views on issues that by definition have no real answer, such as the nature of the enduring Al Qaeda threat. The analysis was, after all, only an interpretation of events by a small group of experts who had the luxury of only a small window into the minds and activities of terrorists. Why not encourage differing views, as long as they were well argued and clearly written? In addition, I should confess that watching the analytic battles appear in print brought occasional amusement. The senior consumers around the briefing table, such as the FBI director, might not know the blood that would have been shed over an analytic argument that was summarized for him in two pages. But a studied reading of some of the intelligence we received, when there were clearly differing analytic views across the intelligence community, was enjoyable for an old analyst who didn't have to write the stuff anymore and didn't have to manage the analytic fights.

⌒

AS WE watched the threat flows during the latter half of the post-9/11 decade, the evolution of Al Qaeda and Al Qaeda-ism, and the threat it posed, was clearly evident. During my years at the Bureau, we would periodically see information about the plans and intentions of the Al Qaeda central organization, located in the tribal areas along the Pakistan-Afghanistan border. Any quality source information about Al Qaeda plans and intentions was, obviously, a high priority. The information we received over the years might run the gamut, from first-hand threat reporting that, while often general, was nonetheless highly disturbing, to around-the-campfire material that was more difficult to respond to.

During the late afternoon threat briefings at CIA in the early days after 9/11, Al Qaeda had not suffered the damage of years of losses, particularly strikes and arrests that eliminated one after another of its operational leadership. The early threat reporting we charted on the daily threat matrix included more Al Qaeda core plotting than you would see today. Also, the Al Qaeda affiliates, particularly the prominent components in the Arabian Peninsula— Saudi Arabia, Yemen, and the smaller states of the Arabian Gulf—proved to complement their focus on attacking local regimes with over-the-horizon plots against America. Some of these plots were serious, such as cooperation between Al Qaeda and Jemaah Islamiyah, headquartered in Indonesia. Both, in the post-9/11 environment, remained committed to staging spectacular strikes, and both wanted to return to the air. Only work in South and Southeast Asia, including operations by Indonesian and other Southeast Asian security services that gutted the Jemaah Islamiyah organization, prevented the group's joining Al Qaeda in a spectacular strike.

Meanwhile, as they plotted to expand their reach to targets in North America, these affiliates focused on Westerners closer to home. Al-Qaeda's Saudi Arabian heartland erupted early in the decade, as groups that were in contact with Al Qaeda, and inspired by it, struck American diplomatic targets and beheaded Americans in 2004 in Iraq (Nicholas Berg) and Saudi Arabia (Paul Johnson). Jemaah Islamiyah targeted cultural icons—tourist locations in Bali, for example—and the Australian Embassy. The homegrown phenomenon we have seen in recent years, youth who have never met an Al Qaeda member but are inspired by the Al Qaeda message of violent extremism, was not as prominent then; instead, the core group, and its closely connected wings, cropped up again and again, month after month, in our threat reports.

What had changed, from the first days of dealing with threat, was the experience that can only come with years of this work. The bureaucracy behind that was far more well-oiled, and less jumpy, than in the first years after 9/11. The initial years were not as smooth. Often, before the evening briefings, we would be discussing how we could pass a new threat to a foreign security partner; the director insisted, rightly, that all threats be passed, but there were still instances where the information hadn't been passed by the time we prepared the threat matrix. And passing off leads and threat information in the daily threat videoconferences, where agencies across town gathered to compare notes and assign duties on threat responses, was still a messy proposition.

The evolution of the threat management bureaucracy is one of the most significant changes I witnessed over the years. It was not just the creation of a new bureaucracy—the consolidation of various agencies as the new Department of Homeland Security, or the creation of a clearinghouse for data and analysis at the new National Counterterrorism Center—but the creation of mechanisms across agencies to share, and share quickly, what they were uncovering. The relatively quiet demise of the color-coded threat scheme that advised the American public when we were shifting from yellow to orange captures this evolution: we moved from inefficient but effective fingers in dikes to efficient and effective bureaucratization of threat. In this case, bureaucracy is good, obviating the need to jury-rig new relationships or intelligence sharing mechanisms every time a new threat unfolds.

This bureaucracy isn't entirely efficient, by a long shot, explained not only by the volume and speed of threat information that still flows through the system but also by the masses of data that threat management agencies in Washington deal with daily. Looking at the data management problem from the outside—the failure to match up bits of data before the attempted takedown of an airliner by the "underwear bomber" over Detroit on December 25, 2009, for example—it is easy to believe that matching such data up should be simple. We all worked on this problem, and the people I dealt with across the community were focused on not missing bits of data. It is just that the volumes and varieties of data across many agencies and around the world, is stunning.

Think not just of a cryptic reference to an individual in a phone call; instead, add in years of phone calls, visa requests at embassies and consulates around the world, CIA cables with our own information and disparate data from other security services, travel data, immigration records, FBI leads, hits at border entry points, and a hundred other bits and bytes. Matching up this information coherently and quickly remains a daunting task, and we will fail again: not just in finding out the true identity of someone who might appear in a database today, but in ensuring that the new information—maybe just a fragment of a name—bounces against a data load that expanded exponentially starting a decade ago.

What also changed, and what was evident at the briefing table as my years at the Bureau progressed, was the steady accretion of larger and larger mountains of data: not just what we could quickly accumulate on an individual case, but what was funneled in through the system that might match a bit of data collected years ago, in another case, from another agency, or from a partner overseas. The accumulation of data meant that we might be able to draw a picture more quickly around a potential terrorist cell—by determining, for example, whether any of the cell members had traveled in the past years—but it also placed a premium, in a city that simply will not accept that you can't always match a bit of information today with a bit from five years ago, on making no mistakes as we designed data management systems and processes. We suffered from data overload, the good and the bad. There was the chance of quick access to information that might clarify a case that would otherwise appear murky, and the risk of sitting on mounds of information that would lead to a front-page investigation, and a congressional inquiry, if we missed something. There was not much room for error. Like everyone who has ever looked at this problem, I believe that we are virtually guaranteed, as we uncover plots down the road, to find a bit of data somewhere that suggests that we should have known about, or investigated, the plot earlier. Part of the maturation process in this country will be realizing that we can learn from these incidents, but that head-hunting in their wake, unless there is serious fault, is not going to solve the problem. Doing the tedious work of closing gaps will, along with an understanding that open societies are inherently easy for small groups of people to operate in, and not every group will be caught.

This was another area that always seemed easier on the outside than it proved to be on the inside, even with the smartest minds we could muster sitting around the table. Take the fictional case of an eighteen-year-old youth who, in 2005, sits in a cluster of other youth who are talking about traveling to Iraq to fight against Coalition forces. He proves unwilling to participate in the discussion, and falls out. He has exercised free speech, and he is not the subject of an ongoing investigation. Should you purge your files of his name?

Or maintain records in a separate electronic file space only accessible for specially designated purposes? What if, four years later and in the midst of intense commentary about the role of Yemeni jihadists in training operatives to come to the United States, he decides to travel to Yemen for Arabic language training. Certainly not illegal, but equally certainly of importance to a security service. What if you had purged his name, as an innocent bystander, and thus didn't know he had earlier shown some interest in jihad? That one fact could change the entire investigation, both in terms of a threat assessment and how many resources this case might merit. That one fact raises questions, too, about the growing expectations of a domestic security service—the FBI, the service charged with preempting attacks, not simply responding to them—in a civil society. If I were that youth, I would expect that a security service in this country would purge my name from any file. If I were another American, knowing what I do about youth radicalization in Yemen, I would be astounded that the same name was inaccessible after that youth came home to commit an act of violence. This is not, under any guise, a suggestion of a "balance" between civil liberties and security: we live in a society that cherishes freedom over security. It is simply to say that the public does not always see practical contrasts between the ideals of a liberal democracy and the expectations of an increasingly security-conscious public.

All these types of questions were emerging in those years, as the Al Qaeda threat grew to slowly envelop youth in America. Court documents detailing a case we knew as "Northern Exposure" highlight the kinds of investigations we saw briefed every morning. One of the main subjects in that case, a young man named Haris Ahmed, hooked into a web of international extremists and began talking about attacks in Washington. As the conspiracy slowly gelled, he traveled to Washington, videotaping several potential targets and researching explosive devices. He also contacted high-level extremists overseas, highlighting the role of the Internet not only in radicalizing people but in allowing for the creation of virtual cells, young men prone to violence who develop loose cells despite never seeing one another. Twenty-first-century terrorism.

The Northern Exposure case underscored the importance of global cooperation among security services; the case quickly spread across South Asia into Europe and the United States. But more important, it also underlined the kinds of activities and clusters of youth that have come to define terrorism in the United States. Once again, what we were witnessing was not a formal cell—a group characterized by tightly knit conspirators with clear targets, cell leaders, operatives, and high-level training and explosives. This is not what I saw evolve in the decade after 9/11. The 2001 attacks were just that: a serious group of 19 hijackers with cell leaders, overseas guidance, foreign financial support, and a sophisticated, years-long process of looking at targets.

As the Al Qaeda revolution spread around the world, though, the kinds of terrorism we saw stemmed more from loose clusters of youth, typically kids who were angry and thought other members of their communities weren't serious about opposing what they saw as a U.S. or Western crusade in Afghanistan, Iraq, and elsewhere. They often did not have training by Al Qaeda, and most members of these clusters had never met an Al Qaeda member. Instead, they were motivated by the ideological message: the lesson of 9/11 was that the United States was vulnerable. And the volatile mix of U.S. policy—support for regimes characterized by Al Qaeda as apostate; photos of prisoner abuse at the U.S.-run prison at Abu Ghraib that became fuel for the Al Qaeda flame; anger at Israeli strikes that left Palestinian citizens dead—all contributed to a global movement of youth who captured the Al Qaeda vision. When bin Laden and Zawahiri created Al Qaeda, they never meant to conduct or even oversee every attack themselves. They wanted to use attacks to spark a global revolution that might take decades or more to reach fruition. These clusters of kids represented the bow wave of that spreading revolution.

⌒

AS I settled into the Bureau, over months and then years, the days took on a rhythm of their own, particularly the first few hours in the morning. As I noted earlier, the director received twice-daily briefings, with a dedicated briefer stepping us through the most significant issues across the field, a group of executives around the conference table, and counterterrorism managers and staff streamed in via secure videoconference. This process was taxing on the staff, who were spending a disproportionate amount of time preparing for the briefings. The morning session would conclude before 8 a.m., and the second would start in late afternoon. You could hardly walk out of the conference room in the morning before analysts and agents began preparing materials for the afternoon session. To ease this burden, the afternoon session was later dropped, but the morning program still remains as a standard process for Bureau executives.

The preparation for these sessions highlighted one of the fundamental differences between the Bureau and CIA. Too often, critics of the Bureau argue that it should have more of a CIA-like culture. I thought this, too, during my first weeks. I quickly came to question the notion, though, when confronted with the foundational difference between the two organizations. The Bureau has a primary responsibility of protecting the fiber of the country, its freedoms and the right of its citizens to live in an open civil society, without the threat of a security service that can look over a citizen's shoulder without a reason to do so. The Agency obviously has fewer restrictions, and its pursuit of intelligence is far less constrained: within limits, Agency officers are driven to answer questions—such as how a potential adversary might be pursuing a nuclear weapons program—by finding the people who know the answers and figuring out how to recruit them so as to help improve our understanding of national security threats. The Bureau also recruits, but its approach to answering national security questions starts with a different question. Does this pursuit violate civil rights or civil liberties? By definition, then, the Bureau—or any American security service—cannot be a purely intelligence-driven organization, because the pure pursuit of knowledge cannot trump its responsibility to protect citizens from violations of their rights.

A case in point: after the attempt to take down an airliner on December 25, 2009, national security decisionmakers rightly might have asked how much the intelligence community knew about Yemen, and particularly Nigerian youth traveling to Yemen for training. The answers to such questions might come from human sources talking about the flow of foreign students to Yemen. But if we were to pose the same questions for the United States, we would start from a different place. Sending sources into Nigerian expatriate populations in America, perhaps into mosques frequented by Muslims born in Nigeria, is a potential start to answering whether radicalization is occurring in those expatriate populations. But those immigrants, as much as any American citizens, have the right to speak freely and to practice their religion freely. Without information indicating that any particular location, including a mosque, harbors extremists talking about violence, a source can't simply walk in and start reporting on what people are saying. Intelligence is subordinate to the protection of rights. Overseas, intelligence trumps: there is not a bar to going into any location to recruit a source. The question is whether it's worth precious intelligence resources—time, manpower, money—to target a location for collection, not whether the investigating agency can prove, to a skeptical public, that there is credible information underpinning the intelligence investigation.

Similarly, debates I had heard about whether the United States needs a dedicated domestic security service were, I slowly learned, too simplistic. After the 9/11 Commission published its report on the intelligence problems that preceded the attacks, many openly questioned whether America needed its own MI-5, a reference to the vaunted British Security Service. In contrast to the FBI, MI-5 has no law enforcement authority. The service has a simpler mission: collecting intelligence about national security threats, and when that information reaches a certain point, passing it to law enforcement authorities for potential investigation and prosecution. The system has the beauty of simplicity: one service collects and produces intelligence; a second takes action based on that intelligence.

The system also has inherent inefficiencies that are often lost in the "grass is greener over there" debates in Washington. Primary is the requirement for a formal process to hand over an intelligence case to law enforcement. Because MI-5 has neither arrest authority nor legal investigatory powers, police have to pursue intelligence cases when they evolve from MI-5's intelligence purview into problems that require law enforcement. When the contact of a suspected terrorist appears on the screen, for example, MI-5 might spend months determining who the contact is, what he's doing, where his money comes from, what his overseas connections are, and so on. But if the contact turns out to be part of a conspiracy—in an immigration fraud scheme, for example—that legal violation has to be adjudicated in a court. And law enforcement, such as London's Metropolitan Police, have that authority, not intelligence. Over time, to close this gap, MI-5 and its law enforcement partners have moved closer together, increasing efficiency by working closely together and collocating their officers.

There are also clear efficiencies, and they are simple. The security service can recruit, train, reward, and promote officers who are solely dedicated to an intelligence profession. And the entire ethos of the service—how to develop sources, penetrate networks, analyze disparate bits of data—is driven by intelligence. The core of intelligence is collecting, reporting, and analyzing information well enough to understand a target; law enforcement has the responsibility to act on the intelligence. MI-5 also has the luxury of working with a relatively limited number of police agencies, several dozen, easing the burden of coordinating with police executives, providing training, and implementing policy.

The Bureau has a mission similar to the combined MI-5/British police responsibilities. It not only collects on an intelligence target, such as a terror cell, but also develops evidence that might be used in a court, and works with prosecutors to make a case that will stand the test of legal scrutiny. This has a critical efficiency: the people sitting around a table in the morning to discuss an emerging case have no need to hand a case over formally to a law enforcement authority. This isn't simply a theoretical distinction: I cannot remember how many instances we were faced with this challenge during our morning threat briefings. Had we learned enough to move? Were there pieces out there we didn't understand, and therefore should we defer disruption until we collecting more intelligence? And, finally, the most significant question: might public safety be threatened if we didn't move? In some cases, plotters might have independent access to weapons or explosives that we didn't control. Even if we felt we did not fully understand the threat, we could not risk allowing plotters, or single individuals whose motives and intentions we could never fully predict, to decide one night they were going to strike a shopping mall while we were still trying to determine the full scope of their conspiracy. Public safety came first, but there was always a risk, even when we thought we controlled a case, that we'd be surprised.

The answer is that there is no perfect answer; both systems have strengths and weaknesses. When I talked to friends from foreign security services, they often would remark about how much they would like the efficiency of combining intelligence operations with enforcement: the ability to understand an intelligence problem combined with the authority to do something about it. Running a highly productive source into a terror cell, who wants to enter a complicated conversation with a sister service about how to extract the source so that a second source, someone comfortable testifying in court, could be inserted? Of course, we had some of the reverse laments at the Bureau:

wouldn't it be easier if we could focus training solely on intelligence, and not worry about agents who also had to be trained on collecting evidence for trial?

It was, to say the least, frustrating to deal with critics who thought that the simple creation of a dedicated domestic intelligence service would solve all our problems. At the same time these criticisms were coming in, sister services were talking about operating more closely with their law enforcement colleagues; they wanted some of what we had. The answer in Washington always seemed to be "you guys aren't moving fast enough, so let's create another bureaucracy, and that will solve everything," as opposed to the simpler answer: working to make what we had into a more intelligence-driven apparatus.

Meanwhile, often left unsaid, in my view, were two virtual certainties in Washington. First, the creation of any dedicated intelligence service in the United States would, in a matter of years, lead to congressional hearings about how the new service was stepping on American civil liberties. And second, bureaucracies in Washington that lose clout as a result of bloody battles simply do not go down without a fight. I thought, based on what I'd seen at CIA and FBI and what I'd spoken about in casual conversations with friends in other security services, that it would take at least ten years, maybe longer, for a new service to get on its feet in the United States with an expensive new bureaucracy and a mandate that inevitably would lead to accusations of looking over Americans' shoulders. The Bureau didn't develop its intelligence program perfectly, but it always seemed that the arguments that we simply needed a new bureaucracy were too simplistic. Just because what we had wasn't working perfectly didn't seem a legitimate argument for making yet another behemoth organization.

This is not to say that we didn't face well-documented resistance, some serious and entrenched, to these efforts to grow the intelligence component of the Bureau's infrastructure and mindset to match the investigative approach the FBI has always had. The resistance was there, it was real, and it continues to this day, often among Bureau personnel who believe that the director and those below him are taking the Bureau away from its strengths, and gutting its ability to do what it does best. For me, some of this resistance was overt— there were a few, but surprisingly few, exchanges with Bureau agents that were heated, when those agents thought we were trying to replicate the CIA at the expense of the traditional Bureau.

Some of the resistance was also behind the scenes. The *New York Times* ran a front-page article, not long after I had joined the Bureau, about some of our efforts to build the intelligence program. In particular, the article focused on a concept called "domain management," an effort to press field offices to know not only their cases but the environment they were working in. What communities have moved into major cities? Do field offices have contact with those communities, enough to understand their concerns? The article had unnamed agents suggesting that this shift would return the Bureau to the domestic intelligence scandals of 50 years ago, when it was involved in devastating efforts to penetrate the civil rights movements and political opposition. It was an example of the kinds of issues that were raised by those who, in some cases, had legitimate questions about where a renewed intelligence focus would take the Bureau, but in other cases simply didn't like moving away from traditional Bureau work. I viewed these kinds of reports, in a way, as positive: if we weren't having an impact, nobody would have bothered to complain. No pain, no gain.

Luckily, we had support from some of the senior executives who helped push the bureaucracy forward. This wasn't a job for anyone who thought Rome should have been built in a day; it required patience and persistence. In my second year at the Bureau, Director Mueller brought on one of the executives I thought brought the combination of leadership skills that helped slowly drive the organization in the direction we had been given by congressional legislation that established the National Security Branch, and by public expectations that we would become as preventive as we were investigative. Willie Hulon came on as the second head of the National Security Branch, with a reputation for savvy and toughness matched by what I saw in practice. He also turned out to have the most incisive eye for people's strengths and weaknesses of perhaps anyone I have ever seen, bar none. It was intimidating watching him size up people who came into the office, even those I knew well but he didn't. Invariably, after the meeting, he'd comment on what he saw transpire, evaluate whom we were dealing with, and assess a personality within 20 minutes in ways that were uncanny.

He was also a great partner, never rattled, never condescending, always positive. "Philly Dog," he would say, "we can make this work," even in the face of tortuous bureaucratic processes or hurdles. And he brought humor into the office. A former college basketball player, Willie T., as I often called him, must have had at least 70 or 80 pounds on me, along with more than a few inches in height. He sized me up one day, after we'd become comfortable with each other, and appraised the size difference in one sentence: "Philly Dog, if we'd been in grade school together, you're the kind of guy I'd walk up to on the playground and ask, 'So, what'd your momma make us for lunch today?'" I am still laughing.

Willie and others were aware of the criticisms of the Bureau for moving too slowly out of a traditional investigative posture. Even Bureau executives who didn't believe in the direction we were taking had to read the tea leaves. First Congress, the White House, and the president's board of outside intelligence advisers were all breathing down our necks. If that wasn't enough, so was the director, who drove the process of intelligence transformation as long as I was at the Bureau.

Congressional committees also frequently asked us how the Bureau was absorbing a more intelligence-driven approach to federal law enforcement. Congressional staff visited headquarters occasionally, and we went down occasionally to meet staff and, less frequently, for hearings with members of Congress on the committees that oversee the Bureau. The legislation that had created the National Security Branch was designed partly to press the FBI to incorporate more intelligence practices, and members of Congress and their staff were often critical of the pace of change as they reviewed our progress in implementing the law they had passed. In one of the more memorable hearings, Willie and I went to answer questions, only to find that Iraq war protesters also had decided to attend. They represented the group called Code Pink, female protesters typically wearing items of pink clothing and speaking out against the war in Iraq.

As we answered questions in the hearing, the whispering among the Code Pink members in the seats directly behind us became so distracting I was tempted to ask the chairman of the hearing to quiet the group. We worked through the hearing, though, only to find the Code Pink group waiting for us immediately outside the hearing room. This was not a subdued bunch. Willie quickly walked ahead, with some of our congressional staff, while I followed too slowly and was instantly surrounded by a few protesters who asked whom they should call to deal with legal problems they were having—apparently, one of the group had been barred from travel to Canada. I assumed that she had been charged with a minor offense, perhaps disturbing the peace, and suggested she contact a lawyer. This suggestion didn't go over too well; the comments quickly turned more confrontational. What I did not know was that one of the protesters was filming the entire episode with a small, handheld camera. Later that day, after we returned to FBI headquarters, I was told the video clip had already been uploaded onto YouTube. I am giving thanks to this day that the exchange never turned ugly. Another learning moment, I suppose, about the pervasiveness of digital culture. And Willie, my partner, was smiling the entire time in front of me, enjoying the show while we quickly made our way to the waiting FBI van.

The Bureau's classic criminal investigative components—those involved in fighting organized crime, cyber porn, white collar fraud—were separate from the national security components, and slower to adopt the intelligence focus that the National Security Branch was growing. This makes some sense, because many of the personnel recruited into the Bureau had either grown up in a different culture or joined for the simple reason that they enjoyed the reward of putting people behind bars, and closing cases. One of the biggest success stories of the past half-century of the Bureau, however, was the fight against organized crime, particularly the decimation of organized crime families in New York. The phrase "intelligence-driven" didn't exist at that time, and there was not the culture of high-end strategic analysis that is slowly moving into the Bureau. Nonetheless, core concepts, perhaps unspoken, drove the organized crime success. Understand the adversary through intelligence, particularly human source penetrations and technical coverage, such as well-placed wiretaps. Focus on the elements of the adversary that will most accelerate its decline—in this case, the leadership of the five families. Continue through a collection cycle: once one series of takedowns occurs, determine the emerging crew of leaders and take them down, cycle after cycle. What we were asking was similar, that field offices identify threats and map them through strategic collection, both human and technical sources, so that we understood the depth and breadth of what we were facing well enough to dismantle a threat. Arrests were a means to an end, a tool to eliminate a threat, not an end in themselves.

⌒

THE MORNING staff meeting, with managers from across the Bureau (criminal, national security, public affairs, congressional liaison, etc.) concluded the several-hour information-collection process every morning. Like many meetings hosted by the director, it was short and to the point, but not without its own amusing moments. We went around the room, about 20 people around a long conference table and a few on the back benches. All were reporting on interesting events of the day: congressional hearings, breaking stories in the media, a large gang bust, a budget battle. The more sensitive issues were deferred to one-on-ones with the boss after the meeting, and rare was the meeting at which someone around the table didn't say "I've got one for you afterward," usually a sensitive political corruption problem, a congressional muddle, or maybe a high-end counterintelligence investigation that was moving forward.

Humor was more common than you would expect, given the brevity of the meetings and the director's well-deserved reputation as a no-nonsense manager. At least once a week, in his dark suit and starched white button-down shirt, he would comment on the invariably colorful combination worn by our pubic affairs coordinator, John Miller. John, a native New Yorker and former ABC news anchor who ran counterterrorism for the Los Angeles Police Department after a tour at NYPD, bucked the Bureau standards for suits, shirts, and ties. Pink pocket squares matching pink shirts with coordinated pink cufflinks. Seersucker in the summertime. A different fountain pen for every occasion. The director never tired of querying John about style: "What do we have today, John?" And Miller played along perfectly, describing some outlandish color combination with his deep, made-for-TV voice and a delivery that suggested this was a normal question for a staff meeting.

At least as amusing as these exchanges on style were the occasional back-and-forth exchanges between the director and the Bureau's general counsel, Val Caproni. Mueller came to the Bureau with a storied reputation as a federal prosecutor, both at the Department of Justice and, before his appointment as FBI director, as the U.S. attorney in San Francisco. Part of the legend was his decision, years before, to leave a prominent law firm and return to prosecuting cases, taking a step down several notches to work murder cases in

Washington. His style matched his resume; matching wits with the boss on problems, you could always assume that he'd step through a series of questions that would, usually quickly, get to the heart of the matter, often without a great deal of subtlety.

Val would occasionally raise a legal issue on a particular investigation, for example, or a thorny policy issue. The Bureau's latitude to collect intelligence in the United States would be the type of topic that might come up, or a pending lawsuit against the Bureau that resulted from a botched case. It took me some time to understand and appreciate Val when I joined the Bureau, but I came to find that she was one of the most impressive executives with whom I'd ever worked, at the Bureau or elsewhere. She was smart, thoughtful, open-minded—and fierce when she went into battle.

At the morning meetings, the director, returning to his attorney persona, occasionally poked and prodded Val about some legal opinion she would offer. Quickly, Val's legal acumen came into play, and she would return fire without hesitation, also in good humor but leaving no doubt that she fully intended to best him at legal argumentation. He almost invariably backed down, or at least dropped the discussion, after enjoying a few minutes of back-and-forth about legalities and technicalities. I'm not certain I ever saw him win. But sitting back and watching these exchanges, and seeing the boss enjoy himself for a bit, was invariably one of the highlights of those short meetings.

As our conversations deepened about developing the intelligence program, and an intelligence mindset, at the FBI, it became apparent that the problem we faced was not the quality of the investigations the FBI undertook. Nor was it whether we looked at these investigations with an eye first on whether we could gather intelligence and only second on whether we could prosecute successfully. In the cases I saw, the initial question at the morning table was never whether we had a case but even simpler: what do we have here? Are we seeing everything, or is there a conspiracy afoot that we don't see? Each serious case raised complicated questions that took time to untangle. Who were the players? How were they radicalized? Who were they recruiting? Had they been overseas? And if so, why? How were they financed? Along with another laundry list of questions as we went through the intelligence and investigative process.

Domestic security and intelligence inevitably bump up against the foremost concern, though: can we continue to paint a picture of what we are seeing, or do we have to sacrifice intelligence because the cluster of people we're watching poses an imminent threat we can't control? The balance is straightforward in practice: if the threat to the public is at all imminent, or unknowable, taking down a cell trumps continuing intelligence collection. You can't sacrifice innocent people for information. In the Northern Exposure case—or in the case of the group a few years later, in 2007, that was targeting the U.S. military facility at Fort Dix in New Jersey—the intelligence we were uncovering clearly indicated that the members of these clusters were looking at committing acts of terrorism, but they weren't ready yet. So we had time to learn, to understand whether there were other conspirators, other avenues of funding, other elements that we couldn't know when the investigation broke. A service with solely law enforcement functions might not need to ask these questions. Find the suspect and determine whether there's enough evidence for a U.S. attorney's office to indict. If not, continue the investigation until it either concludes without charges or the U.S. attorney takes the case.

The bottom line in these complex intelligence investigations, in other words, wasn't whether we were ready to prosecute. It was whether we were comfortable that we could contain the threat to the public—did the subjects, for example, have access to a source of weapons we couldn't control? And if we were comfortable, had we learned enough to convince ourselves that when we went in, there were no additional conspirators, in the United States or overseas, that we didn't know about?

The measures of success used by study groups and the media to look at counterterrorism investigations in the United States sometimes miss this subtle point. These measures often used rely on one simple fact: how many subjects in the United States are successfully prosecuted for terrorism violations? A good question, but not entirely relevant from a security perspective. The first question we faced was this: did we understand a conspiracy well enough to dismantle it? Once we mapped a conspiracy, "dismantling" might include prosecution for immigration violations or marriage fraud, not necessarily prosecution for terrorism violations. In other words, our mission was to map conspiracies so that we could wrap them up.

So statistics showing how many individuals are successfully prosecuted for terrorism violations are misleading. Running full-bore counterterrorism investigations is extremely expensive. Surveillance, technical coverage, human source operations, translation, paperwork are all hugely labor intensive, and expensive. Once we felt we had fully mapped a conspiracy, our question wasn't whether we should spend months or years continuing to collect intelligence. Our mission was to shut down the conspiracy and move onto the next problem. The Department of Justice, the FBI, and major city police departments have a responsibility to protect the public, not to amass terrorism arrests. So when the best disruption tool turned out to be prosecution on other charges, we didn't hesitate. Watching experts characterize the terrorism threat to the United States by counting the number of terrorism convictions, then, always has seemed to me a simplistic measure.

This is not to say we were perfect in transitioning to intelligence-driven law enforcement. We were not, and the long labor of evolution in domestic security goes on at the FBI. But at the senior levels, in daily briefings, the transition was evident. The questions posed every morning illustrate this evolution. Is there an imminent threat? Who are the players? Are we missing any of them? What are their overseas connections? Where are they getting money? Who recruited or radicalized them? Whom did they recruit? And then, once we understood the web around a cell or cluster, the final question, what should we do?

This all sounds simple, almost straightforward. It is not. Lurking behind these conversations, most prominently, was the perennial question whether we were sitting on a plot that, as we mapped it, might move in a direction we didn't understand or couldn't contain. How confident could we be that we understood an individual, or a group, well enough to know that they wouldn't decide, off the cuff, to stage an attack? Or that they didn't have access to weapons or contacts we didn't know about? Every day, for years on end, looking at these problems, all with the expectation that one miss would mean congressional hearings, media scrutiny, and maybe the murder of innocents.

Early on, it appeared to a few of us that one way to inculcate this way of thinking was to create some sort of system to add metrics to intelligence. The Bureau, like other large bureaucracies, tends to measure things. The legacy of law enforcement inevitably led to measurements of arrests, or referrals to U.S. attorneys, or how many agents and analysts were dedicated to particular investigative categories. As we pushed to ask more intelligence questions, it became clear that the lack of clear metrics for intelligence performance was holding us back, on at least two fronts. First, field offices, and senior executives, prepared for a brutal FBI inspection regime that focused on these numbers, and people tend to perform based on how they're evaluated. Second, the lack of metrics on the intelligence side limited our ability to set goals, and to evaluate performance. How could we have a conversation about performance, across 56 field offices, when we didn't have standard methods of measuring performance?

Early in my tenure at the FBI, John Miller, the public affairs coordinator, dropped a *Harvard Business Review* document on my desk. It quickly became apparent that this document, to a newcomer in the law enforcement world, provided some of the answers we would need to move toward intelligence metrics. The report detailed an NYPD-originated process called COMPSTAT, measurements for crime in cities that allowed senior leaders in a department to paint a quick picture of crime trends, to ask questions of precinct chiefs and others about why crime was occurring, why trends were developing, and what was being done to respond. It was a document that allowed for a serious conversation about crime, based not on anecdotal information but on hard facts. Miller had participated in the evolution of COMPSTAT at NYPD, and he was convinced the approach would help on intelligence metrics for the Bureau. He didn't know intelligence work at that time, but he had a good nose for where we were headed.

He was right. Working with a few superb staff assistants, we put together a pilot package for field offices that required answers on such questions as what their human source base was, how many intelligence reports they had disseminated, and how many personnel they had working on different key threats. Before the metrics, though, came the hardest part: a requirement that the offices characterize threats in their domains not by caseloads but by a judgment about which problems were most serious. In other words, the presence of high-tech defense industries and universities with large Department of Defense grants might mean that foreign intelligence adversaries would target those areas for technology theft. The absence of cases didn't mean the threat was absent. The idea was never that the numbers would give us answers, but we knew they would at least provide fuel for a conversation about intelligence performance. I wasn't sure this would work, at the outset, but it quickly caught on.

The first pilot implementation of the COMPSTAT-oriented approach were painful, and sometimes ugly, because both we at headquarters, and our field counterparts, were struggling with a new beast. Senior field managers, sitting in secure videoconferencing rooms while the headquarters team sat in the Hoover Building on Pennsylvania Avenue in Washington, offered assessments of threats that often referred to individual cases. We soon learned to prohibit the mention of cases. Tell us what you're most worried about, we asked, and tell us why. Then tell us what you're doing about it. And, finally, the hardest part for most bureaucracies, tell us what your gaps are—personnel shortfalls? lack of sources? competing priorities?—and tell us what you intend to do about these gaps.

The atmosphere in those early days was also mixed. Some offices performed well, often because they were led by senior field managers who embraced where we were headed. Field offices often packed their conference rooms with dozens of staff, and it was heartening to know that analysts, agents, managers, and support staff who performed well knew it. Poor performances, though, led regularly to tense exchanges about why. Why is your source base limited? Why is this threat so opaque? And what are you doing about it? Having a few Bureau outsiders conducting the initial videoconferences from headquarters probably didn't help, though there were only rarely direct confrontations.

Soon, though, the boss stepped in. At the Bureau, the legacy of powerful directors lives on. Couple this with the fact that many Bureau employees, in an organization dispersed across hundreds of large and small field offices in the United States—and an increasing number of offices overseas—rarely see the director. So when he asked about the initial COMPSTAT pilots, and we told him that they were producing conversations about intelligence that ranged from interesting to fascinating, he said he wanted to chair a few. He did. And he never stopped. I wasn't sure initially that this was a good idea, because it would require of time we weren't sure he had, and it might stifle discussion. But, as it turned out, his presence forced field offices to engage, and take the process seriously. And his engagement left him with a clearer understanding of the problems the field was facing, on everything from re-sources to terrorism to mortgage fraud, at a level of detail he would have gotten nowhere else.

The staffing and documentation for this process grew quickly, and the director and others around his conference table received an inch-high stack of paperwork for each office and its intelligence program. We found that the requirements to prepare for these videoconferences became too onerous: we asked too much, and they overprepared anyway. The initial concept was that these video meetings, scheduled roughly quarterly for each office, should be a conversation, a chance for the director and others (there were maybe 20 people in the room at headquarters) to learn about field operations and problems, and a chance for the field to have in-depth conversations with headquarters. The best of the sessions ended up this way: if an office could explain clearly why a key threat remained a gap—for example, another prob-lem was sapping all their resources—the conversation evolved into a valuable chance to determine whether we should address the resource problem by shifting people around.

Other offices struggled at the start, though. This was partly the transi-tion from cases to threats, from characterizing which federal violations were under investigation—the number of significant white collar fraud cases—to characterizing threats. In the midst of signs of major fraud at mortgage firms, for example, should we be concerned that individual field offices might be sitting on large fraud schemes that hadn't been uncovered? And what could we do to uncover these schemes? Questions about threat were never limited to terrorism. Central American gangs, Mexican mafia, organized crime all gave rise to the same questions. What is the threat? Who are the players? What are they doing? And how confident are we that we have the intelligence coverage—human sources, phone taps, etc.—to understand their networks well enough to eviscerate them?

The conversations improved over time, in some cases dramatically. And field offices, by and large, grew more comfortable characterizing what they knew and what they didn't, and talking to the director about it. When the sessions worked right, the conversations were extremely helpful. During mortgage fraud discussions, for example, we talked about thresholds for action—how much fraud could we investigate, at what levels of financial loss, before this endemic issue consumed too many resources?—and why they differed from field division to field division. Whether there should be a conversation with prosecutors about thresholds for action. Whether there should be a Bureau-wide policy on such issues. The COMPSTAT process, and the statistics that fed the videoconferences, were never intended to provide all the answers. They were intended to provide enough material to start a conversation that was based on data, not suppositions, guesses, or anecdotes. And, as time went on, they started becoming more streamlined.

CHAPTER 8

ONE MORE TRANSFER: INTELLIGENCE AT THE DEPARTMENT OF HOMELAND SECURITY

WHEN THE staff of President Obama arrived at the White House in 2009, they were looking for career professionals to take senior positions. Not long after the inauguration, I received a call about taking one of those positions, head of intelligence at the Department of Homeland Security. This was a rare opportunity for an analyst who started in an entry-level position: to take a presidentially appointed, Senate-confirmed job. In Washington, this is an honor, especially for someone with no political connections. There were clear downsides, as there always are. For one, DHS was legendary among my friends in Washington for being an unwieldy, massive enterprise that might never fully gel as an organization. Further, the intelligence component of the organization, known widely as I&A (Intelligence and Analysis), was rife with problems.

There were minor issues, but they were inconsequential from my perspective. First, I'd relied on the Metro for years, and I no longer had a car. The Bureau was a six-stop, no-transfer commute for me, with the Metro line only 150 yards from my doorstep across the river from Washington in Alexandria, Virginia. DHS would take an hour or more by public transit. Second, because I was transitioning from a civil service job to a presidential appointment, I'd be on a different pay scale. Bizarre as it sounds, this would mean a pay cut. More responsibility, less pay: only in Washington do you get these kinds of choices.

Before we even started the formal nomination process, I had conversations with both DHS secretary Janet Napolitano and her deputy Jane Holl Lute. Both were gracious, as we talked through the challenges of the organization and what might be done to improve. Napolitano was at ease, laughing on a Friday evening as we spoke about Washington and intelligence. Lute was equally engaging, particularly after we quickly determined that both were committed flyfishing addicts.

The nomination process, even for a position as relatively modest as an undersecretary, is byzantine, seemingly endless, and painful. We started with searches of public information about me, such as media mentions. Far more time-intensive, and labor-intensive, was the work on financial records. Because so many nominees are caught up in embarrassing revelations about problems such as unpaid taxes and undocumented nannies, the screening process results in scrutiny of every financial angle that could go wrong. And before the White House is prepared to tell Congress to proceed with scheduling a hearing for the nominee to be considered, that scrutiny has to be completed. After 20-plus years of government service, on a government salary, I didn't have any particularly exciting financial secrets to reveal, but the process nonetheless took a few months.

Preparing for Senate confirmation hearings also was a lengthy process. The most time-consuming element was working through the many documents and briefings provided by the staff of DHS's congressional affairs element and the managers in the Intelligence and Analysis component I was slated to manage. Reviewing mountains of relevant documents and listening to the managers of every element of the DHS intelligence organization present their mission, programs, and personnel took weeks. There were related briefs as well, including meeting with civil liberties advocates who were concerned that DHS might conduct analysis that violated Americans' rights or collect information on innocent people.

The most challenging were the aptly named "murder boards," the groups of people who meet to pepper any nominee with the kinds of hard questions that might be posed during a Congressional confirmation hearing. These questions can start from difficult policy issues—in the case of DHS intelligence, for example, there were persistent questions among many civil liberties advocates, and others, about efforts to compile "Suspicious Activity Reports," documents about suspicious behavior around infrastructure sites, possible surveillance of nuclear facilities, and other such bits of data that might later provide critical pieces in a mosaic of intelligence. But questions also covered personal issues, from questionable financial documentation (I didn't have any) to professional history (I had a lot, including some knowledge of and experience with the third rail of intelligence issues in the early twenty-first century, that of detainees and CIA interrogations).

The latter issue, my professional background at CIA, raised questions early on, and those questions only grew over time. Central to the rising volume of interest among those participating in the confirmation process was what I knew, and when, about CIA interrogation and detention programs, and the "rendition" (transfer) of prisoners captured overseas to CIA detention facilities. I was well aware of these programs at CIA, particularly in my capacity as deputy director of the Counterterrorist Center and briefly as acting director in summer 2004, but the treatment of prisoners and administration of these programs had not been one of my key responsibilities. They were overseen by the director of the Center because of his operational background and experience. During the heated congressional debates in 2009 about the detainee program—including questions about which members of Congress knew what about the program, and when—these were the only questions I was facing. What I knew. (Quite a bit). Whether I had ever briefed members on the program. (Yes.) Whether I would speak in hearings about everything I had witnessed during meetings I had attended within the administration, particularly White House meetings. (No.) Whether I had ever registered opposition to the program while I was at CIA. (No.) Whether I had ever signed an order to "render" (transfer) a prisoner to a CIA facility. (I couldn't remember, which seemed to be a dodge unless you'd been involved in the variety and intensity of activities the Center had underway while I was there.)

Nominees typically have an individual assigned to help shepherd them through the confirmation process, both the tortuous compilation of documentation before the White House issues a nomination and the preparation for the confirmation hearing. The young lawyer assigned to assist me was energetic and competent, and he advised me that he hadn't lost a single nominee yet among the fifty or sixty he had handled. We met for drinks some time after I had withdrawn the nomination, at the historic Hay-Adams Hotel in Washington, and I jokingly told him I was sorry for ruining his perfect batting average. He laughed, and I never sensed, at that time or as the process frayed, that he was anything but supportive.

The issue of my knowledge of and involvement in CIA detention of Al Qaeda prisoners eventually destroyed the prospect of a clean nomination hearing. After consultations with the White House, I knew that the hearing would be difficult. Difficult was fine for me personally, but creating a distraction for the people who had nominated me, on issues that were then already years old, for a position that was a third-tier presidential appointment, seemed inappropriate. I was ready for fireworks at the hearing, for difficult exchanges over difficult questions, and for attacks from senators who would use the hearing to state their positions about the detention and interrogation tactics backed during the previous Bush administration. I even thought the hearings would be an interesting challenge, and maybe an opportunity for public education. But it became increasingly evident that they would instead be a minor circus. It seemed inappropriate, and irrelevant to the DHS intelligence position for which I had been nominated.

Events escalated quickly, with sympathetic—and not-so-sympathetic—Hill staff indicating that the hearing would be unpleasant or worse, and that there would be negative votes. One friend said the committee might decline to confirm me for the job, a prospect I thought was highly unlikely but which nonetheless seemed a sign of the potential vitriol that would emerge at the hearing. In the end, after consulting with a few friends and the White House, I decided the best, and only, course of action would be to withdraw. When a president I had never met nominated me for a position he was not even aware of, I nonetheless took it as an honor. And when that same position might vault from a minor appointment to a political distraction, there seemed only one appropriate step to take. The path seemed clear at the end, when I traveled across town for yet another of the countless murder boards, which at that point included White House lawyers, and the lawyers failed to show up for the meeting or advise us they weren't showing. Even an amateur analyst could read that writing on the wall.

⤝

LATER, FRIENDS and colleagues asked why I'd pulled out too early, a perspective I did not, and do not, share. Other friends asked about bitterness or regrets, seeing the political show as an indication of the age-old lesson of intelligence: involvement in controversial covert action by one administration, even if legal, doesn't absolve the CIA of attacks farther down the road. This, too, struck me as an odd sentiment. Bitter after a career that started at entry-level and ended with a presidential nomination? I was pretty happy. In any case, the political maelstrom surrounding CIA detention and interrogation practices wasn't a personal attack; my nomination had simply come at the worst possible time. My thought was simple: it was a nice run, but now it was time to figure out what to do next. No regrets, no surrender.

I spoke with the White House early on the morning after I'd slept on the decision, and sent a short email indicating that I did not want this minor nomination to become a distraction. Almost instantly, the announcement was out from the White House, and the phone calls and emails started coming in fast and furious. Part of the next few days was easy: I wasn't going to do any press. There wasn't anything to say, and it was better to let the story die anyway.

The flood of contacts from friends and work colleagues was overwhelming, and more heartening than I had anticipated. For days, supportive words came from every direction, including people I hadn't heard from for years. Senior people who didn't need to call—Secretary Napolitano, former Attorney General Mukasey, LAPD Chief Bill Bratton; so many I couldn't keep track. Old Agency acquaintances and newer Bureau colleagues. A few people I'd never met, or didn't remember meeting, just reaching out—believing, I thought, that this had somehow been a far more painful process than it seemed to me. In the midst of this, I took a few days off to smoke cigars on my back patio in Alexandria and figure out what to do next.

The calls and emails could not have been more courteous, but there wasn't much consoling to do. After a quarter-century in Washington, the political process I had seen didn't seem out of the ordinary. My view was that I had enjoyed a great run, seeing corners of the world I never knew existed and meeting people—including presidents and kings—I would never have had the chance to meet. It seemed like a gifted career. Why worry? It just didn't seem that disturbing. In the midst of the plenty I saw, why worry about one job? In a life of adventures, on to the next adventure. There's always another job, and it often turns out to be better than the one you missed out on.

Travel, too, had allowed for perspectives on Washington life that I did not have when I started government service in 1985. Traveling to places like Bangladesh, or driving from the airport past the monumental acres of trash in Calcutta, helps bring perspective. Colleagues I had known in Bangladesh had told me of staff in their houses who struggled because of protein deficiency as children. The few times I passed the trash in Calcutta I had seen young children destined for lives as ragpickers in living environments with feral dogs and human dung. There were other memories. Being approached in Bombay by lepers. Seeing children destined for deprivation in wartorn Kabul. Walking past drug addicts outside the mayhem of Lagos airport. And, closer to home, drunk bums sleeping near the waterfront Torpedo Factory art galleries, and homeless people asking for money at streetcorners all over downtown Washington, the nation's capital. Worrying about a lost job that would have meant less salary and a commute four times longer seemed a bit much.

I had worked for a series of senior managers at the Bureau who were supportive, people who had grown up in the Bureau field but who now had the responsibility of developing a more intelligence-driven program. In the day or two after I withdrew my nomination, Art Cummings, the supervisor I was working with at the Bureau, sent a note I will never forget: "Come on home, Phil," it read. Four words, and I knew it was time to return to the Bureau and figure out next steps.

The preparatory work for the congressional hearings had taken more than a few weeks, and in that time, the Bureau had rightly gone forward with choosing my successor, another officer from the Agency's senior executive service. Director Mueller knew I had no follow-on assignment, and without a word, he politely told me that I could stay on as the Bureau's senior intelligence adviser, continue to attend the morning's briefings, participate in the periodic COMPSTAT exercises, and figure out what to do next.

It took awhile to develop a clear vision of next steps. Years of analysis, I suppose, led me to break down the problem into constituent pieces, and the picture I saw was a major step, but almost inescapable. There seemed to be three options in government: stay at the Bureau, as a loan from CIA; return to the Agency; or find something else. The first, remaining at FBI, didn't make sense: I'd already been there more than four years, something of a record for an officer on detail, and I had no permanent home there. The Agency was still paying my salary, and making noises, understandably, that I should find a position somewhere back at Langley. With the time I'd been out of sight, though, the only options that cropped up were positions I thought were going back to the future, assignments that did not seem especially interesting. Finally, there seemed to me nothing exciting elsewhere in government: I would probably never receive another presidential appointment, and assignments that didn't require this process seemed like a step backward. There didn't appear to be an opportunity to grow anywhere. A lateral move would have been fine, it just wasn't something I was interested in.

Staring in the mirror one morning, I knew the answer. And I think it had been clear all along: it was time to leave. Part of this decision was daunting because, after nearly a quarter-century of government service, I had no idea how to make a living on the outside. Perhaps at least as important was how I'd pay the mortgage: I was forty-seven years old, eight years shy of retirement age of fifty-five. With a little checking, I found that, if I left early, I'd delay my retirement benefits until age sixty-two. In other words, it wasn't just finding a job, it was finding something I could land in immediately that would replace my federal salary. It is not surprising how the need to earn a living focuses your attention.

There was one other problem, entirely self-inflicted. Suddenly, there was the prospect of finding a life outside the confines of bureaucracies. After years of working for other people, in huge organizations with countless rules and regulations that sometimes didn't make sense, I knew I wanted to avoid bureaucracy at almost any cost. This meant sidestepping what would have been the most straightforward route: joining one of the many companies around the Beltway that sold services back to the government. I didn't want to get swallowed up into another bureaucracy, and I didn't want to walk the halls of Langley as a "green badger"—the inside term for people who left the Agency and came back under private contracting companies.

The months started to move. I talked to every friend I had, and got advice—much of it extremely useful—from friends I didn't even know I had.

Many had similar counsel. Don't move too fast. If you're going out on your own, take at least a year to let the initial dust settle. Don't spread yourself too thin. Only work with people and projects you like. Talk to everyone you know, but understand that at least 90 percent won't lead anywhere. But don't refuse any conversation. You never know.

After about six months of this, I did know. I'd talked to enough friends and colleagues, in the United States and overseas, to know I could make a go of it. With a lot of risk, but manageable risk. And what was the option? Avoid the biggest job change I'd had since 1985 out of fear? Not an option.

I called the Agency and advised them that the openings we'd discussed would not work, and that I would resign, since retirement wasn't even a close option. The process was remarkably simple, after more than two decades of accumulating promotions, transfers, personnel evaluations, polygraphs. Just a few sessions at Langley to fill out how I would designate my government retirement plan, a few security documents, and that was it. I turned in a badge and walked out.

The crowning moment of a fascinating few decades, and overwhelmingly positive experiences in two large bureaucracies, occurred when I walked out to the parking lot at CIA headquarters for the last time. There was construction at one of the lots on the vast compound, and parking was at a premium, as it always is around the suburban facility. After driving around for about 15 minutes looking for a spot, I had left my car at the end of a parking lane, in a no-parking zone.

And, of course, I walked out, after twenty-four years, to find a security officer writing a ticket. "Is this your vehicle?" he asked. "Yes," I answered. "I couldn't find a spot, and I wasn't in for long. You are not going to believe this, but this is my last day, after 24 years. So I don't even have a badge." He looked at me for a moment, clearly not believing any of it. It felt absurd even to offer the excuse; who could come up with that one? But we spoke for a moment, and I told him I no longer had an identification badge because I'd handed mine in not 15 minutes earlier. And, like the opportunities and chances and breaks I'd gotten for an entire career, from people I'd known and people I hadn't, he let it pass. "Have a nice day," he said. "Thank you," I responded. After living the last chapter in this book, and off to live another.

And drove home.

Index

Abbottabad 24, 77

Abdullah, Abdullah, 18

Abu Faraj al-Libi, 23

Abu Ghraib, 175

Abu Yayha al-Libi, 23

Abu Zubaydah, 57–62

Adl, Sayf-al, 79–80

Ahmed, Haris, 174

Al Qaeda of the Arabian Peninsula (AQAP), 82

Al Qaeda of the Islamic Maghreb (AQIM), 85

Aum Shinrikyo, 64

Awlaki, Anwar, 85–86

Atta, Mohammed, 93, 99

Bagram Airfield, 13, 20

Bald, Gary 148, 150

Bashir, Abu Bakr, 74

Berg, Nicholas, 171

Bharot, Dhiren, 135–36, 148

bin Laden, Osama, 23, 57, 70, 72, 77, 79, 83, 175

Bojinka, 77

Bonn, Germany, 15–17

Bratton, Bill, 195

Brennan, John, 168

Brokaw, Tom, 128

Burgess, Ron, 107–9

Bush, George W., 36, 45, 168

Caproni, Val, 183–84

Cheney, Dick, 45, 95–96

Code Pink, 181

COMPSTAT, 187–88, 190, 196

Crumpton, Hank, 12

Cummings, Art, 196

Dobbins, James, 6–8, 11–18, 20, 22, 24, 27, 30–31

Fahim, Mohammed, 18

5 o'clock (meeting), 43–44, 48–51, 69, 73, 111, 159

Fort Dix, 185,

Fort Hood, 79, 85–86

Goss, Porter, 128, 148

Hariri, Rafiq, 155

Harlow, Bill, 123–25, 127

Harvard Business Review, 187

Hayden, Mike, 149

Hulon, Willie, 180–81

Jemaah Islamiyah (JI), 74, 76, 143, 171

Jordan, Paul, 171

July 7, 2005, 139

Kappes, Steve , 49

Karzai, Hamid, 11, 14–15, 17–18, 24–25, 27

Khalilzad, Zal, 16–17
Khan, Ismail, 24
Kindsvater, Pattie, 32–33, 35–37, 40, 51,
    104
Krongard, A. B. (Buzzy), 50

Libby, Scooter, 96
Lincoln, Abraham, xi
Lute, Jane Holl, 192

McLaughlin, John, 12, 44–45, 48, 50, 137
McVeigh, Timothy, 77
Miller, John, 183, 187
Miscik, Jami, 105
Mohammed, Khalid Shaykh, 23, 59, 77,
    79
Mowatt-Larssen, Rolf, 68–69
Mubtakar, 65
Mudd, Dr. Samuel A., xii
Mueller, Robert, 50, 137, 146, 147–50, 153,
    155, 180, 183, 196
Mukasey, Michael, 160, 195
Musharraf, Pervez, 10

Napolitano, Janet, 192, 195
National Counterterrorism Center
    (NCTC), 51, 115, 133, 145–46, 167–69,
    172
New York Times, 34, 180
Northern Alliance, 6, 11–13, 15, 18, 24–25,
    45
Northern Exposure (FBI case), 174, 185

Obama, Barack, 168, 191
One Percent Rule, 67–68

Pease, Bruce, 105–6, 112
Powell, Colin, 92, 97–104, 161
President's Daily Brief (PDB), 34–37, 45,
    47–48, 51–52, 55, 59

Rabbani, Burhanuddin, 13–14
Rabia, Hamza, 23
Redd, Scott, 146
Ridge, Tom, 131–33
"Rob," 111
Rice, Condoleezza, 99
Rodriguez, Jose, 105–9, 141–42, 149

Shah, Zahir (king), 9
Shahzad, Faisal, 86
Sharif, Sayyid Imam al- (Dr. Fadl), 83–85
*Starfish and the Spiderweb: The Unstop-
    pable Power of Leaderless Organizations,
    The*, 156
Sun Tzu, 88
Swing's, 2

Tenet, George, 44–45, 48, 50, 54, 58, 68,
    73, 93–95, 98–103, 111–12, 123–24, 133,
    138, 146, 159
Terrorist Threat Integration Center
    (TTIC), 145–46
Threat Matrix, 33, 41–43, 51, 53, 62, 79, 171
Times Square, 85–86
Tora Bora, 22

"Underwear Bomber," 112, 172
USS *Cole*, 75

Virginia, University of, ix, 28

Washington Post, xi
Weapons of Mass Destruction (WMD), 41,
    49, 64–69, 95, 97–100, 103–4, 121, 132
Wiley, Winston, 27, 29, 31–32

Zarqawi, Abu Musab al-, 82, 85, 88
Zawahiri, Ayman al-, 22–23, 29, 70–72, 77,
    79, 82–85, 175
Zazi, Najibullah, 65

CPSIA information can be obtained at www.ICGtesting.com
Printed in the USA
BVOW070735160513

320450BV00002B/2/P